14.99

EFFECTIVE

PERSONNEL

MANAGEMENT

Effective Management
Series Editor: Alan H. Anderson

Effective Personnel Management
Alan H. Anderson

Effective Business Policy
Alan H. Anderson and Dennis Barker

Effective General Management
Alan H. Anderson

Effective Organizational Behaviour
Alan H. Anderson and Anna Kyprianou

Effective Labour Relations
Alan H. Anderson

Effective Marketing
Alan H. Anderson and Thelma Dobson

Effective International Marketing
Alan H. Anderson, Thelma Dobson and James Patterson

Effective Marketing Communications
Alan H. Anderson and David Kleiner

Effective Entrepreneurship
Alan H. Anderson and Peter Woodcock

Effective Enterprise Management
Alan H. Anderson and Dennis Barker

Effective Accounting Management
Alan H. Anderson and Eileen Nix

Effective Financial Management
Alan H. Anderson and Richard Ciechan

EFFECTIVE

PERSONNEL

MANAGEMENT

a skills and activity-based approach

ALAN H. ANDERSON

The right of Alan H. Anderson to be identified as author of this work has been asserted in accordance with the Copyright, Designs and Patents Act 1988.

First published 1994

Blackwell Publishers
108 Cowley Road
Oxford OX4 1JF
UK

238 Main Street
Cambridge, Massachusetts 02142
USA

British Library Cataloguing in Publication Data

A CIP catalogue record for this book is available from the British Library.

Library of Congress Cataloging-in-Publication Data

Library of Congress data has been applied for.

ISBN 0-631-19116-X

Designed and typeset by VAP Group Ltd., Kidlington, Oxfordshire

Printed in Great Britain by T. J. Press Ltd, Padstow, Cornwall

This book is printed on acid-free paper

This book is dedicated to my wife Maureen whose immense effort and support have sustained me in writing not only this book, but my contribution to each of the first twelve books of the series.

Contents

Figures

Boxes

Activities

Introduction to the Series

❝ He that has done nothing has known nothing. ❞

Carlyle

The Concept

In this series 'effective' means getting results. By taking an action approach to management, or the stewardship of an organization, the whole series allows people to create and develop their skills of effectiveness. This interrelated series gives the underpinning knowledge base and the application of functional and generic skills of the effective manager who gets results.

Key qualities of the effective manager include:

- **functional expertise** in the various disciplines of management;
- an understanding of the **organizational context**;
- an appreciation of the **external environment**;
- **self-awareness** and the power of **self-development**.

These qualities must fuse in a climate of **enterprise**.

Management is results-oriented so action is at a premium. The basis of this activity is **skills** underpinned by our qualities. In turn these skills can be based on a discipline or a function, and be universal or generic.

The Approach of the Series

These key qualities of effective management are the core of the current twelve books of the series. The areas covered by the series at present are:

People	*Effective Personnel Management*
	Effective Labour Relations
	Effective Organizational Behaviour
Finance	*Effective Financial Management*
	Effective Accounting Management
Marketing and sales	*Effective Marketing*
	Effective International Marketing
	Effective Marketing Communications
Operations/Enterprise	*Effective Enterprise Management*
	Effective Entrepreneurship
Policy/General	*Effective Business Policy*
	Effective General Management

The key attributes of the effective manager are all dealt with in the series, and we will pinpoint where they are emphasized:

- *Functional expertise.* The four main disciplines of management – finance, marketing, operations and personnel management – make up nine books. These meet the needs of specialist disciplines and allow a wider appreciation of other functions.
- *Organizational context.* All the 'people' books – the specialist one on *Effective Organizational Behaviour,* and also *Effective Personnel Management* and *Effective Labour Relations* – cover this area. The resourcing/control issues are met in the 'finance' texts, *Effective Financial Management* and *Effective Accounting Management.* Every case activity is given some organizational context.
- *External environment.* One book, *Effective Business Policy,* is dedicated to this subject. Environmental contexts apply in every book of the series: especially in *Effective Entrepreneurship, Effective General Management,* and in all of the 'marketing' texts – *Effective Marketing, Effective International Marketing* and *Effective Marketing Communications.*
- *Self-awareness/self-development.* To a great extent management development is manager development, so we have one generic skill (see later) devoted to this topic running through each book. The subject is examined in detail in *Effective General Management.*
- *Enterprise.* The *Effective Entrepreneurship* text is allied to *Effective Enterprise Management* to give insights into this whole area through all the developing phases of the firm. The marketing and policy books also revolve around this theme.

Skills

The functional skills are inherent within the discipline-based texts. In addition, running through the series are the following generic skills:
- self-development
- teamwork
- communications
- numeracy/IT
- decisions

These generic skills are universal managerial skills which occur to some degree in every manager's job.

Format/Structure of Each Book

Each book is subdivided into six units. These are self-contained, in order to facilitate learning, but interrelated, in order to give an effective holistic view. Each book also has an introduction with an outline of the book's particular theme.

Each unit has *learning objectives* with an overview/summary of the unit.

Boxes appear in every unit of every book. They allow a different perspective from the main narrative and analysis. Research points, examples, controversy and theory are all expanded upon in these boxes. They are numbered by unit in each book, e.g. 'Box PM1.1' for the first box in Unit One of *Effective Personnel Management.*

Activities, numbered in the same way, permeate the series. These action-oriented forms of learning cover cases, questionnaires, survey results, financial data, market research information, etc. The skills which can be assessed in each one are noted in the code at the top right of the activity by having the square next to them ticked. That is, if we are assuming numeracy then the square beside Numeracy would be ticked (✓), and so on. The weighting given to these skills will depend on the activity, the tutors'/learners' needs, and the overall weighting of the skills as noted in the appendix on 'Generic Skills', with problem solving dominating in most cases.

Common cases run through the series. Functional approaches are added to these core cases to show the same organization from different perspectives. This simulates the complexity of reality.

Workbook

The activities can be written up in the *workbook* which accompanies each book in the series.

Handbook

For each book in the series, there is a *handbook*. This is not quite the 'answers' to the activities, but it does contain some indicative ideas for them (coded accordingly), which will help to stimulate discussion and thought.

Test bank

We are developing a bank of tests in question-and-answer format to accompany the series. This will be geared to the knowledge inputs of the books.

The Audience

The series is for all those who wish to be effective managers. As such, it is a series for management development on an international scale, and embraces both management education and management training. In management education, the emphasis still tends to be on cognitive or knowledge inputs; in management training, it still tends to be on skills and techniques. We need both theory and practice, with the facility to try out these functions and skills through a range of scenarios in a 'safe' learning environment. This series is unique in encompassing these perspectives and bridging the gulf between the academic and vocational sides of business management.

Academically the series is pitched at the DMS/DBA types of qualification, which often lead on to an MA/MBA after the second year. Undergraduates following business degrees or management studies will benefit from the series in their final years. Distance learners will also find the series useful, as will those studying managerial subjects for professional examinations. The competency approach and the movement towards Accredited Prior Learning and National Vocational Qualifications are underpinned by the knowledge inputs, while the activities will provide useful simulations for these approaches to management learning.

This developmental series gives an opportunity for self-improvement. Individuals may wish to enhance their managerial potential by developing themselves without institutional backing by working through the whole series. It can also be used to underpin corporate training programmes, and acts as a useful design vehicle for specialist inputs from organizations. We are happy to pursue these various options with institutions or corporations.

The approach throughout the series combines skills, knowledge and application to create and develop the effective manager. Any comments or thoughts from participants in this interactive process will be welcomed.

Alan H. Anderson
Melbourn, Cambridge

The Series: Learning, Activities, Skills and Compatibility

The emphasis on skills and activities as vehicles of learning makes this series unique. Behavioural change, or learning, is developed through a two-pronged approach.

First, there is the **knowledge-based (cognitive)** approach to learning. This is found in the main text and in the boxes. These cognitive inputs form the traditional method of learning based on the principle of receiving and understanding information. In this series, there are four main knowledge inputs covering the four main managerial functions: marketing/sales, operations/enterprise, people, and accounting/finance. In addition, these disciplines are augmented by a strategic overview covering policy making and general management. An example of this first approach may be illustrative. In the case of marketing, the learner is confronted with a model of the internal and external environments. Thereafter the learner must digest, reflect, and understand the importance of this model to the whole of the subject.

Second, there is the **activity-based** approach to learning, which emphasizes the application of knowledge and skill through techniques. This approach is vital in developing effectiveness. It is seen from two levels of learning:

1 The use and application of *specific skills*. This is the utilization of your cognitive knowledge in a practical manner. These skills emanate from the cognitive aspect of learning, so they are functional skills, specific to the discipline.

   For example, the learner needs to understand the concept of job analysis before he or she tackles an activity that requires the drawing up of a specific job evaluation programme. So knowledge is not seen for its own sake, but is applied and becomes a specific functional skill.

2 The use and application of *generic skills*. These are universal skills which every manager uses irrespective of the wider external environment, the organization, the function and the job. This is seen, for example, in the ability to make clear decisions on the merits of a case. This skill of decision making is found in most of the activities.

There is a relationship between the specific functional skills and the generic skills. The specific functional skills stand alone, but the generic skills cut across them. See figure SK.1.

In this series we use activities to cover both the specific functional and the generic skills. There are five generic skills. We shall examine each of them in turn.

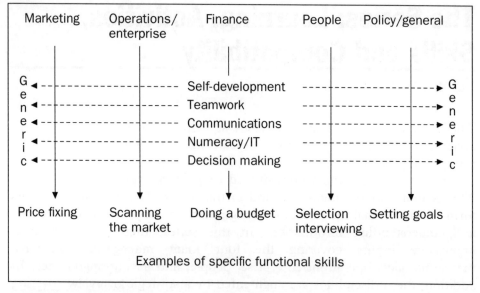

Figure SK.1 Series skills matrix: functional and generic skills.

Self-development

The learner must take responsibility for his or her learning as well as 'learning how to learn'. Time management, work scheduling and organizing the work are involved in the procedural sense. From a learning perspective, sound aspects of learning, from motivation to reward, need to be clarified and understood. The physical process of learning, including changing knowledge, skills and attitudes, may be involved. Individual goals and aspirations need to be recognized alongside the task goals. The ultimate aim of this skill is to facilitate learning transfer to new situations and environments.

Examples of this skill include:

- establishing and clarifying work goals;
- developing procedures and methods of work;
- building key learning characteristics into the process;
- using procedural learning;
- applying insightful learning;
- creating personal developmental plans;
- integrating these personal developmental plans with work goals.

Teamwork

Much of our working lives is concerned with groups. Effective teamwork is thus at a premium. This involves meeting both the task objectives and the socio-emotional processes within the group. This skill can be used for groups in a training or educational context. It can be a bridge between decision making and an awareness of self-development.

Examples of this skill include:

- clarifying the task need of the group;
- receiving, collating, ordering and rendering information;
- discussing, chairing and teamwork within the group;
- identifying the socio-emotional needs and group processes;
- linking these needs and processes to the task goals of the group.

Communications

This covers information and attitude processing within and between individuals. Oral and written communications are important because of the gamut of 'information and attitudinal' processing within the individual. At one level communication may mean writing a report, at another it could involve complex interpersonal relationships.

Examples of this skill include:

- understanding the media, aids, the message and methods;
- overcoming blockages;
- listening;
- presenting a case or commenting on the views of others;
- writing;
- designing material and systems for others to understand your communications.

Numeracy/IT

Managers need a core mastery of numbers and their application. This mastery is critical for planning, control, co-ordination, organization and, above all else, for decision making. Numeracy/IT are not seen as skills for their own sake. Here, they are regarded as the means to an end. These skills enable information and data to be utilized by the effective manager. In particular these skills are seen as an adjunct to decision making.

Examples of this skill include:

- gathering information;
- processing and testing information;

- using measures of accuracy, reliability, probability etc.;
- applying appropriate software packages;
- extrapolating information and trends for problem solving.

Decision making

Management is very much concerned with solving problems and making decisions. As group decisions are covered under teamwork, the emphasis in this decision-making skill is placed on the individual.

Decision making can involve a structured approach to problem solving with appropriate aims and methods. Apart from the 'scientific' approach, we can employ also an imaginative vision towards decision making. One is rational, the other is more like brainstorming.

Examples of this skill include:
- setting objectives and establishing criteria;
- seeking, gathering and processing information;
- deriving alternatives;
- using creative decision making;
- action planning and implementation.

This is *the* skill of management and is given primary importance in the generic skills within the activities as a reflection of everyday reality.

Before we go about learning how to develop into effective managers, it is important to understand the general principles of learning. Both the knowledge-based and the activity-based approaches are set within the environment of these principles. The series has been written to relate to Anderson's sound principles of learning which were developed in *Successful Training Practice*.

- *Motivation* – intrinsic motivation is stimulated by the range and depth of the subject matter and assisted by an action orientation.
- *Knowledge of results* – ongoing feedback is given through the handbook for each book in the series.
- *Scale learning* – each text is divided into six units, which facilitates part learning.
- *Self-pacing* – a map of the unit with objectives, content and an overview helps learners to pace their own progress.
- *Transfer* – realism is enhanced through lifelike simulations which assist learning transfer.
- *Discovery learning* – the series is geared to the learner using self-insight to stimulate learning.
- *Self-development* – self-improvement and an awareness of how we go about learning underpin the series.

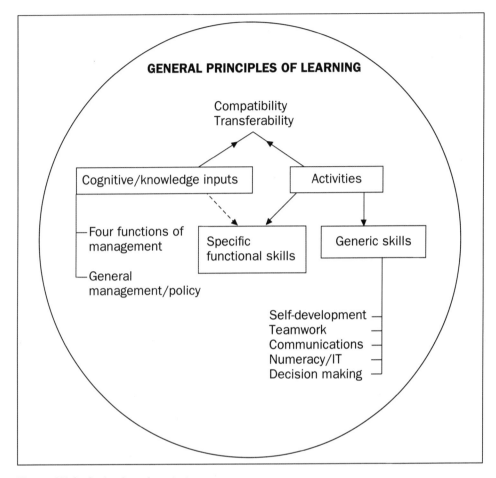

Figure SK.2 Series learning strategy.

- *Active learning* – every activity is based upon this critical component of successful learning.

From what has been said so far, the learning strategy of the series can be outlined in diagrammatic form. (See figure SK.2.)

In figure SK.2, 'compatibility and transferability' are prominent because the learning approach of the series is extremely compatible with the learning approaches of current initiatives in management development. This series is related to a range of learning classification being used in education and training. Consequently it meets the needs of other leading training systems and learning taxonomies. See figures SK.3–SK.6.

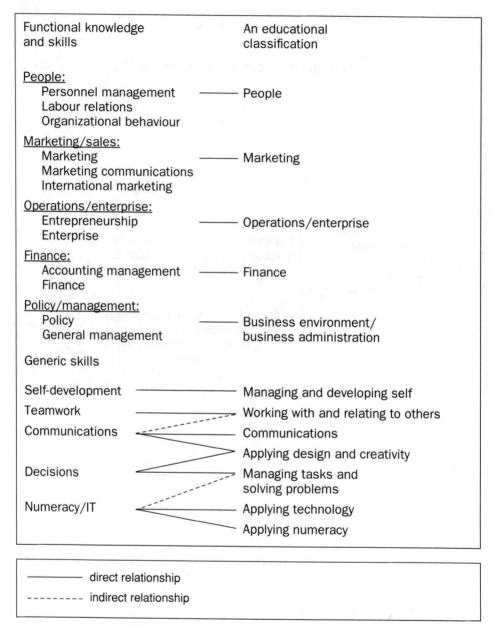

Figure SK.3 Series knowledge and skills related to an educational classification.

Source: Adapted from Business Technician and Education Council, 'Common skills and experience of BTEC programmes'.

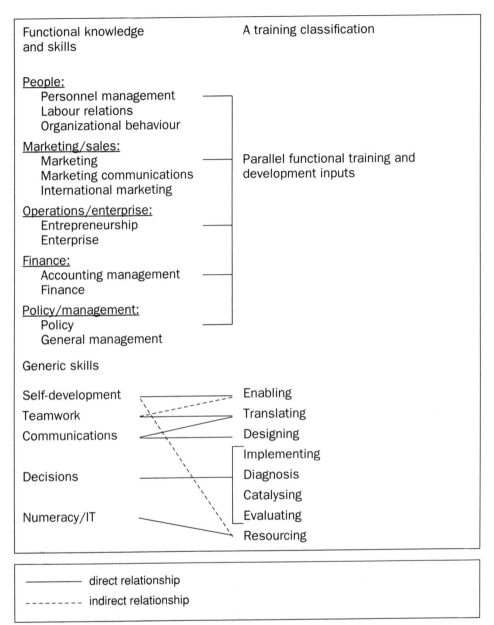

Figure SK.4   Series knowledge and skills related to a training classification.

Source: Adapted from J.A.G. Jones, 'Training intervention strategies' and experience of development programmes.

Functional knowledge and skills	MCI competency
People:	Managing people
Personnel management	
Labour relations	
Organizational behaviour	
Marketing/sales:	Managing operations and managing information (plus new texts pending)
Marketing	
Marketing communications	
International marketing	
Operations/enterprise:	
Entrepreneurship	
Enterprise	
Finance:	Managing finance
Accounting management	
Finance	
Policy/management:	Managing context
Policy	
General management	

Generic skills

Self-development	Managing oneself
Teamwork	Managing others
Communications	Using intellect
Decisions	Planning
Numeracy/IT	

—————— direct relationship

- - - - - - - - indirect relationship

Figure SK.5 Series knowledge and skills related to Management Charter Initiative (MCI) competencies.

Source: Adapted from MCI diploma guidelines.

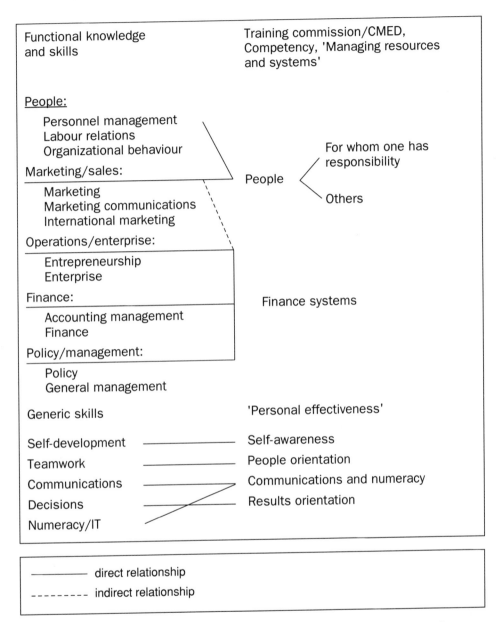

Figure SK.6 Series knowledge and skills related to Training Commission/Council for Management Education (CMED) competencies.

Source: Adapted from Training Commission/CMED, 'Classifying the components of management competencies'.

Preface

❝ It is the kaleidoscope of personnel management which has always made it so attractive to me. How boring it would be to pursue other dull professions.❞

    L. Peach, Director of Personnel and Corporate Affairs, IBM UK Ltd.[1]

Outline Themes

Books need a theme if not a plot. The effectiveness theme with its diverse strands has been covered in the introduction to the series; now we need to look at the distinct themes of and approaches to personnel management.

Personnel management aims to maximize the contribution of people to the world of work. This involves meeting the task or operational objectives of the organization and coming to terms with, if not fully meeting, individual and group needs and aspirations. Particularly during the 1980s, the emphasis of the subject tilted in favour of management at the expense of people. The occupation has become more managerial*ist* in its philosophy and in its priorities, setting a business agenda rather than taking a caring approach to people's welfare. Human resource management (HRM) has increasingly become the 'in' view of people management.

Inherent in this new approach is the view that people are a resource. This is preferable to seeing people as machines, but it can degenerate into seeing them as the extension of the machine. People are also an asset. With nurturing, like capital, people can accumulate interest and increase their contribution to the organization, provided that their needs and wellbeing are catered for by the enterprise. This concept of people as an asset is important, for viewing people purely as a resource depersonalizes their unique contribution to the competitive advantage of an organization, and can lead to the use of overtly manipulative people strategies.

Some of the priorities of the HRM perspective cover the practitioner's tasks of the 1990s. For example, a strategic overview, closer ties with business objectives, an emphasis on change management, flexibility, quality and a customer orientation are all contemporary issues.[2] The flatter organizational structures, greater individualism through appraisals and reward systems linked to anti-collectivism, and a unified culture expressing overtly managerial norms and value systems are used as the means to meet these HRM goals.

In themselves the ends of HRM are not dissimilar to those of personnel management, although the business orientation is far stronger in HRM, and it is more manipulative. The difference may involve the means of achieving these goals, but fundamentally it lies in the philosophical approach. In essence HRM pursues a unitarist or neo-unitarist perspective of one team with one (managerial) core value system, while personnel management can accept more of a pluralistic vision of competing and conflicting group/individual interests and beliefs within the organization. This is not to argue that personnel management is not manipulative, for all management is manipulative; but there is more scope for an acceptance and tolerance of difference within a traditional personnel management framework.

The theme here is to attempt to fuse individual and organizational need. This is not advocating a return to welfarism. Of course, complete fusion of interest would lead us back to a unitarist perspective, and a more pluralistic view of organizational reality is being advocated.[3] We are more concerned with organizational task objectives being in line with the overall dignity of labour and the quality of working life. We need to allow for conflicts of interest and of right between these business and people objectives. It is because of this approach that the book is entitled *Effective Personnel Management*.

However, the perspectives of staff management and people are insufficient. So many books on the subject are written from the perspective of the staff specialist, yet the management of people is very much a line role involving staff advice and guidance. The approach taken here is to 'operationalize' the function of personnel management to give a line manager's frame of reference to day-to-day issues. A strategic insight is given, but only as a context.

Yet it is not a prescriptive, 'how-to-do' type of approach. It needs cognitive awareness – an understanding of concepts and principles before action is taken – and this prevails here. At the same time, the book attempts to address the action orientation of busy managers. As such the book is geared to non-specialists, but students of the subject, new entrants to the specialist personnel management occupation and those taking professional examinations will find it helpful. Unlike many books in the area, it simplifies the message without losing sight of the complexity of the subject matter. As in *Effective Labour Relations* in this series, consideration of legality and legislation, although they are important contexts, has been minimized in order to facilitate cross-cultural and national transferability.

The main themes have been outlined, but of course the subject is far from static. So we will attempt to outline some future priorities (which is always a risky business) and to relate the aims and content – the subplots – of the text to these priorities.

Proposals: Future Priorities in Personnel Management

Some future priorities will be as follows:

- There is a great need to anticipate and to react to the environmental influences on the organization.
- Social responsibility and ethical aspects of management in the community and in the organization will increasingly become an issue.
- Coping with change, from internal flexibility to external adaptability, is going to be a constant factor.
- People will expect more and more out of the working relationship, will resist 'coercive' management and organizational conformity, and will expect a fair reward for their efforts.
- Trade unions will remain an influence in spite of their relative decline.
- Discrimination practices in employment will become less and less acceptable.
- The quickening pace of the competitive environment will demand increased flexibility and efficiency from labour as well as reward systems that have in-built incentives.
- The need for planning will be writ large, with contingency options to manage the changing environments.
- Skilled, competent staff will be essential (and may be difficult to recruit or select) to meet competition from within an industry sector and particularly from abroad.
- People's self-developmental needs at work will have to be met in order to provide intrinsic motivation.
- The design of jobs and work itself will be increasingly questioned as automation increases.
- Some degree of flexible working looks to be here to stay, assuming no radical changes in full employment policies, and this will have an impact on skill and training practices.
- The contribution of people at work to organizational objectives will be seen as critical in managing labour.
- Personnel management, specialist and non-specialist, will be important in acting as a catalyser and facilitator of change at the place of work, so the function will need to be able to evaluate its contribution to the wellbeing of the organization and to think of the individual.

This book builds these proposals into its aims, format and content.

Learning Aims

The learning aims of this book are:
- to provide an understanding of the various perspectives on the roles of personnel management;
- to place personnel management in the context of the organization, its objectives and the changing external environment;
- to place personnel management in the context of meeting individual/group needs at the place of work;
- to develop a range of personnel techniques in order to maximize the contribution of people at work;
- to identify the principal priorities of personnel management and current issues facing the discipline;
- to evaluate the contribution of personnel management to meeting organizational and employee needs.

Format and Content

The activity-based approach implements these aims and underpins the knowledge input. Specific techniques and approaches of personnel management permeate each of the six units of the book and are aligned to the five generic or universal skills outlined in the introduction to the series. The knowledge or information inputs with their respective sub-themes are as follows:

Unit topic	Sub-theme
1 Roles and functions of personnel management	It is argued that a hierarchy of roles exist but the concept of partnership between the line and staff personnel managers is critical. The professionalization of the occupation is also debated.
2 Manpower planning, recruitment and selection	The systematic approach, in spite of its mechanistic limits, is put forward as the most suitable way to maximize success and minimize failure.
3 Money and rewards	The trend to individualize payment is noted and the view of rewards and incentives rather than 'compensation' is pursued.

Unit topic	*Sub-theme*
4 Training	The merging of task and people needs is seen here through a new approach to a training model, taking account of external environmental and internal organizational variables.
5 Development	Individual, management and organizational change and development are covered in this section, with the argument that all three are critical to successful change, flexibility and adaptability.
6 Evaluation and audit	The various perspectives of the different clients of personnel management are adopted as a baseline from which to evaluate effective personnel management.

An Outline of the Units

To conclude this introduction, the summary that follows gives an outline of the six units of the book:

- *Unit One* demonstrates the functions and roles of professional personnel management.
- *Unit Two* considers the manpower plan and internal labour 'resourcing' of the organization from job analysis through recruitment to selection.
- *Unit Three* relates internal payment levels and systems to the external environment and considers a range of payment methods and techniques, particularly incentives and job evaluation.
- *Unit Four* conducts an analysis of training from needs analysis and design to implementation, with reference to particular functions and skills.
- *Unit Five* considers the development of the individual, management and the organization through a variety of techniques and methods.
- *Unit Six* evaluates the strategic and operational input of personnel management in the organization and considers its input to individual/group needs at work.

Notes

1 Peach, 'A practitioner's view of personnel excellence'.
2 These examples of issues of the 1990s are pursued in part in this book and elsewhere in the series. See the further reading list below.
3 See Fox, *A Sociology of Work in Industry*.

Further reading

Strategic overview: see Anderson and Barker, *Effective Business Policy*.

Change management: see Anderson, *Effective General Management*; and Anderson and Kyprianou, *Effective Organizational Behaviour*.

Flexibility: see Anderson, *Effective Labour Relations*.

Quality: see Anderson, *Effective General Management*; and Anderson and Dobson, *Effective Marketing*.

Customer orientation: see Anderson, Dobson and Patterson, *Effective International Marketing*; Anderson and Dobson, *Effective Marketing*; Anderson and Kleiner, *Effective Marketing Communications*; Anderson and Woodcock, *Effective Entrepreneurship*; and Anderson and Barker, *Effective Enterprise Management*.

Organizational structures: see Anderson and Kyprianou, *Effective Organizational Behaviour*; and Anderson, *Effective General Management*.

Individualism, reward and collectivism: see Anderson, *Effective Labour Relations*.

Acknowledgements

I would like to thank all my friends at Blackwell Publishers for their work assistance, commitment and encouragement. Thanks go to Fiona Sewell and Brigitte Lee on the editorial front, and to VAP on the production front. To Tim Goodfellow and to Richard Jackman I owe an immense gratitude not only for this book, but for the whole series.

The author and publisher would also like to thank Delia Goldring, Brenda Jarman, Samantha Jenkins and Evelyne Lee-Barber for their advice and assistance in the development of this book.

Unit One

Roles and Functions of Personnel Management

Learning Objectives

After completing this unit you should be able to:

- place personnel management in a historical context;

- distinguish the various roles and functions of personnel management;

- allocate staff and line responsibilities;

- examine the degree of professionalization that has occurred within the occupation;

- apply the generic skills.

Contents

Overview: A Rose by Any Other Name

Management Roles

The Job Over Time

▶ Trade unions

▶ Welfare

▶ Scientific management

▶ Human relations philosophy

▶ The behavioural sciences

▶ The organizational context

▶ The wider environment

▶ Management

The Job Itself

▶ Pigors and Myers

▶ Anthony and Crichton (1)

▶ Anthony and Crichton (2)

▶ Livy

▶ Tyson

The Person In the Job

The Degree of Professionalism

Line–Staff–Functional Relationships

Unit One

❝ Every aspect of a firm's activities is determined by the competence, motivation and general effectiveness of its human organization. Of all the tasks of management, managing the human component is the central and most important task, because all else depends on how well it is done. ❞

R. Likert[1]

Overview: A Rose by Any Other Name

Personnel management is concerned with the human aspects of the organization. The UK Institute of Personnel Management (IPM) currently defines it as: 'that part of management concerned with people at work and their relationship within an enterprise'. The aim of this people management, according to the IPM, is to build an 'effective organisation' while 'having regard for the well being of the individual and of working groups'. So the primary aim is seen to be to meet organizational aims, while people's aspirations should not be ignored, but are subordinated to these wider goals. This contrasts with an earlier (1963) IPM definition: 'Personnel management aims to achieve both efficiency and justice, neither of which can be pursued successfully without the other.' In this definition the organizational or task aims seem to be equal to the people aims. This shift in emphasis is very significant. The later definition is task-oriented, with people being seen to be part of that task; the earlier view talks of both task and people aims as being intertwined. The 1963 definition goes on to say:

> It seeks to bring together and develop into an effective organisation the men and women who make up an enterprise, enabling each to make his own best contribution to its success both as an individual and as a member of a working group. It seeks to provide fair terms and conditions of employment and satisfying work for those employed.

This definition is more acceptable and is used as a basis for this book. This is not advocating a relaxed style of country-club management: it is emphasizing that without people's needs and aspirations being appreciated, the task aims will not be fully met.

The latest trend (see Box PM1.1) is to portray personnel management as human resource management (HRM). In this view, people are a

3

BOX PM1.1

Personnel management v. human resource management

This is not a barren academic debate. It is a discussion about the whole nature of people management, the relationship between task (business need) and individual aspiration, a traditional UK approach and creeping 'Japanization', and ultimately between differences in philosophy. It has an impact on the whole subject.

The first idea to dispose of is that there is some holistic view of personnel management (PM) and one approach to human resource management (HRM). PM covers a whole spectrum of philosophies: from the paternalism of some retail organizations, with their chiropodists looking after the feet of their workers, to the 'commercialese' of 'hire-and-fire' newspaper firms that recruit and dismiss sales people almost on a weekly basis; from the developmental perspectives of some local authorities, with their 'investors in people' awards, to the hard-nosed labour relations of the education, coal, steel and transport 'industries'. A common philosophy is difficult to pin down. Equally, within HRM, there is a 'soft' approach, with an emphasis on leadership, communication and motivation, which responds to the call of the human relations school that permeates many personnel functions; and there is a 'hard' variation, with an emphasis on qualification, calculations and business needs, which mirrors the labour relations sections of many personnel departments. This is not to say that PM and HRM are the same old wine in two new bottles, for their aspirations, philosophy and approaches are different – although the last of these may be a difference of degree.

The aspirations of PM revolve around the optimum use of people to benefit the organization, the individual and the community. Some integration of people and task has always been an aim of PM. Crude capitalism has been tempered by aspirations concerning social responsibility, justice, the dignity of labour and the needs of people for some job satisfaction. The socio-legal obligations come from inside and outside the organization. But we need to be clear: when the task needs are in conflict with the people needs, there is no contest; the task is the usual champion.

There seems less dignity of labour involved in the HRM approach. The aspiration of the HRM vision is the optimum use of people to benefit the business organization. Of course socio-legal obligations must be met, but the aim is 'business excellence'. The approach is managerialist.

Although both PM and HRM draw upon a human relations philosophy and that of the behavioural sciences, the philosophical basis looks different and the value systems are different. PM tends to recognize the various 'constituents' of an organization, including trade unions and their collectivity; HRM looks to more of a team effort, without such an 'opposition' from trade unions. The HRM approach is more unitarist, although many in the PM approach in non-union firms may also subscribe to this philosophy. The HRM people are business- or market-led while the PM people tend to be more people- and business-led. The HRM people wish to alter norms and the culture of whole organizations by changing the value systems; under PM, only the organizational development and management development specialists would tackle such a revolution. Both groups have a strategic view of things, and it would be incorrect to suggest that PM is merely an operational or administrative function. Equally, both see people as important contributors to the organization, but they become a resource like other resources in the HRM view, to be used and put aside as required.

In practice, both PM and HRM seek top management support, although it becomes part of the 'cascade' effect (percolating down from the top) for HRM, while PM may still use an 'intervention strategy' (creating and managing change) for given problems. PM needs to focus on all employees; HRM looks to the commitment of the core workers, perhaps to the detriment of the peripheral labour force. Collectivity is recognized by some in PM, while 'mutuality', harmonization, co-operation and integration are the policies adopted by HRM.

On paper, people are no longer an 'unco-operative cost' but a 'co-operative resource' to HRM, but when recession bites the costs are dominant and the resources are 'sold off' whether they co-operated or not.

Changes in workplace norms are possible under PM and critical under HRM.

Finally, the role of line management changes or, rather, becomes more blurred under HRM. The line–staff division is the norm under PM, with the line implementing and the staff advising; with HRM the line assumes more of an HRM vision, while the perspective of the HRM specialist becomes more that of a line or business manager.

In this book, 'personnel management', with its emphasis on task and people, is preferred.

resource like other organizational resources. High-level strategic planning is inherent in this perspective, and a greater task or organizational orientation comes to the fore. In a word, it aims to put personnel management on the same business footing as finance, marketing and operational management. In itself this is not a bad thing, but people are more than a mere resource to be manipulated by management, and the implication is that the task needs dominate the people needs even more fully than in the later IPM definition. Hence the philosophy of this book is reflected in the term **personnel management**.

The organizational boundary does not limit the subject either, for political, economic, social and technological changes in the wider community and the external environment impinge on, and often make for, the organizational agenda of personnel management. This agenda is not the sole preserve of the staff specialist working in the personnel or training department. Quite the reverse: the people specialist should be an advisor to the mainstream line management, who must have the ultimate say over 'their' people management. So effective personnel management is a partnership between the staff specialist and the line or operational executive, with both parties taking heed of individual and group needs and aspirations.

Before looking at the roles and scope of current personnel management, we need to go back a little, for a knowledge of the past gives us a perspective on the present – if not the future.

Management Roles

A role is a pattern of behaviour associated with a position. As most societies and work organizations have some hierarchical basis, roles can be placed in a pyramid, prompted by the wider society or the organization itself. Equally, the individual managers bring to their work roles their own distinct personalities and attitudes, which may modify their prescribed organizational roles.

At the same time, roles are quite fluid, as they are based on constant interaction with others, and perceptions of 'what is' and 'what should be' differ. The manager has many such 'interactions'. For senior managers, in particular, the needs and wishes of the owners or stockholders or 'membership' must be met. Customers, clients and suppliers can modify prescribed roles as well. Perhaps a wider view of 'social responsibility' and the ethical considerations of the community outside of the organization needs to be mentioned in this mixture of roles. Other ingredients include the expectations of others within the organization: boss, peers and subordinates.

Mintzberg[2] adds the dimension of time to give the four variables impacting on work roles:

- the job in the environment
- the job over time
- the job itself
- the person in the job

We will address the 'job over time' by looking at historical themes and specific job aims at given times. The 'environmental influences' follow on in separate units. The 'person in the job' is difficult to determine, although individual differences are thoroughly examined in another book of this series.[3] Consequently, we look at a series of role sets and ask you to complete your preferred selection (and your views on your organization's selection as well). *The bulk of this unit is concerned with 'the job itself' and its responsibilities and work allocation.*

Before we do this, Mintzberg's vision of managerial roles as they affect personnel managers (specialist and non-specialist) need to be teased out. Some ten roles are seen to exist in three 'clusters':

- 'interpersonal' – derived from the formal authority vested in the individual by the organization;
- 'informational' – derived from 'interpersonal roles';
- 'decisional' – made possible by the informational role.

The roles themselves form a gestalt, or integrated whole, but there may be differing emphasis on one or more roles (from whatever source).

Box PM1.2 gives more detail on these roles as they apply to people managers. This role classification is useful in giving the main aspects of management. It also helps to address the executive–line division from the advisory and support services of the specialists. The specific responsibilities on 'pure' personnel issues will be picked up later in this unit.

BOX PM1.2

Managerial roles and people managers

Role	Description	Application to non-specialist people manager's personnel duties	Application to specialist people manager
Figurehead	Symbolic function	Top managers may be called upon to 'open' colleges/schools/ events, etc. in local labour market.	May have to represent organization at external events, e.g. IPM etc.
Leader	Staffing, training and motivation	Line authority to lead and motivate subordinates.	Advises on same: key function.
Liaison	Contact maintenance	Day-to-day contact with staff: prefers an 'open-door' philosophy.	'Manages' through other managers: critical role.

Role	Description	Application to non-specialist people manager's personnel duties	Application to specialist people manager
Monitor	Nerve-centre of information	No need to be an organizational spy, and too much control over staff can demotivate: some monitoring sought.	Should beware of 'policing' the organization: needs constant information/intelligence, not gossip.
Disseminator	Transmitting information internally	Important in maintaining motivated staff and not keeping them in the dark over relevant organizational information.	Co-ordinates organization-based communications systems, e.g. house journals.
Spokesperson	Transmitting information externally	Usually gives bad news (e.g. lay-offs, redundancies, strikes etc.) to the specialist; often tells good news (e.g. new opening) him or herself.	Can end up in a PR role justifying the unjustifiable, so beware.
Entrepreneur	Opportunity seeker	'Natural' to some functions, e.g. sales/marketing, more than others, e.g. finance/ accounting; but a 'live' organization needs to be aware of opportunities.	Needs to be able to initiate structured change strategies rather than being purely opportunistic.

Role	Description	Application to non-specialist people manager's personnel duties	Application to specialist people manager
Disturbance handler	Takes corrective action	Many non-specialist labour managers would prefer to pass this hot parcel to the specialist, but this is an error of judgement – advice can be sought.	Gives uniformity; should beware of being the 'hit man'. Conflict is easier to stem or channel at root – advise line on policies and tactics.
Negotiator	Representative role	Day-to-day 'negotiations' with staff and with his or her boss over manpower.	May be chief negotiator with unions or advisory service provider.
Resource allocator	Makes and approves decisions	Decisions on staff should be vested in line management whenever possible.	Advises and guides, but approval (e.g. manning levels) may be sought as cost-effective strategy.

Source: Adapted from Mintzberg, *The Nature of Management Work*

The Job Over Time

Resisting the temptation to write a historical tract, we will instead take a thematic approach, noting some of the main influences on the specialist activity of personnel management, which in turn influenced non-specialists as well. 'Still photographs' at key times will be given to illustrate the changing role emphasis within the UK. Minimizing detailed British history will also facilitate transferability to other cultures.

Some of the main themes are:

- trade unions
- welfare
- scientific management
- human relations philosophy
- the behavioural sciences

- the organizational context
- the wider environment
- management

(See also the appendix on 'The personnel function' for a brief historical overview of the specialist function in the UK.)

Trade unions

The trade union movement aims to maintain and improve the working lives of employees. As such, it shares the people and operational side of the enterprise with personnel managers (line and staff). The other functions of management – marketing, finance, general management and policy – tend solely to be the prerogative of management.

The late 1880s in the UK witnessed a phenomenal growth of trade unionism among the unskilled and semi-skilled classes, and an increase in overt conflict between workers and owners or managers. This conflict was the most direct means by which the relatively unskilled could attain their objectives, and contrasted with the less radical route of the better-heeled artisan class of craftworkers, who had greater skill and expertise in the labour market, the administrative and organizational backup of established unions, and more conservative leaders. Either way, employers were faced with some tough 'negotiations' on their own or through their employers' associations. The blacklisting of strikers, the lock-out, the requirement for workers to sign a document declaring that they would not become trade unionists, and the use of blackleg labour illustrate one coercive approach by employers. According to many trade unionists, a more subtle strategy would have been the establishment of personnel or welfare officers.

This is not to deny the genuine, often almost religious belief in 'industrial betterment' of the pioneers of personnel management. However, it cannot be denied that the origins of the movement coincided with a very 'active' (militant) period of trade union history.[4] The accommodation of trade union aims and aspirations can be seen going on under the 'labour officer' mantle right up to the 1970s – if not beyond.[5]

The attempt to neutralize trade unions by a form of employer-based paternalism is another sub-plot running through this theme. Manifestations can be found in famous retail stores and multinational American computing companies as well as in the 'Japanization' trends going on in both north European and North American companies. Indeed, as we have seen, the human resource movement owes some of its philosophy to this 'unitarist' perspective.[6] Briefly, the unitary viewpoint is based on the extended family or team concept, with all partners, associates and employees pulling together, in the same direction as management, to meet the organizational goals. The aim is harmony, and conflict, where it exists, is seen as a short-term aberration. In a pluralist perspective, the organization is made up of diverse competing groups probably with diverse aims. Consequently, conflict is likely to resolve these interests. The radical perspective assumes there will be more conflict between labour and management, with little or no real common interest between the parties.

Welfare

It is very easy to be cynical about the welfarist traditions of personnel management. It is clear that the movement emerged at the same time as a turbulent period of union growth, but welfarism is more than a mere ploy against 'militant' unions. There was a sound belief in 'industrial betterment', a genuine concern for the lot of your fellow human being, and a positive reaction against the worst excesses of the 'sweated trades'. Both Quaker and Christian Socialist ideologies permeated the actions of these 'founding mothers' – for they were usually female and often quite well-heeled.

Perhaps this 'class collaboration' went back further:

> *The reasonable employer and the reasonable trade unionist worker;*
> *the fair capitalist and the fair worker, the big-hearted bourgeois,*
> *friend of the workers, and the narrow-bourgeois-minded proletarian*
> *condition one another, and are both corollaries of one and the same*
> *relationship, whose foundation was the economic position of Britain*
> *from the middle of the nineteenth century.*[7]

The philanthropists had a captive 'market'. According to Niven,[8] the basic working week in the late 1870s to early 1880s was some 60 hours; children could be employed at the age of 12; one-third of the population at the turn of the century was below the poverty line, with no pensions, benefits or unemployment monies.

The welfarist views of the pioneers of personnel management have found a natural home in paternalistic organizations. An anecdote may give a perspective: when I joined a company as a personnel manager, it was expected that I should attend all the funerals of staff, former employees and pensioners of the firm. Employees lived in company houses, and a welfare-cum-sports club organized cheap beer and family events such as sports days.

The 'cradle-to-the-grave' paternalism of some American and Japanese firms can be cited in this context. A useful analysis of the Japanese phenomenon is provided by Palmer[9] (see Box PM1.3).

Even outside of these overtly paternalistic firms, the term 'welfare' has moved on to become 'employee services'. Assistance with house removal, stress counselling, discussion groups, personal counselling and work-outs in the gym may all come under this banner. Hence the welfarist tradition, although modified, is still an influence on present-day UK personnel

---

BOX PM1.3

Japanese paternalism and personnel management

To Palmer much of management of the employment relationship is concerned with control. She distinguishes between physical control over the 'task performance', through detailed work schedules, authority allocation and divisions of labour, and more remote controls through 'personnel policy'. Written rules, covering entry to exit, contractual relationships, fixed salaries and career structures, facilitate this latter, 'hands-off' method of control.

In the Japanese context, the core tenets of the large firms can be seen as follows:
- There is a lifetime commitment to employees, to give permanent status.
- A group responsibility is given for a specific task.
- The salary scales and career structures are reward-oriented.

She concludes her review on the Japanese influence by stating: '[In Japan] the emphasis has been on the construction of bureaucratic personnel policies, not bureaucratic control over task performance.'

Source: Adapted from Palmer, *British Industrial Relations*

---

management. Further, the 'Japanization' of industry looks to be a force of the future,[10] so the philosophy may permeate across cultures. We will return to this area later.

Scientific management

Altruism was not the only motive for paternalism. Part of the scientific management originally propounded by Taylor was a realization that the wellbeing of the employee was linked to business efficiency. This is not the pure 'contented cows give the best milk' philosophy of the later human relations views, but efficiency and the results of philanthropy and enlightenment may merge. The scientific managers may not have implemented Taylor's vision fully, but his overriding principles did give some cognizance of people which is often ignored. The principles were that:

- management should be scientific and methodical, to avoid rule-of-thumb judgements;
- each job had a right way and right method;
- there should be a division between mental work (management) and manual work (employer);
- 'scientific' selection and training should occur;
- there should be a 'co-operative system' between managers and managed.

Yet it was left to a more enlightened philosophy to guide personnel managers throughout the years, with the views of the human relations theorists.

Human relations philosophy

It is a matter of great debate whether ideas galvanize people into action or whether the action occurs and the philosophical trappings are used to justify or rationalize events. In the case of personnel management, the human relations approach to people has provided a positive counter to the task-specialization and people-negation views of scientific management, as well as providing a liberal umbrella for self-expression – if not self-actualization – at the place of work.

The basic principles of this philosophy are these:

- The organization is a social entity with real people, not just a machine.
- Group norms can set standards of behaviour and of performance or group output.
- Non-economic incentives, such as people relationships, are an important part of the job.
- People do not just work independently; groups can make decisions as well.

Examples of this approach will be developed later.

The behavioural sciences

If human relations philosophy provides a backdrop to personnel management, the social or behavioural sciences have provided the tools and the methods of putting the philosophy into effect.

The work of Lupton can be cited in this regard,[11] for he believed that the personnel practitioner had to have a stock of social scientific techniques which he or she could call upon. In *Industrial Behaviour and Personnel Management*, he advocated the duality of the social scientist's work: not only did he or she have to satisfy human needs at work, but the analysis and functioning of the 'social structure' (organization) was equally important. This diagnosis could minimize the 'friction' between labour and capital.

The behavioural science approach can be summarized as follows:[12]

- A logical and systematic approach is used.
- At the outset, a more creative or brainstorming type of problem solving may be used in conjunction with this systematic vision.
- The issue is often given the focus of a problem or perceived problem to management.
- From these early steps a hypothesis may be formulated.
- The data, views and analysis are next carried out in the field and at a desk.

- Next comes the inference phase, when the problem and research are combined and conclusions are drawn from them.
- A report, seminar or public presentation should occur to give a wide audience to the findings and recommendations.

Some of the tools or approaches of the behavioural sciences which may assist the manager of personnel have been described by Lupton:[13]

- clarity of roles and allocation of responsibilities;
- models of 'dynamic' organizations;
- communication and problem-solving 'networks';
- incentives and motivation of the labour force;
- needs and their satisfaction;
- labour relations.

As an aside, this useful checklist gives some insight into how the behavioural sciences can be applied for the mutual benefit of the various actors.

However, scientific knowledge and skills cannot be fully insulated from an organizational context. The behavioural scientist, or the external researcher coming into the organization from a consultancy or business school, may have more of a purist's approach, but for the practitioner manager the organizational context becomes the organizational reality, and 'scientific' detachment may be more difficult.

The organizational context

Organizations differ. No two institutions are identical, and even in the same company we find significant differences between subsidiaries and between plants and cost centres. Goals, aims, ownership, leadership, the labour force and its mix, the product, the predominant technology, the workflow, the degree of union penetration, the organizational type and structure, the predominant style of management, the degree of delegated decision making, etc., all contribute to this uniqueness.

One example will suffice: the size of a firm has a definite impact on the personnel management within the organization. Small to medium-sized firms (under 200 employees) will tend not to have a specialist personnel person, and personnel management, if it exists, will be the preserve of the line manager. With increased bureaucratization and size, organizations develop a more specialist function, and the personnel department can begin to monopolize much of the people management, often to the detriment of line management. I worked for one firm where there were several hundred personnel specialists.

The wider environment

Organizations do not exist in a vacuum. Managers involved in sales, marketing and business policy are very conscious of the fickleness of the external environment; but they are not alone in their interaction with it.

Changes in political, economic, social and political features of the external environment have an impact on the management of labour. Take one example: the role of the state. The twentieth century has witnessed greater state involvement in all aspects of our lives. Even under *laissez-faire* governments such as Thatcher's and Major's administrations, the state does intervene in the work relationship; for instance, in legislation between 'master' and 'servant'. There has been protectionist legislation such as that for redundancy payments, employment protection, and health and safety. There have been more radical acts, such as equal pay and equal opportunity, in an attempt to remove the worst abuses of discrimination in employment. There has been legislation to advance the interests of trade unionists (the Trade Union and Labour Relations Act 1974) and other acts to curb collective union power (1982) if not to strengthen individual rights.

The history of state involvement in pay regulation is another good example of its 'interfering' in the relationships of people at work. For instance, at the time of writing, the Conservative government in the UK has recently installed a pay limit (if not freeze) on all employees within the state sector.

Management

If the early phases of personnel management were dominated by welfarism, the later phases since the 1980s seem to be dominated by managerialism. Personnel managers are no longer the people in the middle, and they join their line colleagues as managers first, with knowledge of and skills in how to handle, if not manipulate, labour for the benefit of the organization (see Activity PM1.1).

The Job Itself

Clearly, there is both a specialist job of personnel management and also a non-specialist operational management function, combining that functional specialism with that of, say, finance, production or sales. A lot of the research on roles focuses on the specialist activity. In part this recognizes the historical dichotomy of business need versus individual need, the search for a role and an obsession with professional status. A useful way forward is to examine the research on roles, noting constraints and opportunities as well as the degree of transferability to non-specialist labour managers.

ACTIVITY PM1.1

A NEW MANAGEMENT TAKES OVER

Activity code
- ✔ Self-development
- ✔ Teamwork
- ✔ Communications
- ☐ Numeracy/IT
- ✔ Decisions

Malmö Communications, a Swedish-based organization with its core business in telecommunications, had recently taken over an established peripheral systems company in the United Kingdom.

Peripheral (UK), the systems firm, employed 220 people. It had a strong marketing and customer liaison section based at Peterborough. Indeed, 123 people were involved with services, software support, testing and in-house repair work under the banner of 'customer care'. The products range from powerful minicomputers with economical standard configurations and built-in expansion capability, suitable for introductory levels, to the powerful System 95, ideally suited for signal conditioning, process control and mass data applications.

The firm was unionized and the relationship with the white-collar union was reasonable, while the technicians and craftworkers in the manual engineering union had experienced a more troubled relationship with management over the years.

Malmö decided to clear out some of the top managers, and Heidi Hardnut was put in charge of the personnel function. Her background was that of high technology, local government and academic 'management' at a business school. The operations director, Bill Marsh, came from a Japanese plant in the north of England. Between them they were in control of the human resources of the firm.

Malmö had a hard, cost-effective philosophy and a reputation for being tough to their subsidiaries. Costs were seen as a problem. They decided on a policy of cost-cutting on labour, linked to 'good' personnel management policies. After consultation with the new management team at the top (the junior managers remained in post) they decided that personnel management should have a new profile. The unions would be totally ignored or bypassed, flexiworking would be introduced, salaries would be incentive-based, a new appraisal scheme would provide motivation for all, the management would go direct to the workers, quality would be emphasized and customer care would mean what it said. 'Attitudinal training' would reinforce these changes in status so that the firm could become one happy family – and one fit family, with little 'slack', so that it could fight off the competition.

The programme went into effect. Compulsory redundancies at the beginning did little for morale. The personnel section was now the 'HR advisors' and all line managers from director to supervisor were 'HR managers'. Restructuring occurred, with subsequent job changes, role reallocation and redundancy. The labour force had been cut by almost one-third in the first year and was now (in the second year) down to 110.

The communications section of the HR department (i.e. the new graduate trainee) put out a monthly newsletter direct to the staff, entitled *Open System*. It was seen as a propaganda sheet by some, ignored by others and read avidly by some supervisors, for it was the first time ever that top management had bothered to communicate with them.

A quality programme was run with the help of external consultants. All staff members attended a two-day session in batches of ten people.

Next there was an assault on the unions. Seriously weakened by the dismal economic conditions outside the firm, they were in no position to offer much resistance. Allowances were consolidated into basic rates, and overtime stopped being paid, although it could still be worked as all employees were now called 'staff associates'. Grades were now being revamped so that career streams could be made for all employees.

Tom Smith, a normally affable fellow with a bilingual ability, was the MD and the liaison point with Sweden. He called his normal monthly report meetings and opened the session by saying to both Hardnut and Marsh:

> Malmö are not happy. I'm not happy. Our output is falling. Morale is at an all-time low. In spite of this quality programme both Malmö and I are still getting complaints on customer service. Our costs have certainly tumbled but our profitability is falling as well. Our productivity per person has dropped. We've just missed the huge Aerospace contract, and the contract with Construction Inc., that new American firm, looks to be a non-runner. The troops are not happy and you are my officers.
>
> Look, call me old-fashioned if you like, but I think that all this new-fangled people stuff has alienated our people. We need change but not this change. Both of you – get out – and justify your position in a report by tomorrow. This is serious. I've got to get back to Malmö and they are not very happy.

The people managers left the room.

1 Analyse the personnel issues in this case.
2 Itemize and analyse the HR strategies being pursued. Can you justify the activities of the people managers?
3 Assuming some change is required, on reflection how would you tackle some of these areas? (Report sought: max. 200 words.)

Pigors and Myers[14]

The conventional role was seen as one of advice and *service to others*. In addition, the specialist would have some 'line' authority heading his or her own department, and hence an *executive role*. The more intangible advisory role was used to demonstrate the level or type of service, so he or she became an *educator.*

Finally, setting up and monitoring processes within the organization led to the role of a *controller.*

Anthony and Crichton (1)

Four distinct roles were seen to exist: (1) management of part of the organization; (2) part management of the whole organization; (3) liaison officer between parts of the organization; and (4) a public relations role. To all intents and purposes, the specialist personnel managers become 'line managers' when they co-ordinate the activities of their own department, and this is 'management of part of the organization'. 'Part management' is the sharing role with their non-specialist colleagues in line management. The 'liaison' and 'public relations' roles mean servicing committees and providing a public face inside and outside the organization. The non-specialist can identify with most of these roles, although ambiguity exists as to the boundaries of 'managing part of the organization'.

Anthony and Crichton (2)

Another scheme has been proposed, covering a whole role set:

- **consultant** – conducting research into the structure etc. of the organization and recommending improvements;
- **employment planning** – still doing some diagnostic evaluation but also ensuring that the procedures were in line with the policies;
- **maintenance** – combining the existing procedures while minimizing any disruption to the operation;
- **operational** – a more standardized approach with specific routines and specific procedures;
- **clerical** – more mundane, statistical and routine administration.

These roles are not necessarily mutually exclusive, for in my experience a busy personnel department, often understaffed and under-resourced, means that the personnel manager may have to move up and down this hierarchy on the same day. Larger organizations usually mean smaller jobs, so the specialist practitioner may stay at one level for a far longer period.

If we use the terms 'strategic', 'maintenance' and 'operational' as in decision-making theory, the line manager or non-specialist manager of labour could relate to this role set. The planning of employment would have to widen out and the clerical role would have to be dropped to be meaningful to most line managers.

Livy

Another role set is provided by Livy:

- **analyst** – acts on own initiative and diagnoses problems;
- **consultant** – gives specialist advice to others;
- **problem solver** – more of a pragmatic role (if not political);
- **resourcer** – finds, deploys and maintains people;
- **executive** – implements agreed policies and does more routine work.

With the exception of the consultant role on people, this set would be transferable to most line managers of labour.

Tyson

Although writing in a different context, Tyson argues for the organization context to be taken into account to determine the 'model' of personnel management being used:

- **administrative/support** – a supporting act to line management with a focus on the basics of a routine activity; welfare evident;
- **systems/reactive** – a more sophisticated version with a strong industrial relations flavour, aiming to maintain some stability;
- **business manager** – more of a strategic role with a longer time scale and integration with the top management's view of the business.

Tyson goes on to relate these models to various organizational types.

The line manager of labour can clearly identify with the business manager role and the systems role depending on the degree of unionization and the dominant industrial relations system within the organization. The support role is, of course, less relevant to this line official.

For my own part and from the perspective of the line–staff relationship, where it exists, the division between 'management of part of the organization' and 'part management of the whole organization' is useful when allied to Livy's classification.

In another context[15] we find 'pure' trainer roles which may be transferred and amended:

- **consultant/problem solver** – an interventionist who enters perceived problems and facilitates solutions in conjunction with the line manager;
- **designer** – follows on from the problem-solving vision with recommendations on policies, procedures and techniques;
- **implementer** – puts the designs into effect and monitors them accordingly; has to be a shared role with the line manager of labour for things to be put into effect;
- **administrator/manager** – involves the personnel department or section and its overview as well as more routine and potentially tedious statistics and record keeping, etc.

This training hierarchy of roles seems to be transferable both to the specialist and the line labour manager (if we drop the term 'consultant' and use 'problem solver').

Yet in spite of all these role classifications of the job itself, or indeed as a reflection of them and their dichotomy, there are some difficulties with the specialist job which also have an impact on line management. Wilson, for example, sees various signs of actual and potential malaise:[16]

- The function is fragmented, with artificial distinctions between the likes of salary administration and management development resulting in different approaches to people.
- Systems become a fetish and maintenance of administrative efficiency becomes a goal in itself.
- Low professionalism equates to low credibility, with the function being used as a dumping ground for failed line managers.
- Bureaucratic, not people, roles develop, with overelaborate policies and procedures.
- A reactive 'bush-fire' mentality ensures that little time is available for either preventative medicine or longer-term planning.

An example from my own experience may be illustrative of Wilson's points. This particular firm had several hundred personnel people on a site and divisional basis with a duplication of jobs at head office. Each specialism kept its own 'territorial integrity', which meant there was a powerful personnel director who could divide and rule. Standing instructions on an army-like basis also existed. If professionalism is linked to IPM membership as a rule of thumb (it does not fully equate of course), only a handful of the multitude were professional. Interestingly enough, the senior personnel people were ex-line managers rather than personnel professionals, so the 'dumping ground' vision may apply, although 'failed line managers' looks to be a little harsh. The environment was certainly quick-moving and reactive.

Legge is equally critical.[17] The specialists tend to be less than positive in their approach, which is typically prescriptive and always looking for the 'best way'. This lack of analysis spreads to the wider environment, for many lack a context for what they are doing. Initiative taking is out, while reaction to events is in vogue. Conventional wisdom dominates at the expense of new precepts, while 'maintenance' not 'change' governs the philosophy of work. Little action research seems to occur.

Hopefully the critiques of both Wilson and Legge have been overtaken by events. I am not sure, though: my anecdotal evidence in consultancy and in supervising many work-based postgraduate dissertations in a variety of organizations seems to reiterate some of this critique. However, change is emphasized more now, and professionalism (see below) seems to be improving. The fragmentation, systems and bureaucratic fetish still remain while the function, like training, seems to grasp the latest fad or technique with an alarming lack of discrimination. So change in the later 1980s and early 1990s may have altered Legge's vision in some organizations. Either way, the jobs need to take account of these critiques.

To work meaningfully alongside the line manager of labour, the personnel specialist needs to run and maintain the 'systems' and deal with day-to-day problems. But the context is fluid and becoming even more so. The dynamics of change (external and internal) need to be understood, and a 'maintenance vision' is not adequate for managing these changing scenarios. Equally, the personnel specialist needs the assistance and the partnership of the line manager of people, and a working understanding of the labour force and its needs and aspirations as well. Equally, the person in the job must take a professional approach to the tasks being undertaken.

The Person In the Job

The individual manager will have his or her own concept of personnel management, style and approach to the management of labour. These may tally with those of the organization to give what Pettigrew and Reason would call a cultural 'fit'.[18] Individual differences in personnel specialists and line labour managers will be evident in the aspect of the role they emphasize, and in how they act in their role. Personality, attitudes, value systems, motivation and diverse styles will be to the fore. Watson,[19] an experienced practitioner and academic, examined the world of the personnel manager, the individual experiences and the role within employing organizations. For example, he looks at occupational entry, which gives some clue to orientations, values and judgements. The career was more or less the initial choice for 24 per cent of his sample. During a career, an employee-initiated move into personnel was largely seen as 'career advancement' by 29 per cent. About 20 per cent had moved, usually at the initiative of the employee, through rejection or incapacity in their previous work. Hence, occupational entry was not initiated in the main by the individual 'professional', but was more often stimulated by the organization asking, or demanding, the new entrant go more into personnel management.

The contribution of the individual line labour managers will be examined in more detail under the section on the line–staff interface below, but so far as this role theme is concerned it may be of less significance, as the people aspect is only one part of their job while it is the whole job of the specialist. Both types of manager, though, will clearly have personal views of their work.

The diverse subjective experience of work of these personnel people will clearly have an impact on their view of their role. However, if a professional approach is taken to the task, the subjective experience may be constrained by a more universal objectivity. We shall now examine this professional approach and see to what degree it modifies the subjective approach to the job role.

The Degree of Professionalism

The concepts of a profession and professionalism are important facets of the role of people managers. Arguably these concepts provide a fifth dimension to Mintzberg's four factors influencing the job role. If not, at least they provide some gauge of the concept of personnel management, and mechanisms for evaluating the actions and functions of people management. Indeed, they should give the budding manager something to aspire to and meet.

To assess this professionalism, we need some criteria. The traditional professions of law and medicine are useful in this regard. The common factors defining a profession can be seen as follows:

- Expertise is necessary, involving the passing of formal examinations and tests of competence.

- Formal education up to degree-level standard is necessary.

- An ethical code of practice is followed. In the UK, the Law Society and the British Medical Association provide semi-independent guardians of such morality.

- Transgressors to this code can be expelled and lose their licence to practice. Job security and promotion are clearly affected.

- A licence to practice is sought. This gives relative freedom of movement within the country to set up a practice.

- A client relationship exists. The professional gives independent and objective advice to the client.

- The individuals can join organizations or act as 'independents'. The professional is not necessarily bound by the organization as he or she can set up on his or her own account.

- Clients have a right of redress if the service is not satisfactory. This provides an external regulation of the profession.

- Ongoing training and development occurs. 'State-of-the-art' knowledge needs to be maintained.

- The groups are perceived generally by their clients and the public to be 'professional'.

It is useful to transfer these principles to both the staff specialist personnel manager and the line labour manager (see Activity PM1.2). A full discussion on this activity can be seen in the handbook.

ACTIVITY PM1.2

PROFESSIONALISM

Activity code

- ✓ Self-development
- ☐ Teamwork
- ☐ Communications
- ☐ Numeracy/IT
- ✓ Decisions

Rank each of the following criteria 1–5 for line labour managers and staff personnel managers. Ring the number you choose for each, and total the score.

Code:

1 = Does not meet the criterion.
2 = Marginally meets the criterion.
3 = Partly meets the criterion.
4 = Meets most of the criterion.
5 = On a par with medicine/law.

Line labour manager: non-specialist manager of labour operating in finance, operations, etc.
Staff personnel manager: specialist in personnel management.

	Line labour manager	Staff personnel manager
Expertise including passing normal tests of competence	1 2 3 4 5	1 2 3 4 5
Specialized degree-level education	1 2 3 4 5	1 2 3 4 5
Must follow ethical code	1 2 3 4 5	1 2 3 4 5
Ethical code deviants 'punished'	1 2 3 4 5	1 2 3 4 5
Needs licence or qualification to work	1 2 3 4 5	1 2 3 4 5
Client relationship with users of the service	1 2 3 4 5	1 2 3 4 5
Can act as an independent	1 2 3 4 5	1 2 3 4 5
Can act within organizations	1 2 3 4 5	1 2 3 4 5
Undertakes ongoing development	1 2 3 4 5	1 2 3 4 5
Right of redress by client against deviant 'professionals'	1 2 3 4 5	1 2 3 4 5
Seen as professional by others	1 2 3 4 5	1 2 3 4 5
Total		

The summary proposition is this: although there is a greater trend towards professionalism, as managers, neither the staff specialist nor the line labour manager is a full professional according to the established criteria.

We have considered the concept of managerial roles and related them to roles within personnel management. We have touched upon the line–staff relationship, and it may be useful to relate this division of responsibility, if not authority, to what people managers have to do in practice. We will conclude this unit by examining the constraints upon their job roles as well as the opportunities which exist and which can be exploited by the effective manager.

Line–Staff–Functional Relationships

Various types of relationship exist within organizations: lateral, functional, line and staff.

The **lateral** relationship exists across an organization, often between those of equal status. When the boss says 'This is best discussed outside of the meeting by Jill from Accounts and Tom from Sales', he or she is advocating such peer collaboration.

The **functional** relationship is more specialized, yet removed from the main chain of command as well. The corporate planner may need the assistance of the market researcher to provide intelligence on the competition. The planner can only 'manage' the researcher through the researcher's boss, so this is a functional relationship which necessitates line help in order to manage. The staff personnel person is usually in this position *vis-à-vis* the subordinates of the line manager.

A **line** relationship tends to be vertical down the organization from the chief executive to the supervisor. There is a direct chain of command with formal authority being vested by the organization in the line manager.

The **staff** manager is there in more of an advisory role. This line–staff division has its origins in the armed forces, where the line arm is made up of those who are paid to kill, while the staff or support arm is there to interpret the orders and diktats of the high command in more detail. The staff also advise the executors (or executives in non-military parlance). So the specialist personnel manager will have a foot in this staff camp as well.

Most organizations seem to start off their lives with line relationships predominating. Growth and increasing size and complexity mean that more 'lines' are added, all leading to the chief executive. The span of control can become unwieldy, and specialist assistance is sought from production controllers, lawyers, personnel managers, etc. There is a view that, with the onset of human resource management (HRM), the specialist

HR professional's business orientation and fuller identification with the organizational aims mean that the relationship between staff and line is no longer an issue. I would accept that it has become more blurred in this case, but the fundamental view remains: line managers execute policy while staff managers, such as personnel managers with their functional expertise, are primarily there as advisors to the line and to senior management. Hence the line–staff division is still relevant – albeit less rigid in some HR types of organization.

We could embark on a long philosophical debate about the nature of the line–staff relationship and how it works out in practice. We will not do so. Suffice it to say there is a great potential for conflict between line and staff managers, with contrasting philosophies towards people, differing visions of priorities (such as economic v. social aspects), and different perspectives on what the specialist manager should actually be doing.

It is this 'part management of the whole organization' that has potential for further conflict between the advisors and the executives, as the advisors can be seen as interlopers in the line manager's 'territory' (i.e. his or her people). The potential for conflict is heightened not so much in advisory matters, where the staff manager's views can be rejected or accepted (in spite of memos and 'I told you so's from the staff manager after the event), but where the staff specialist attempts to 'police' policies and agreements.

A trivial real-life example will illustrate the point. You are working in a busy office and have a diktat from head office to contain labour costs. Recruitment and selection have been singled out as potential areas of saving. 'Establishment' figures are agreed, and if these are exceeded the personnel department will come in with a heavy stick. You have been using a simple A5 form to trigger the recruitment process. The system falls apart in one line department when the manager refuses to use this simple procedure. He gets what he wants on one occasion, and thereafter exceeds the establishment figures as he pleases. Many arguments and much ill-feeling result, and ultimately he does start to adhere to the procedure, but only after his senior management has got involved. Your advisory and policing roles do not go together.

Livy[20] notes other conflicts within the specialist's role. For example, as resourcer and problem solver, the specialist is often involved in fire-fighting, yet is asked to make decisions that have wider ramifications. Similarly, as consultant and executive the advisor may have difficulty doing or putting a thing into practice. The analyst and problem solver would be a more acceptable role to line managers, while the analyst and executive would need the direct reporting relationship of the MD to make the role workable.

In another context, Pettigrew and Reason[21] looked at roles within an organization. They listed the following three dimensions of a 'workable' relationship:

- **role** – the behaviours and attitudes expected by both 'client' and role holder;
- **culture** – the history, style, values, rituals and typical modes of prevalent behaviour (e.g. towards the staff specialist);
- **person** – the role occupant's skills, aptitudes, hopes, knowledge, abilities and enthusiasms.

They suggest that a 'fit' or congruence is required between these person, culture and role variables. If there is no fit, much energy will be wasted in just surviving. Personal experience, particularly in education, holds this to be the case where academic freedom and integrity can be limited by the fickleness of so-called 'line managers'. For both the staff specialist and the line labour manager, this vision of congruence is useful, for both need to be able to:

- identify the congruence;
- try and manage it without it getting on top of you;
- move between various subcultures (particularly important for the staff specialist);
- fit in without becoming an organizational clone or sycophant and without prostituting any basic principles.

The aim is not to be too prescriptive, but to give some clarity in order to avoid ambiguity and minimize friction between line and staff specialists; see Activity PM1.3.

ACTIVITY PM1.3

LINE AND STAFF MANAGEMENT WITHIN THE TRAINING SECTION

Activity code
- ✓ Self-development
- ✓ Teamwork
- ☐ Communications
- ☐ Numeracy/IT
- ✓ Decisions

Who should do what in training? From the list of 'actors' and the levels of management below, role allocation in training may seem complex. To avoid this complexity, while not putting aside its results, focus on the line–staff interface. For your benefit the nature of the training functions has been summarized on the left-hand side. Your primary task is to allocate the staff managers and give a weight to the responsibilities of each. Allocate A, B, C or D to each of the 'actors' for each role.

Code:

1 = Senior line management
2 = Senior staff management, e.g. personnel director
3 = Training manager/controller
4 = Staff trainers
5 = Line trainers/managers
6 = Trainees
7 = External advisors
8 = Trade unions
A High level
B Medium level
C Low level
D Nil/virtually nil

Type of role	Trainer roles	1	2	3	4	5	6	7	8
Framework for activities	Training policy formulator								
Goal determination	Training need identifier and diagnostician								
	Generator of ideas for training initiatives								
	Formulator of training objectives								
Preparing initiatives	Researcher and curriculum builder								
	Materials designer and developer								
	Training administrator and organizer								
	Training marketeer								
Implementing initiatives	Instructor								
	Direct trainer								
	Organizational development agent, catalyst, facilitator								
	Coach, mentor								
	Training advisor, consultant								
	Agent of learning transfer to the job								
Associated activities	Manager of training resources								
	Trainer and developers of trainers								
	Liaison officer								
Evaluation	Assessor of training quality								
	Evaluator of training contribution								

Source: Type of role adapted from Leduchowicz and Bennett, *What makes an effective trainer?*

As we can see, the specialist advises and the line manager executes. It should be a partnership but the final decision should rest with line management. This basic formula can be applied to the whole range of functions of personnel management, namely: manpower planning and strategic management; recruitment and selection; placement and termination; education, training and development; terms and conditions of employment; labour relations; appraisal and promotion; communication and consultation; health, safety and welfare, etc. At the same time, the degree of input may differ according to expertise and skills, and we will touch upon this as we go on. On the subject of skills, Pigors and Myers[22] tell us that the people manager needs the following 'traits' or skills:

- integrity
- statesmanlike intelligence
- diplomacy or persuasiveness
- analytical skills
- objectivity and open-mindedness
- flexibility
- common sense
- perceptiveness and sensitivity
- decisiveness
- democratic attitude

It looks to be a tall order. Equally, people managers need a sound appreciation of personnel management. Before concluding this unit we will look at constraints and opportunities for personnel management.

The **external environment** provides both constraints and opportunities. Some examples will suffice:

- *Political:* in the UK, the legislation on labour made by Conservative administrators in the 1980s and early 1990s has made heavy if not punitive inroads on collective rights. This can be both an opportunity to build up one-to-one relationships with employees (rather than to smash unions) and also a constraint, as employees can become quite disillusioned with such heavy-handed ideological outputs from the state.

- *Economic:* the recession-cum-depression makes for pools of unemployed people, redundancy, short-time working and wage freezes. Fuller employment also causes recruitment and cost difficulties as more job choice is available. The task culture as opposed to people culture may also predominate.

- *Social:* in education, for example, more and more young people are staying on at college or university to take degrees. It seems to be one of the few growth industries in a recession. The calibre of this group can raise some eyebrows amongst the personnel profession in the UK, including as it does semi-literate 16-year-olds and a wholesale output of first-class degrees from the college system.

■ *Technological:* technological change is a constant, and the response to such change, from paperless offices to semi-automated factories, provide opportunity for greater flexibility in working, job redesign, more leisure – and more conflict if it is not handled properly.

The **internal environment**, within the organization, has also become more fluid in recent years. People needs should be more fully integrated with business needs – without compromising on either. Senior management must become more imbued with the view that people are an asset. Personnel specialists and non-specialists need to become less reactive and better at diagnosing and solving problems. We need to understand fully the importance of personnel management to the individual and the organization. Equally, we must be able to justify its existence to the non-believers and the sceptics. The remaining units will address these issues.

Appendix: The personnel function: an historical overview

Dates	*Roles*
1913	Welfare Workers Association:
	• canteen overview
	• evening class enlightenment
	• not really involved with managing the workplace
1915	Welfare Section in Ministry of Munitions:
	• protective clothing and first aid
	• rest, recreation and transport facilities
	• recruitment and selection
	• record maintenance
1917	Central Association of Welfare Workers:
	• 'wellbeing' of those engaged in business was the main concern
	• specialist but very subordinate to line authority of management
1925–39	'Labour management'/labour relations to the fore:
	• welfare in relative decline
	• employment more of an issue
1939–45	Accommodation
	Training the unskilled entrants to the labour force
	'Labour officers'/relations
1945–c.55	• Attracting and retaining employees (relatively full employment)
	• Welfare and employees' interests to be looked after as part of the retention strategy
1955–63	• Business efficiency
	• Justice at the place of work
1963–94	• Business efficiency to the fore, with people being seen increasingly as a means to that end

Notes

1 Likert, *Human Organization: its management and value.*
2 Mintzberg, *Nature of Managerial Work.*
3 See Anderson and Kyprianou, *Effective Organizational Behaviour.*
4 Thomason, *Textbook of Personnel Management.*
5 See Anderson, *Effective Labour Relations.*
6 Fox and his pluralist/unitarist debate with Clegg can be cited in this context. Clegg, *Changing System of Industrial Relations*; Fox, *Sociology of Work in Industry.*
7 Hobsbawm, quoting Rosa Luxemburg (1899), in 'Trends in the British Labour Movement'.
8 Niven, *Personnel Management, 1913–1963.*
9 As a former MBA student of Professor Palmer, I can thoroughly recommend her innovative sociological perspectives on the employment relationship. See G. Palmer, *British Industrial Relations*. See also Littler, 'Deskilling and changing structures of control', and Littler, *The Development of the Labour Processes in Capitalist Societies.*

10 Oliver and Wilkinson, *The Japanization of British Industry.*

11 Lupton, *Industrial Behaviour and Personnel Management.*

12 The literature on research method is vast. It is covered in Anderson and Kyprianou, *Effective Organizational Behaviour*, and in Mitchell, *People in Organisations.*

13 Lupton, *Industrial Behaviour and Personnel Management.*

14 The role sets and critiques of various writers have been classified under this reference:

Pigors and Myers, *Management of Human Resources.*

Anthony and Crichton, *Industrial Relations and the Personnel Specialist.*

Livy, *Corporate Personnel Management.*

Tyson, 'Is this the very model of a modern personnel manager?'.

15 Anderson, *Successful Training Practice.*

16 Wilson, 'The role of the personnel function in a changing environment'.

17 Legge, *Power Innovation and Problem Solving in Personnel Management.*

18 Pettigrew and Reason, *Alternative Interpretations of the Training Officer Role.*

19 Watson, *The Personnel Manager.*

20 Livy, *Corporate Personnel Management.*

21 Pettigrew and Reason, *Alternative Interpretations of the Training Officer Role.*

22 Pigors and Myers, *Management of Human Resources.*

Unit Two

Manpower Planning, Recruitment and Selection

Learning Objectives

After completing this unit you should be able to:

- relate personnel management to the concept of manpower planning;

- conduct a manpower plan;

- carry out job analysis;

- formulate recruitment policies;

- apply a range of in-depth selection methods for both the organization and the individual;

- apply the generic skills.

Contents

Overview

Manpower Planning

Job Analysis, Recruitment and Selection

▶ Job profiles

▶ The person for the job

Recruitment

Selection

▶ References

▶ Psychometric tests

▶ Interviews

▶ Group selection and assessment centres

The Individual and Recruitment or Selection

Unit Two

These doubts must occur to anyone who thinks for one moment about the 'personality inventory', particularly the 'personnel practitioners' who have been responsible for the huge increase in its use in the past decade. Still, one can see why they might not question it too closely. Personality tests have the one advantage of creating enormous amounts of paperwork, something which is always welcome to this profession and which seems to me to add little to the sum of human happiness. It is no wonder one test I found linked the career of personnel officer with prison administration.❞

H. Porter[1]

Overview

This is very much a practical unit, based on a systematic approach which is seen as a critical component of manpower resourcing. This systematic vision permeates the manpower plan which sets out to reconcile the supply of and demand for labour, the recruitment process, making potential candidates aware of a vacancy, and the selection itself – physically choosing the most suitable candidate. This unit also looks at selection from the candidate's perspective. This is in line with the ethos of the book; moreover, sooner or later we all face the potential trauma of job hunting.

The flowchart in figure 2.1 gives an outline of the unit.

Manpower Planning

The organization must be placed in its environment. The political, economic, social and technological opportunities and constraints are well covered in other books in this series[2] and we have touched briefly on them in Unit One. The manpower plan is very much concerned with this interaction with the wider external environment, and we will now turn to this area of planning for people and the business – assuming some environmental knowledge.

Planning is formulating a course of action to meet a desired result. It has been said that planning is making a decision today in the context of what you forecast for tomorrow. Equally, it necessitates some control mechanisms to ensure that the plans are continuous and flexible enough to meet changing needs. In manpower terms, this planning function should

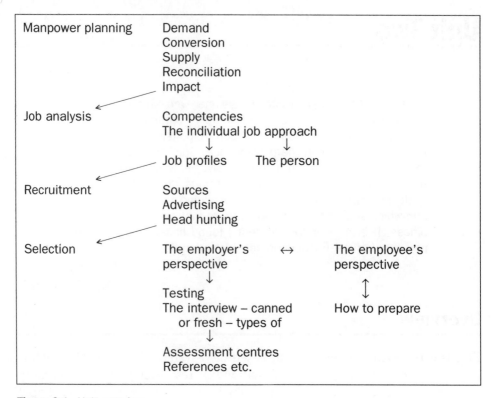

Figure 2.1 Unit overview.

be centre stage: the 'acquisition, utilization and retention of human resources' is perhaps the most critical function of personnel management.[3] Manpower planning is important to all organizations for the following reasons:

- Labour is a significant cost to the organization and the plan allows greater control.
- Business planning is a key ingredient of organizational success, and financial marketing and corporate planning must be augmented by manpower planning.
- The labour supply is neither constant nor flexible and people's (growing) social aspirations must be taken into account.
- Environmental changes, from technology to political and economic turbulence, mean that management is becoming more complex, so planning is essential.
- The changing product demands have social implications for labour, from redundancy to retraining, and planning can help accommodate these demands.

Manpower planning essentially means reconciling the demand for and the supply of labour.[4] It involves calculating the demand for labour via corporate, marketing and financial objectives, then deriving the supply of labour. This needs an internal audit or 'stock take' and an external review of the labour sources from the labour market, coupled with a 'productivity index' of what level of work is being achieved. A reconciliation occurs through a forecasting process and the manpower implications from recruitment to retirement to labour relations can follow on.

The core principles of planning can be applied to this manpower reconciliation:

■ Basic objectives need to be translated into workable targets.

■ Policies should be determined.

■ Resources must be effectively deployed.

■ Flexibility must be built into the plan.

■ Control mechanisms must monitor the implementation of the plan.

■ There must be ongoing feedback in order to alter the plan if necessary.

Putting the principles of planning and this labour reconciliation together we end up with the flowchart in figure 2.2. We will develop this flowchart in a little more detail below.

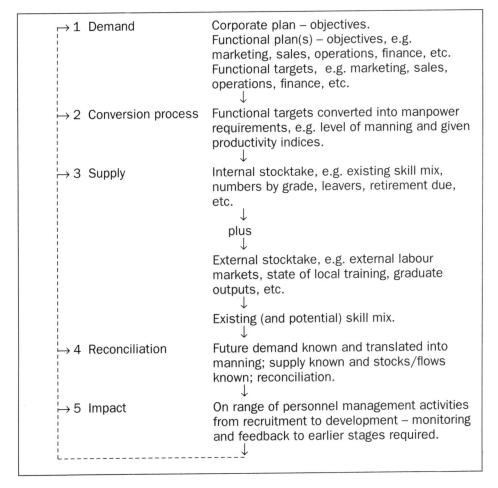

Figure 2.2 Manpower planning process.

The **demand side** is forecast by considering the corporate plan and the likely demand for labour. New product development, investment or 'disinvestment', changes in technology, organizational growth or contraction, decentralization or centralization of decision making, etc., are all factors which have an impact on the demand side. The chances are that most organizations will have some overall corporate or organizational plan. The difficulty often lies in taking manpower into this overall plan and/or converting the objectives of the plan into manpower targets.

A management view can be taken and a calculated guess can be made on the **conversion of targets to manpower**. The chances are that sales, power consumed, number of customers and level of production can quantify the whole process to some degree, and staff numbers can be worked out. For example, a retail store related its manning levels to sales turnover. The established manpower pitch was related to turnover, initially by the experienced views of the managers in each subsection advising the section head of their views on staffing levels. These were summated and top managers took a view on the overall staffing level. After some time, work pressures, Saturday work and late-night shopping gave demand fluctuations and short-term contracts, overtime and part-timers were used. Gradually a crude relationship was established between sales turnover and staffing levels, which could then be fine tuned.

In other areas, work study could be applied to 'direct' operational staff and a calculation used for 'indirect' administrative staff. The production or sales schedules can be related to man hours and man days. A costing perspective can be added to this 'demand' figure. A productivity factor can be introduced at this stage to give an index on the output of labour, or it can be related to the supply side later on (see Box PM2.1).

BOX PM2.1

Manpower demand

Purkiss usefully analyses some approaches to working out the demand for manpower, which in many ways, is the key to effective manpower planning:

- *Workload analysis:* a very detailed study of a particular job can be made, and specific 'core work situations' can be isolated in jobs, e.g. dealing with the public. A broader perspective is to examine productivity ratios. Purkiss notes that 'standard levels of manning' on each unit of business operation tend to occur. These 'standards' are often derived from work study. A statistical vision is also given and regression analysis is advocated by some to calculate the manning levels.
- *Training analysis:* differing rates of learning and training times may also have an impact in manning levels.

■ *Business activity:* an attempt can be made to relate a set of management ratios (business activity) and labour levels.
■ *Productivity analysis:* all the factors contributing to business efficiency are related. The role of labour productivity in this equation is seen as a key aspect.
■ *Extrapolative methods:* the projection of trends needs great care as past patterns may not have future relevance. Time series analysis has been used by some researchers.
Source: Adapted from Purkiss, 'Manpower planning literature'

So various methods can be used. The managers' views (top-down, bottom-up, or committee) can set the ball rolling, and once a plan has started, such opinions can modify forecasts with a touch of hard-nosed reality. The extrapolation of past employment trends, the use of regression or correlation analysis and some econometric model may be applicable – if costs allow. Variables need to be built into such a model. The use of work study can give the best mix between machines and people, while output per man hour or day and productivity indices can give measures of labour efficiency (existing and proposed).

The **supply side** should be easier to accommodate.[5] The aim is to build up an accurate picture of your resources and to estimate 'stock erosion' by the end of the forecast period. The 'audit' may include:

■ all occupations;
■ all skills/status;
■ qualifications;
■ those undertaking training;
■ age/sex profile;
■ changes in the labour force;
■ labour turnover analysis;
■ changes in working practices, e.g. overtime, holidays, retiral policies, hours of work, etc.;
■ productivity indices (if not already covered).

Labour turnover is critical.[6] 'Natural' leavers from illness or death, discharges or dismissals, transfers and promotions can be shown via trends. The real problem concerns voluntary wastage, which cannot be legislated for fully. The labour turnover index of:

$$\frac{\text{Number of leavers}}{\text{Average number of employed}} \times \frac{100}{1} = \%$$

can be used for occupational groupings and age/sex analysis. It can be linked to the labour stability index of:

$$\frac{\text{Numbers of employees with 1 year's service}}{\text{Number employed a year ago}} \times \frac{100}{1} = \%$$

(See Activity PM2.1.)

ACTIVITY PM2.1

MANPOWER PLANNING: THE PROBLEM OF LABOUR TURNOVER

Activity code
✔ Self-development
✔ Teamwork
✔ Communications
✔ Numeracy/IT
✔ Decisions

The company spent a fortune on recruitment, selection and initial training, but to no real avail, as labour turnover was crippling and turned any concept of planning into dust. The results of the company's 'exit survey' are shown below (percentages are ratings of the views of staff who left in the last year).

Initial discussions with management showed that Saturday work, poor prospects and some managerial 'style' difficulties could be key issues.

Your task is to make brief recommendations on issues which you feel may reduce the labour turnover from the data given.

		Very Satisfied	Satisfied	Dissatisfied	Very Dissatisfied
1	Were you happy with the information given by the management?	6%	32%	43%	19%
		All of the time	*Most of the time*	*Some of the time*	*Never*
2	Did we make use of your abilities?	7%	31%	52%	11%
		Very good	*Good*	*Poor*	*Very poor*
3	What are your thoughts on our payment policy?	3%	30%	44%	24%
		Very interested	*Interested*	*Uninterested*	*Very uninterested*
4	Were you interested in what we were selling?	26%	63%	8%	3%
		Very good	*Good*	*Poor*	*Very poor*
5	How would rate your ex-manager?	13%	41%	32%	14%

	Far too much	Slightly too much	Slightly too little	Too little
6 The volume of work given to you was:	20%	37%	34%	9%

	Very well	Well	Poorly	Very poorly
7 How did you get on with your colleagues?	45%	42%	12%	1%

	All of the time	Most of the time	Some of the time	Never
8 Did your management have a consistent approach and style?	22%	27%	33%	17%

	Very good	Good	Poor	Very poor
9 The job training here was:	14%	28%	31%	27%

	Very satisfied	Satisfied	Very dissatisfied	Dissatisfied
10 How do you feel about your initial training?	30%	30%	18%	22%

	'Saturdays'	'Colleagues'	'Money'	'Challenge'	'Prospects'	'Other', e.g. domestic
11 Give the main reason for leaving	10%	1%	25%	17%	29%	18%

The external labour market provides a key aspect of the supply side of the equation. For example, at local level some factors worth noting may include:

- population density;
- local unemployment levels;
- availability of labour;
- views of the skills mix;
- competition from other firms;
- movements of labour;
- 'outputs' from local education;
- transport;
- new housing planned, etc.

At national level the market is also important:

- state initiatives in training;
- population trends;
- redeployment schemes;
- development schemes;
- unemployment levels;
- 'outputs' from national education, etc.

On one of these issues, population trends, there is a considerable ongoing debate in the UK. There is a so-called UK demographic timebomb. Atkinson argues that labour shortages will occur over the next few years; that an ageing workforce will mean fewer young people entering the labour market; that the sexual composition of the 'activity rate' will alter to absorb more women into the labour market; and that there will be distinct skill shortages in some areas, particularly among the more highly skilled.[7] Continued recession and slackening demand for labour may have camouflaged the trends noted by Atkinson but the underlying message still seems to be there.

To return to the manpower process: the demand and supply sides need to be *reconciled*. We have manpower targets from the demand side. On the supply side, our human inventory will have given the numbers by skill and occupation at the start of the year, the normal intake of trainees/apprentices, the transfers in and the anticipated levels of wastage. So we have both the starting stock and the finishing stock (movement out). We know the demand and the additional requirements sought during the year through the plan, so we have a total demand and the existing supply. Reconciliation is thus achieved.

So manpower planning is a key element of effective personnel management. It needs the following for successful implementation:

- total integration with the corporate and other functional plans;
- flexible target setting;
- commitment from management;
- a sound database within and good intelligence from outside the organization;
- reasonably accurate forecasting techniques;
- constant monitoring and feedback.

The implications of the manpower plan can be seen throughout the function of personnel management and nowhere more so than in recruitment and selection. Do we need to replace the job? Do we need to replace the person? Should we merge the jobs or create a new one? Is there pressure to replace or not from managers, unions or staff? Labour is costly, so assuming that these questions are answered, we next need some form of control mechanism or 'switch' to activate the whole thing.[8] This requisition or switch can take the form of an informal chat between the personnel specialists and the line manager, or it can go to great lengths, as in one bureaucracy I worked in where different coloured forms in triplicate were issued. Bureaucracy apart, this written requisition is important, as it:

- gives a check on labour turnover;
- allows 'exit' interviews to follow on automatically;
- gives the opportunity for some budgetary control;
- involves more senior people in the process, which can trigger approval to recruit;
- gives an opportunity to analyse the job and the potential person that we are looking for in that job.

Job Analysis, Recruitment and Selection

Towards competencies

Increasingly there is a trend towards listing a range of desired skills and knowledge for given job levels. To some extent these standardized core competencies bypass the need for the detailed job analysis that we are proposing, but competencies are being made organizational and culture-specific, so the tools of traditional job analysis may still have to be employed. Again, some firms may not fully absorb the competency vision. The concept for recruitment is similar whether we use competencies or a traditional individual job approach: first analyse the job, then derive the qualities of the person to fill the job.

The standards and outline competencies can be seen elsewhere,[9] so we will focus on the 'do-it-yourself' method of traditional individual job analysis.

Individual job approach

The traditional method of job analysis has been to study the job and then extrapolate the 'qualities' required to do it.[10] With the advent of the competency movement, job analysis may become easier, assuming that the core standards are adopted, but even then industry and organizational slants will have to be taken into account in the analysis of work. We will focus on job analysis through the individual study of jobs but also examine the core competency technique as well.

Job analysis through the study of a job in a systematic fashion not only aims to get a statement of all the facts about specific tasks, but looks to the job context and the constraints and opportunities which modify the stated job. Extrapolation of the ideal person who can meet a 'reasonable' (however defined) level of performance follows. So the process is one of fitting the person to the job. However, the cynical would comment that, first there is a job, then the person adapts to it, and then the job adapts to the person.

Job analysis has a whole range of uses in personnel management and it is not just restricted to recruitment and selection, although our focus will be in these areas.

The uses of job analysis include:

■ *Manpower planning* – whole 'job families' can be identified where common denominators outweigh differences to allow the skill mix of the labour supply to alter.

■ *Selection and promotion* – it helps provide an indication of the kind of person to be recruited or promoted, and facilitates career planning, as logical paths of progression may become more self-evident.

■ *Transfers* – again, similar tasks can be highlighted in different sections to facilitate easier transfer.

- *Safety* – particularly hazardous tasks and working environments can be pointed out.
- *Job evaluation* – for equitable salaries or wages and productivity schemes, work measurement and job analysis are critical.
- *Training* – the performance standards and norms required can be noted through job analysis.

There seem to be three main perspectives to job analysis: physiological, engineering and psychological. The *physiological* view is concerned with a scientific method. It can measure the energy or the muscular activity of the job holder. It may have relevance in the work of a pilot or an astronaut. The *engineering* perspective breaks the job down into component parts in a machine-like format; the writer picks up the pen, hesitates, writes a key word on the paper, hesitates, and puts the key word into a sentence. This gives a step-by-step approach and may be useful for training or safety. The *psychological* approach is more face-to-face and seeks the individual's perceptions of the job and its environment. It paints a more dynamic picture, particularly when applied to a factual analysis. (See Box PM2.2.)

BOX PM2.2

Job analysis: methods and pitfalls

Methods include the following:
- *Observation* – physically watching the employee at work can give insight into the job (but see 'pitfalls' below).
- *Experience* – actually doing the job can give exposure to the conditions of work, but may not be appropriate for the analyst.
- *Questionnaires* – for large groups of people, a survey is useful.
- *'Testing'* – looking for the 'ideal' employee and working out the requisite skills and knowledge is another possibility.
- *Activity sampling* – assuming that it is representative, a study of jobs or a group may give a 'feel' for their task.
- *Interviews* – this useful method can include the job holder and his or her immediate manager.
- *Diaries* – these are particularly useful where the job alters, as in management or supervisory positions. The employee is asked to record times, meetings, actions, etc., on a pro forma.

Pitfalls include the following:
- The experienced job holder knows his or her job inside out and takes things (often key things) for granted.
- When making a description of duties, it is useful to restrict yourself to a range of key tasks, or to put the main duties into a flowchart or process chart, as this minimizes endless lists of duties.
- The experienced job holder can make a job look very easy – or very difficult.
- The manager is often too removed to give detailed analysis of the job, but the job holder and manager can give keen insights into, if not different perspectives on, a given job.

Job profiles

We must start with a job profile or job description. Accuracy is important, but doing countless minute tasks must be avoided, and the document needs to be flexible for the interests of all concerned. Over-rigidity will enshrine aspects of the job that make labour inflexible and grading appeals more likely, while a blank sheet of paper can make for an autocratic manager developing the spirit of a latter-day Genghis Khan. We need a balance, which is why the term 'profile' is preferred to 'description'.

The job profile puts the job in context, and states its aim, the specified duties and responsibilities, the relationships involved and the opportunities and constraints within the job. A checklist is used to give a guide to such a job profile. Of course the depth and level will vary according to the job type, the responsibility and the organization. (See Activity PM2.2.)

ACTIVITY PM2.2

HOW TO CONDUCT A JOB PROFILE

Activity code
✓ Self-development
✓ Teamwork
✓ Communications
✓ Numeracy/IT
✓ Decisions

The job profile must be a clear account of the purpose of the job; of the context of the job, from the reporting relationship to the departmental structure; of the work situation, from physical conditions to relationships with others; and, most important of all, of the actual duties and responsibilities in some key task format. Some companies add the financial benefits and terms and conditions as well to this document.

Possible information:

Job title	Section, number employed and the current job title
Aim(s)	The purpose of the job with perhaps four or five key objectives
Tasks	The main duties
Responsibilities	Resource implications re people, machines, plant, equipment, money, etc. (quantified or qualified)
Relationships	Liaison role(s), and with whom – to include both internal and external relations
Working conditions	To include both social elements (group or solitary) and physical ones (health, hazards, etc.)
Terms and conditions	Money, perks, etc.

Using the job profile format below, and from your knowledge to date of personnel management, conduct a job analysis of a personnel manager in a generalist personnel position reporting to the managing director.

Job title

Aim(s) (include four or five objectives)

Tasks (outline main duties only)

Responsibilities

Relationships

Working conditions

The person for the job

To recruit and select the right person, we need a pen portrait, a form of an ability chart or a person specification. The ideal individual attributes must be relevant to the job. These **'essential'** features must be kept to a minimum. For example, while recruiting a telematics specialist for a client, I was given the specification for a bright honours graduate in computing, with in-company and consultancy experience, with an MBA and aged under thirty. These 'essential' features must also be capable of being assessed, and **'desirable'** characteristics can be added to the specification as well.

There may be **contra-indications** as well which would make potential candidates unacceptable. For example, we may not recruit the best person for a job because he or she may be too qualified for the discretion and latitude in that post; hence we go for the most suitable person.

In extrapolating the ideal person for the job derived from the individual job or competency analysis, we can usefully employ one of several plans:

■ a seven-point plan;

■ a five-point plan;

■ an ability or motivation plan.

(See Box PM2.3.)

BOX PM2.3

Summary of a seven-point plan

Physique	Health/fitness standards?
	Height, vision, hearing, strain on limbs, strength, etc.
	First impressions?
	Appearance, voice, cleanliness, manner, social graces, etc.
Attainments	Education level
	Specific training
	Relevant experience – type, sector and level
General intelligence	In relation to the population as a whole
Special aptitudes	Does the job require a faculty in figures, drawing, dexterity, artistic ability, a knowledge of mechanical principles, etc?
Interest	How far does the job need an interest in the following: social, practical, active, intellectual or artistic spheres?
Disposition	Does the job require the following: reliability, acceptability to people, the need to lead or influence and for the individual to accept responsibility?
Circumstances	Age, geography, etc.
Contra-indications	Negatives

Source: Adapted from Rodger, *The Seven Point Plan*

A variation upon the theme which gives a useful selection checklist is to follow this scheme:

Work experience	The type, nature, duration, function, industry, geography and special techniques, etc.
Training	Level; type; duration; on or off the job; skills, knowledge and attitudes required; craft, technical and professional qualification; etc.

Education (including professional)	The formal level of education sought, from craft technicians certificate to a master's degree
Personal background	The motivation, the type of person sought; how he or she adapts to circumstances, etc.
Future plans	How much scope or latitude exists in the job, and does it tally with the individual candidate's expectations at selection?

The work experience and the personal factors should be given more weight than the other items.

Ability and motivation analysis

Irrespective of the plan being used, there is a need to determine the required **ability** and the scope or degree of **motivation** within the job. This will prove critical in the actual selection process, as we need to match up the capability or capacity of the individual with his or her natural inclination or drive. Together, this ability and motivation should result in a more effective performance.

In both the ability and motivational analysis we need the classification of: essential, desirable and contra-indications:

- *Essential* – There should be very few of these; we should not be seeking Superman, and specific industrial or commercial exposure, functional expertise and capability with a given technique should suffice. On motivation, a high need to succeed may be required.

- *Desirable* – The thirty-year-old BSc, or the MBA with years of industrial experience and in-depth consultancy exposure to telematics, can fit into this category. These are add-ons which may help to differentiate candidates but are icing on the cake.

- *Contra-indications* – These are the discouragers if not disqualifiers and may be the polar opposites of the essential abilities.

Recruitment

We have now a picture of the ideal candidate. We need to attract individuals to meet this specification.[11] The first port of call should be internal to the organization. This may result in a form of 'internal labour market' forming, and we see examples of this in large firms and in particular in local authorities and health boards, who seem to recruit from within their own sector at the expense of candidates from other industrial or commercial sectors.

Other external mechanisms can be employed depending upon the job being filled, the budget, and the perceived availability of labour. A checklist (not exhaustive) can summarize these sources with an appropriate commentary. (See Box PM2.4.)

BOX PM2.4

Recruitment sources

Source	Comment
Internal to the organization	Should be first port of call as it acts as a tremendous motivator and individuals have a good knowledge of the firm
	Cheaper, although a replacement will be required
	Useful if a 'keep-in-mind' file of good external applicants is retained so that replacements can be slotted in
	'Bounty' often paid to existing staff to attract outsiders.
External:	
Colleges/schools	Critical for updating stock of trainees/apprentices
	Cheap (free)
	Training costs relatively heavy and longer learning times
	Neglected?
State sector, e.g. Job Centres	Cheap (free)
	Wide range of skills available
	Not just the unemployed and the unemployable – quite the reverse.
Agencies (temporary/permanent)	More expensive (10–16 per cent of starting salary for permanent staff)
	Need a tight specification as some are marketeers, not personnel professionals
Forces resettlement, etc.	Good for technical people
	Cheap
	Underutilized
Search consultants	Expensive ($c.\,33\frac{1}{3}$ per cent of starting salary)
	Useful for senior people and for finding specialized skills
Advertising	Useful – can be relatively expensive

Sooner or later an advertisement may be required. Copy writing is almost an art form and the large organization may be better advised to use a specialist agency. The following criteria need to be considered:

- *Business status* – how well established, etc.?
- *Expertise and in-house facilities* – do they match your needs?
- *Client list* – review past examples of work.
- *Management* – structure, procedures, accountability for the service.
- *Previous success* – review of past campaigns.
- *Fee structure* – changing methods, etc.

Whether we use an agency or do it ourselves, excluding television and radio, which are still quite marginal types of media for recruitment advertising, we tend to use national and regional newspapers or specialist magazines/journals. The rates reflect the media and their coverage.

When it comes to the actual design of an advertisement,[12] sound job analysis quickly pays dividends, for the 'meat' is already there on company details, the job, the person sought and the rewards. (See Activity PM2.3.)

The advertisement needs to be monitored. A copy will be retained and notes taken on the following: the setting; classified or display; size; cost per medium; timing – day of the week and time of the year; and the insertion details in publication or other media. Once the advertisement has been placed, we need to quantify the whole process: number of replies, firm applications, suitable applications, interviews or other selection mechanism, firm offer(s), accepted offer(s) and number of firm starters. Ratio analysis can be used to gauge the impact of advertisements over a longer time span. This may trigger the need for better copy writing, media placement, setting, timing, etc. It will also keep a vision of cost-effectiveness in the eyes of your management and the agency, if used. Before we start sifting through the applications we should also consider executive search or 'head hunting'. (See Box PM2.5 and Activity PM2.4.)

Selection

Once we have a pool of potential candidates who on paper meet the specification, the assessment process begins. Where recruitment stops and selection begins is a moot point, but as soon as the c.v.s, resumés, application forms or letters start arriving on the desk and the sifting process starts, the selection procedure has actually begun.

Again, the right person specification comes into its own. The separation of the 'probables', 'possibles' and 'no-hopers' starts. This should be a joint exercise between line and staff personnel managers. In effect, the sifting is often delegated to the specialist personnel manager. The standard reject letters often go out at this stage but the 'possibles' are retained by the company until later.

ACTIVITY PM2.3

ADVERTISING

Activity code

- ✔ Self-development
- ✔ Teamwork
- ✔ Communications
- ☐ Numeracy/IT
- ✔ Decisions

A typical format is as follows:

Job title:

Rewards: approximate

The *job outline* is given. The scope and potential may be noted. Do not oversell.

The *organization details* are given. If the organization is well known, these facts are usually crisp and succinct. Growth, expansion, new product lines, etc., may be mentioned.

The *person specification* must mention the essential requirements – abilities, qualifications, experience, age (?), etc. A balance is required: we must attract a qualified pool of people but the wording should not be so bland as to attract hundreds.

The *rewards* may include approximate salary and any perks being offered.

The *action* must include the contact name within your organization and perhaps the means to get more information. The address, telephone and the required reply format must be given, e.g. write, telephone, send c.v., write for application form, send a handwritten letter, etc.

Company logo

Action

Using the format above, design a job advertisement for the stress consultant's position in Pyramid Psychology. Refer to the case study that follows.

Pyramid Psychology

The ideas of a pyramid's meticulous craftmanship, the physical and mental mobilization of resources needed to build the edifice, its status as monument to human achievement as a thing of beauty, and of Maslow's vision of self-fulfilment at the apex of the pyramid or hierarchy of needs were all behind the naming of the firm. It had been started eight years ago by two occupational psychologists, Kurt Stinger and Marie Anders. Both had qualified from a prestigious university and had practised abroad, Stinger in Frankfurt and Anders in California. The British view of occupational psychology seemed less developed.

They had met up again at the annual dinner of their old university. Anders was writing and Stinger was in the process of being offered a senior lecturing position at a university in the north of England which had a strong presence in the field of occupational counselling and stress management. Anders shared many of these interests with Stinger. To cut a long story short, they had formed a partnership at a prestigious Cambridge address (Anders had carried out her doctorate there) and had prospered over the years – not that either of them had gone into the partnership solely for money.

Of course there were many occupational psychologists about, but most were in the land of psychometric testing and personality measurement for selection while others focused on training. The large business schools had stress specialists, other consultants existed and there were various stress, meditation, positive health units and relaxation centres dotted around the country. Few firms combined the counselling skills of Pyramid with its stress management techniques and tools. Pyramid did not believe in 'packages': they took to their work a humanistic philosophy based on the approach of Rogers (see Unit Four) and a professionalism that most senior clients readily absorbed and believed in.

Their clients were predominantly corporate. Some individuals at the executive level would pop in to see them on a regular basis for a chat, but this was an extra. Their bread and butter came from large corporations which had identified an efficiency or productivity problem with individuals or with staff in general. If it was an individual problem, the counselling tended to occur in Cambridge; if it was a group matter, the counselling would occur off-site at a nearby hotel. They would not counsel people at the place of work itself. With a charge rate of £900 per day, inclusive of state taxes, and a busy schedule, Pyramid kept growing.

Clients became more demanding and there did not seem to be any time between assignments. They had estimated a 60 per cent work rate over the 230 working days in the year but this last year it had come nearer 90 per cent. Dr Anders had commented, 'If this goes on we'll both be in need of stress counselling.' Stinger agreed. It was decided that they would recruit 'stress consultants', who could not only be professional counsellors but also good sales and marketing people, as both Anders and Stinger wished to focus on their research and the occupational psychology side rather than build up the business. 'While we are looking for these people, perhaps we should employ a marketing professional from an established consultancy firm,' suggested Dr Stinger. 'He or she can co-ordinate all of the sales and marketing while you and I concentrate on our psychological research.'

Both sat down and came up with some requirement in a systematic fashion:

Physique   Must be well groomed and 'clean', with good dress sense. Must be presentable to major clients.

Attainments	Must have a degree in psychology with some postgraduate exposure to occupational psychology or some business qualification at diploma (DMS) level.
Intelligence	Needs to be a bright spark. Not too concerned about past job history as we can train him or her.
Aptitudes	Numerate for testing, etc., and personable. Must like people.
Interests	Not concerned.
Disposition	Must get on with a small team and be acceptable to others.
Circumstances	Not concerned really. Aged 25 +.

BOX PM2.5

Up the Amazon – in search of head hunters

❝ Employment agencies: care should be exercised in dealing with these firms, the majority are swindlers.❞

(from an 1888 edition of Titbits*)*

Most search consultants, or head hunters, and agencies would not subscribe to this quotation on their morality. However, care should still be exercised to ensure a cost-effective service. The careful selection of such head hunters is an important exercise for people managers.

Why bother with search (the term head hunters prefer)? Search means what it says: it takes a vacancy to an individual, unlike advertising, which attracts individuals to a vacancy. Advertising can be quite transitory (yesterday's newspaper is confined to the dustbin of history), but search can go on for months. Search is target-oriented – the telescopic high-powered rifle rather than the scatter-gun technique. Consequently it is useful where skills are in short supply, as in senior management, or where some unique technical experience is sought. The alternative of the old boys' or old girls' network may produce an individual who can pass the social acceptability test – but competence may be another matter.

The real advantage with search is that the 'hunted' are 'caught' and these people may not have been actively seeking a job, and hence not looking in the display columns of newspapers and journals. On paper, this approach should mean that the full specification is met, and it can be confidential, with the client's name not coming to the fore until the last moment.

However, there are potential problems with search. To many, it is immoral – poaching in all but name. As a deliberate ploy to sabotage a rival by pulling out the new product development director, the concept is indeed unethical; but if you genuinely need and want such a person and he or she is the most suitable, perhaps it becomes less so.

The cost is high – up to $33\frac{1}{3}$ per cent of the total remuneration can be charged as a fee. Guarantees are often absent in spite of this fee and many search consultants are better at marketing and selling than they are at personnel assessment. At the wider economic level, search may discourage training and development, as an organization's investment in its management can go the way of asset stripping in all but name. It may result in inflated remuneration as well, as organizations pay over the top to hold on to their best players and will meet any external offer from other firms. However, like love, business is competitive and it is fair to get the edge over your rivals, so search will stay with us.

ACTIVITY PM2.4

IN SEARCH OF A SEARCHER

Activity code
✔ Self-development
✔ Teamwork
✔ Communications
✔ Numeracy/IT
✔ Decisions

Anderson Associates, personnel and management advisors, are conscious of the ethical aspects of head hunting.

Your role is to read through the case material, particularly on executive search, and derive some working guidelines on search as a medium of selection from the client's perspective. These views would equally apply to the search consultancy.

You may wish to consider and expand upon the following guidelines:
■ when to use search
■ the professionalism of the search firm
■ uniqueness
■ payment of fees
■ specifications
■ a working brief
■ guarantees etc.

Refer to the case study on AApma that follows.

AApma

The Andersons, husband and wife, started a consultancy firm in 1982. Both had considerable administrative and managerial expertise and were well qualified for the task ahead. The plan to go it alone had been in gestation for some time. A disillusionment with the restrictions of large bureaucratic organizations and, more importantly, a strong entrepreneurial feel meant that they were psychologically prepared for such a move.

The state of the marketplace was well researched, too. While in his job as a senior manager in personnel development, on behalf of the large bureaucracy, the husband had contacted every single known UK consultancy firm in the area of human resource management. The big name of the firm pulled in an overwhelming response. Fees, format, unique selling points, distinctive approach and expertise were all collated for the large bureaucracy. The research would do no harm to the husband-and-wife team either.

Their core expertise lay in human resource/personnel and general management. The research showed that the work of the competitors tended to be in recruitment, selection, salary administration, benefits, training, development and general personnel management. Some specialists existed as well in less mainstream areas, such as health and safety, counselling, welfare and employee communications. Labour relations seemed to be represented only by a minority. Both the Andersons had internal organizational perspectives from the public and private sectors, so they were aware of the buying process and the needs of the client.

The market was decided as being small businesses, recruitment, selection, training and development. The niche was seen as small to medium-sized firms without specialist personnel help on site. A retainer would apply rather than a daily rate, for this would give security to the firm and financial stability to the consultancy. The recruitment and selection would be aimed at management and would dovetail into the needs of the clients of these small to medium-sized businesses. Other research had noted the absence of personnel specialists in firms of fewer than 200 people. The training and development, although management-oriented, could include all staff from clerks to technicians in the needs analysis, and others would be brought in for the 'delivery' aspect.

The market was to be attacked with this three-pronged offensive. Considerable advertising was done, and much time and effort (and money) were spent contacting and visiting local firms in Cambridgeshire, Hertfordshire, Bedfordshire and north London. There were also mailshots and visits. The 'small to medium-sized business' approach was not working. Both the Andersons agreed that marketing and business policy with some finance might be the order of the day, but state aid and local government initiatives as well as expertise prevented entry into such markets. Maureen said, 'The fact that these people haven't got a personnel department in the first place shows that it is not a niche market at all. There is no such market, because they don't recognize the importance of personnel management. We either try bigger firms or stop throwing good money at it.' The big firms were sophisticated and had resources which the consultancy could not match. The personnel side of things was slowed down and the emphasis went elsewhere.

The recruitment and selection side of things looked attractive. Experience with a city head hunter had given keen insight into the mechanics of such work. The specialist knowledge again lay in the management side of things.

Competition was ruthless. 'Agencies' chased up every advertisement in the press and bombarded personnel officers with neatly packaged but unwanted c.v.s. The 'temporary' market was a growth area. A survey showed sales of some £400 million, with a split between permanent placements and temps of some 10:90 per cent, within these agencies, a considerable market. The return on capital of a typical agency was considerable: on sales of £2,400,000 in the first year an expected loss of c.£30,000 could be reversed the following year. After some four or five years of operation such an agency would have a turnover of c.£4,700,000 with c.£300,000 net pre-tax profit. The company did not move into this segment, however, as it looked crowded. Instead it moved into management search and selection.

It had three arrows to its recruitment and selection bow: search, recruitment advertising and a contingency register. The company's leaflet describes these:

Overview

High-calibre managers are critical to the success of organizations. The selection of effective managers, although time-consuming, has to be right as it has serious consequences both for the individual and the organization.

Through executive search or advertising, or a combination of both, we provide an impartial assessment and shortlist of external candidates for the client. We are involved also in the internal assessment of management, development programmes and personnel consultancy. Our services are completely confidential to both our clients and candidates.

The services

1 Executive search and selection

Search, finding management without recourse to advertising, can be very useful when the job is specialized or where confidentiality dictates a discreet approach. Perhaps above all, search finds managers who are not actively job hunting. We have adapted the process to finding both senior and middle management:

■ *Client briefing:* the initial discussion centres on the client's specific needs. Full account is taken of our potential conflicts of interest with existing clients before undertaking an assignment.

■ *Profiles: job and person:* an exact definition of the appointment is discussed with the client, and a person specification of the ideal candidate is derived. This specification, once agreed, forms our working brief for the assignment.

■ *Search:* by means of an original search plan, applied research and a wide network of contacts, we call forward potential candidates for initial interview.

■ *Shortlist:* after in-depth interviews, qualitative reports and background checks are forwarded to the client on shortlisted candidates.

■ *Guarantees:* existing clients are strictly 'off limits' for the purpose of search. If the individual leaves within an agreed time, we do the search again without any additional fees being incurred.

2 Management selection – advertising

Where a wider range of individuals can be considered, advertising can be effective. A wider range of candidates can mean higher response rates to advertisements, with subsequent time, money and management effort being spent on the assessment process.

Our service frees client management from this time-consuming process and, by advertising or by a combination of advertising and search, we provide the important shortlist for the client's final selection.

Our recruitment service starts with drawing up a comprehensive brief and recruitment plan. Once agreed with the client, advertisements are inserted in the appropriate media. We review applications, invite people to the initial interview and reject unsuitable candidates. In-depth interviews are held and detailed candidates' reports are prepared for the shortlist.

If required, we have a testing facility. Background checks are made on shortlisted candidates. We continue to work with the selected candidate and client to bring about a successful and early conclusion.

3 Personnel Management – advisory service

Unlike many recruitment advisors, we are personnel consultants advising on organizational reviews, compensation programmes, personnel strategy and management development:

■ *Organizational reviews:* we audit the quality and performance of the management team and advise on the structure best suited to the needs of the organization.

■ *Compensation:* salary and benefit packages and structures are developed by the consultancy for individual organizations.

■ *Strategy:* we review the present practices and advise on the scope and application of personnel strategy.

■ *Management development:* the planning, resourcing and assessment of management form the basis of the design of our development and training programmes.

The search side is extremely lucrative. The industry trend is some 30–5 per cent fee retainer based on the initial remuneration of the executive. On average a job with a £30,000 salary would be filled in a company and a retainer of £10,000 would apply. The Andersons thought this was expensive, so their fee was 25 per cent, and they notified the licensing authority accordingly. On recruitment advertising, the fee norm was *c.* 18–20 per cent plus the full cost of the advertisement. The husband-and-wife team went for 16 per cent. The contingency register with people writing in would give a commission of 10 per cent – this is instead of 12 ½ per cent used by the other firms. On price they could beat the competition and on quality they could more than match the expertise of most firms, which tended to employ sales people as consultants rather than personnel specialists.

Although the rewards are lucrative the business is time-consuming, with initial meetings, specification taking, writing up, clearing, agreeing, recruiting, searching and interviewing, with heavy reports on the candidates. More importantly, the work is fickle – the economic downturn of the late 1980s and early 1990s has destroyed many of the competitors who were in the market in the early 1980s.

It was agreed not to push this area given the depressed market. Instead a focus on overseas shorter-term assignments was instigated with a pro forma for organizations and one for potential or actual expatriates. Keeping track of these expatriates on contract proved to be a headache, and keeping up to date on their availability was difficult. However, it is working, and working quite well, with clients from engineers to managers and from petrochemical plants to catering institutions.

Assuming that if it worked for abroad it should work here, they designed a format for organizations in the UK and their firm AApma receives c.v.s on a daily basis. Companies are still tight on labour but the firm has stuck with permanent managerial jobs in the UK, and some come through the register. The process is shown in the flowchart in figure 2.3.

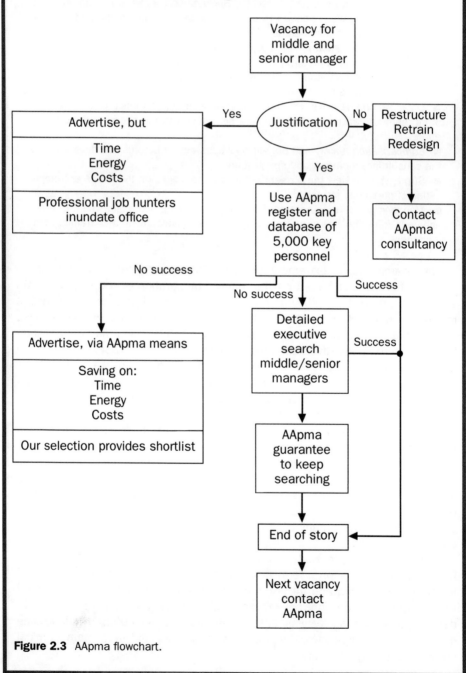

Figure 2.3 AApma flowchart.

BOX PM2.6

Selection methods: usage

Table 2.1 shows the usage of selection methods for some 108 organizations in 1986 (figures rounded for simplicity).

Table 2.1 Percentage of employers using different selection methods.

Method	Used for all	Never used	Used for under half of vacancies	Used for about half of vacancies	Used for more than half of vacancies
Interview	81	1	10	5	2
References	67	4	14	3	11
Psychometric tests (personality)	4	64	24	3	5
Cognitive tests	5	71	20	3	1
Assessment centres	–	79	15	5	2

Note that this covers usage, not validity or reliability.
The interview allied to references seems to be the most popular. Testing of personality has some use, as do cognitive tests. The assessment centre does not fare well.

Source: Adapted from Makin and Robertson, 'Selecting the best selection techniques'

There are various key methods of selection:
- testing
- interviewing
- references
- assessment centres

The work of Makin and Robertson[13] give us some perspective on the usage of these methods for management selection (see Box PM2.6).

Before we consider these mainstream approaches, a brief word is needed on some alternatives. **Handwriting analysis** is used by some firms, which insist on a handwritten letter to accompany a typed c.v. or resumé. Handwriting analysis looks to be in the same category as astrology and it is not a real alternative to the other methods. **Biodata** is a more serious contender. A questionnaire is used and the bio (life history) is analysed against some derived score. The two dimensions of measurement include 'things that were done to a person' and 'the kinds of experience the individual underwent'. The scheme lends itself to a person classification.

As we have now seen, the majority of users still tend to stick with some combination of interview, reference and test, so we will develop these themes. Let us look at references first.

References

Personal references from friends, the local vicar, etc., tend to be meaningless; most people are not going to nominate an individual who will give a negative feedback on them. **Work references** may be more meaningful, but beware of glowing tributes or serious omissions – for example, 'he was a good timekeeper' (but no mention of what he actually did during the time at work). A pro forma mini-questionnaire may be useful, or a brief job outline with a person specification may facilitate a more structured response. 'Difficult' or more 'sensitive' feedback can occur over the telephone, as some employers may not be as forthcoming or truthful when it comes to writing the thing down.

In spite of their usage, then, I have mixed feelings about the value of references. A testimonial or written reference from a previous employer, carried by the applicant, may give some insight into the individual and his or her old job, and may be better than nothing.

Psychometric tests

These are used by a minority, according to the research noted in Box PM2.6. Tests have considerable value in supporting the selection process provided that they are:

- *reliable,* with a parallel test at another time giving similar results to the original;
- *valid,* testing whether testee possesses the characteristics being measured;
- *standardized* – the same for all, with established norms.

Tests should not be the sole criterion of selection. The value of tests really lies in measuring attributes that are difficult to quantify at interview, and in that they provide an 'objective' view, and hence reduce subjective judgement and human error. They can provide additional information and can come into their own when dealing with younger people with limited track records of work. When the numbers are large, they can cut down interview time if used as a 'screening' device.

However, the use of tests for selection purposes does presuppose that the 'success characteristics' are known beforehand. Tests require trained hands to administer them. Bias, racial or sexual, may be inherent depending upon the norms being used. Candidates may find the whole experience unacceptable – particularly senior managers and more mature people. The tests must give some reasonable comparative analysis, and there is now a move to **meta-analysis**, which takes into account other factors such as the size of samples and variations in results.

More specifically, tests aim to predict the behaviour of individuals,[14] and this must be the acid test of their utility. Various tests are available:

■ intelligence

■ aptitude/interests

■ achievement/attainment/typical performance

■ personality

The staff specialist from personnel will need to undertake specific training to undertake such testing, while the line manager needs a nodding acquaintance with what tests can do for him or her, so the discussion will be generalized to cover these needs. (See Box PM2.7.)

BOX PM2.7

A testing time

Intelligence

The idea here is that the test measures the speed of uptake, the capacity to learn and the facility of knowledge retention. The mental capacity does not determine success but its absence would inhibit any chance of success. Yet even though the test does measure intelligence, however so defined, the critical thing to note is this: is intelligence really a key factor in job performance?

The concern is that these tests may show the capacity to perform on a standard series of mental tasks but fail to show the degree of use of intelligence in a real-life situation, or the person's ability to learn from experience and to adapt to new situations. These tests need to be coupled with probing examples in a discussion or interview. So intelligence tests show a 'potential to' rather than an 'actuality of'. Few reach their real potential in intelligence and the test may measure those who have tried to maximize this potential or who are good at doing intelligence tests. The application of this potential at the workplace is critical, and the track record of the candidate may be a better predictor than this capacity analysis.

Aptitude/interests

We are all different animals, and interests and aptitudes differ. Mental ability, clerical aptitude, numerical awareness, spatial aptitude and creativity can all come under this heading. Once the skills and abilities of the job are established, a test can be bought in to gauge the applicants' suitability for the task. This is particularly useful for younger entrants with little or no track record and can also be used for career counselling, etc. Leisure interest may not correlate with work interest and caution needs to be exercised.

Achievement/attainment/typical performance

These tests aim to test the range and depth of attainment and to give a feel for performance on the job. To a great extent the achievement/attainment dimension has been overtaken by standardized examinations by various bodies, colleges and universities. The interview itself can also prove the depth of specific attainment/achievement. Standardized tests in these areas would be difficult to administer and perhaps too costly to buy in or develop. The typical performance is more geared to trade tests or the speed and accuracy of a typist doing a letter. The problem-solving approaches of the assessment centre may enter this category.

Personality

Definitions of personality abound. It can refer to all aspects of the individual, to the ability to adapt, to hereditary factors, to patterns of behaviour or traits, and to a more nihilistic view that we are all so fundamentally different that measurement is impossible.

The **psychodynamic** theories emphasize upbringing and its long-term effects. Without a couch and a clinical psychologist, we may be in the land of projective tests. Ambiguous stimuli will delve into the deeper chasms of personality so that we will **project** some deeply held tendencies. Ink blots, for example, have been used and scored on the basis of content (human, inanimate, object, etc.). As one would expect, variations are wide. To the **social learning** theorists, personality is more mechanistic, a result of learned reactions. Self-ratings of how we view ourselves, assuming self-insight, may be useful in this context. The **phenomenological** perspective is concerned more with an immediate happening and an interaction with a unique personality. Tests of ability to cope with stress and conflict can be derived but this perspective looks difficult to accommodate through testing. The **trait** approach is most widely used. An 'introvert–extrovert' dimension is coupled to an axis based on stable–unstable dimensions. Another route is to look for personality trait clusters, such as temperament, moods, state of mind, etc. So these trait tests may give us objective and measurable factors but the results may be situation-dependent and less than stable. The crux seems to be the stability of our behavioural patterns, and if they are stable, this trait approach is useful.

Interviews

For the average manager, the selection interview is probably of more relevance than psychometric testing – in spite of its many potential pitfalls.[15]

The selection process is still dominated by the interview, so our role must be to make it as 'scientific' and systematic as possible. The selection interview is a conversation with a purpose, not a social chat, for the aims of selection will be all-pervasive and both parties will be on their guard. It is a tense conversation, potentially very stressful, even for experienced interviewers; so skills of ice-breaking, rapport building and destressing the meeting will be required by both the candidate and (more so) the interviewer. It is also more of a one-sided conversation than the normal chat, as the candidate is likely to do most of the talking.

The purpose of this 'conversation' can be seen as:

■ a confirmation period to check over the written details of the candidate;

■ an opportunity to amplify or clarify any written details of the candidate and of the firm;

■ a buyer:sales opportunity to discuss the potential purchase (the interviewee can be both selling him or herself and buying the company spiel, and vice versa);

■ an opportunity to get some information on the social skills and physical attributes of the candidate which cannot be gleaned from a paper application;

■ a test of social acceptability and for some organization–individual 'fit' or congruence;

■ a 'test' which puts the candidate into several real or hypothetical situations.

With these various aims in mind and with the constraint of time allied to the potential for stress, careful planning, relevant content and sound interpersonal skills are needed by both the 'actors' – but even more so by the interviewer. The content and skills will be considered later, but first comes the format, the 'plan of campaign', which needs to be worked out well in advance of the discussion.

Negotiations in labour relations have been termed 'the ritualistic dance of death', with both parties taking up preconceived stances, and using ploys and moves in some preordained plan. There is little room for such a dance in selection, but overpreparation can lead to an over-rigidity and a mechanistic approach by the interviewer and to a glib, overprepared, unspontaneous effort by the interviewee. The ritual remains, but flexibility in the plan is of the essence for both parties.

The plan: canned or fresh?

Should a checklist of canned questions be used or should the plan be freshly picked for each candidate? Equally, should the candidate give the same response to different company interviewers or should it be adapted?

The canned approach looks a little robotic. Each interview will be different and should be treated as such. Of course, you need your own specification and you must ensure that key issues are being met, so it is legitimate to have some set questions to ensure some uniformity of approach between candidates.

Fresh goods

Check the paper details on the candidate from the c.v., application form, covering letter, references, etc. Test results, if applicable, can be used, but I prefer to put them to one side until after the shortlist, or use them as a sifting aid prior to the event, depending upon the numbers involved. Either way, I do not feel that they should be part of the interview proper.

Compare and contrast the paper details with your specification: education, training, work experience, personal, future plans, etc. You can pencil in answers to your specification (although they may need probing at interview), clarify points and note gaps which must be covered. Perhaps linking questions are needed between your main categories – from education to training, etc.

So the interview needs some form of plan to ensure that the specification is met. Indeed, it needs a balance between the systematic planned approach and some time for probing and free-wheeling.

The structure

One approach is to ask all candidates the same job-centred questions which emphasize the special characteristics of the job. The person-centred questions can flow from the paper details or from the 'conversation' itself.

Another approach is to use the 'past–present–future' scenario. The 'past' is a historical narrative of previous jobs, education and early life. The 'present' has a focus on current attitudes, beliefs and approaches to a range of current affairs and problems. The 'future' revolves around the aims, personal goals, lifestyle sought and longer-term career objectives.

The seven-point and five-point plans can also be followed.[16] The main areas in whatever plan you choose must be covered while leaving time for follow-up and more lateral thinking. The plan adopted here is a biographical one – an historical one – probing the past and noting the achievements in the context of opportunities and constraints. One aspect of the plan is future-oriented, to give a view of where the individual feels he or she should be going. The weighting in importance of the five factors will differ according to job and potential job holder. For example, education will be emphasized for the young college leaver, the aspiring executive needs to have some career plan, the manual worker in the parks department of a local authority should have a focus on work experience, the researcher in an academic institution would have a focus on education and training, and so on.

The alternative route is to use the time-honoured seven-point plan. Activity PM2.5, later in the unit, looks at this plan from the perspective of the candidate, and asks him or her to pencil in his or her own profile. It would be repetitive to say the least to go over these questions from the interviewer's perspective but they can easily be turned round to that (original) perspective.

Apart from the questioning technique, there are other aspects of the interview content that we need to consider.

Content

The content of the interview is going to differ interview by interview, and we must avoid being over-prescriptive. What we can do is to give a feel for what can be termed good practice, so that both parties can have a meaningful, if not a totally relaxed, conversation (see figure 2.4).

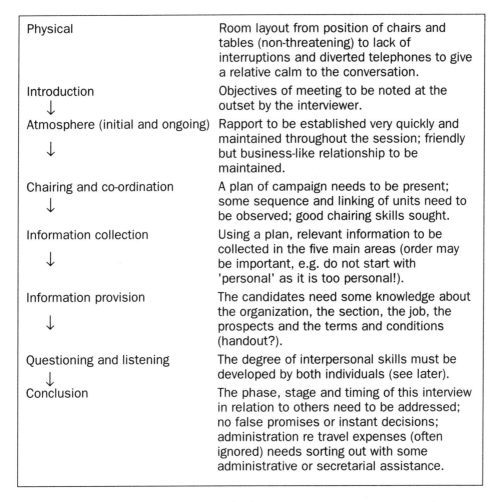

Physical	Room layout from position of chairs and tables (non-threatening) to lack of interruptions and diverted telephones to give a relative calm to the conversation.
Introduction ↓	Objectives of meeting to be noted at the outset by the interviewer.
Atmosphere (initial and ongoing) ↓	Rapport to be established very quickly and maintained throughout the session; friendly but business-like relationship to be maintained.
Chairing and co-ordination ↓	A plan of campaign needs to be present; some sequence and linking of units need to be observed; good chairing skills sought.
Information collection ↓	Using a plan, relevant information to be collected in the five main areas (order may be important, e.g. do not start with 'personal' as it is too personal!).
Information provision ↓	The candidates need some knowledge about the organization, the section, the job, the prospects and the terms and conditions (handout?).
Questioning and listening ↓	The degree of interpersonal skills must be developed by both individuals (see later).
Conclusion	The phase, stage and timing of this interview in relation to others need to be addressed; no false promises or instant decisions; administration re travel expenses (often ignored) needs sorting out with some administrative or secretarial assistance.

Figure 2.4 A flowchart for selection interviewing.

Skills

The skills of interviewing include the administrative skills, particularly at the preparation stage and at follow-up.[17] The preliminaries and the outcomes must go like clockwork, as they can otherwise vitiate the benefits of sound interviewing skills. The timing and arrangements of interviews, the job analysis and specification derivations, the availability of managers, the writing up of notes immediately after the event, the notification to candidates, and the use of a reserve 'list' when offering one person the job are all common-sense attributes, but without them, the process will become an unmitigated disaster. The candidates must exercise some administrative competence as well. However, the key skills in this transaction (which apply to both interviewer and interviewee) concern questioning, answering and listening (see Box PM2.8).

BOX PM2.8

Interview skills: questioning and answering

Type	Example	Value
Open	Tell me about . . .	Useful for getting the individual talking. Too many used in succession will lead to a very general discussion.
Probe	Why, what, how or in what way, etc.	Useful when linked to open questions. Too many in sequence will lead to an interrogation.
Hypothetical	What would you do if/in the following circumstances?	May test creativity. Value in selection seems to be mixed (see later).
Multiple	What happened then and why did you do that at that time as opposed to later?	Unhelpful. Series of questions should not run together. Cause confusion with listener.
Link	That's interesting, did you try the same approach with J. Bloggs?	Helps the flow of things. Can open up new areas of discussion.
Summary	Well, if I read you correctly, Mr Bloggs, . . .	Shows that you are listening (if correct summary is given). Useful at end and pulls the meeting together.

The questions are directed from the interviewer's perspective but a knowledge of what they are trying to achieve will be useful for the interviewer's response.

Negative questions must be avoided, including trick questions seeking an edge on the candidate ('Do you drink?'), boastful attempts to confuse the candidate by asking some rambling or ambiguous question, and questions about ethnic or sexual backgrounds which may indicate bias.

Listening skills

Listening skills must be allied to sound questioning technique. Non-verbal skills are very important when linked to these questions. For example, smiling and being open, particularly through hand movements, indicate 'warmth', as do a relaxed tone of voice, smiling, interested looks, proximity, helpful comments like 'and then', etc. Active listening is more than this, though, for you need to check for ambiguity, listen without making judgements, and be conscious of your own bias, as it can be destructive.

A brief note on bias is necessary: we tend to hear what we want to hear. Ideological bias can be countered by self-awareness and a sound knowledge of our own preferences. Expectational bias, from stereotyping to making judgements based on one or two attributes, can be avoided by a disciplined approach to the subject. Deliberate omissions and camouflage by the candidate can also give a biased perspective. Sound skills and good procedures should eliminate most of this. The panel interview or group session may also be beneficial in reducing this. (See too Appendix 1: Effective interviewing.)

Group selection and assessment centres

We can use groups to assist us with the selection process. We will examine the **panel interview**, which has a long association with the armed services, central government, local government, the police and other civilian services. This type of selection panel often occurs after the initial one-to-one screening and is the last stage of the process whereby the final selection is made from the shortlist. In a variation on the theme, the panel interviews a list of one-to-one interviews and reconvenes later to discuss the applicants. Makin and Robertson give us some feel for the prevalence of such methods in the UK for management selection (see table 2.2).

We can distinguish between a panel session and a **board session** by the numbers of selectees involved (there are more on a board) and by suggesting that the panel can see individuals on a simultaneous one-to-one basis while the board would not tend to do this. We will group both together, however, for the advantages and disadvantages are not dissimilar.

The panel interview does allow various interviewers access to the candidate at the same time. The inexperienced can be trained and specialized questions may be forthcoming through some division of labour. Leads missed by one interviewer can be picked up by others on the panel, so in theory more information can be derived. As a team effort, it may lead to a team acceptance of the chosen candidate once on board. Rapport is

Table 2.2 Percentage of employers using different interview formats (figures rounded)

Format	Never used	Used for under half of vacancies	Used for about half of vacancies	Used for more than half of vacancies	Used for all vacancies
Number of interviews:					
One only	50	15	11	12	12
More than one	2	12	4	16	66
Participants in interview:					
Personnel dept	11	10	2	17	60
Line managers	3	7	4	9	77
Specialists	43	41	8	4	4
Type of interview:					
One-to-one	17	18	13	28	24
2–3 interviewers	8	27	8	22	34
Panel	66	27	1	2	4

Source: Adapted from Makin and Robertson, 'Management Selection in Britain: a survey and critique'

lost, though, and personality and power rivalries may flourish at the expense of the selection exercise, so good chairing is required, and it can be a very stressful experience for the candidate.

Perhaps this stress-inducing facility is deliberate. If one takes the view that the candidate is there to distort past realities, it is best to put him or her under some form of test in his or her current situation. Hence judgements are made on the candidate's behaviour *on that day*, as they are seen as more representative of reality. **Stress** or **situational interviewing** can be applied. The stress does little for the panel, however, and even less for the candidate. The idea of replicating some situation in which the candidate may find him or herself at a later stage is developed later.

The other view of the interview is based on a **stability model**. By adulthood, most of our behavioural patterns are relatively stable, hence past experiences, adjustment and motivation are the key. To get the candidate talking, rapport and a stress-free situation are sought. If this perspective is taken, the panel interview begins to look somewhat suspect, unless tight control is exercised by a good chairperson who co-ordinates the whole thing and asks colleagues to come in unobtrusively at certain points in the proceedings. But even so, stress dominates at the expense of rapport.

Another variation on this theme is to put the candidates in a **group** with the selectors observing it in a 'goldfish bowl' environment.[18] Such scenarios are constructed to gauge social interaction, influence skills, and produce a spontaneity if not creativity, ideas, and some form of group role and leadership. It is very competitive and potentially stressful again. An example is shown below.

Problem diagnosis provides a different but related technique. A case or an issue is given the night before and the individual has to 'present' his or her recommendations on this simulation of reality. The candidate has to defend the recommendations before the peer group, and the assessment is ongoing.

Rankings of intellectual skills, attitudes, problem-solving capacities, team spirit, and the ability to command and get on with others can all be graded, according to the adherents of this approach. Costs, time, trained assessors, self-consciousness and unwillingness to participate by older people need to be balanced against the 'revelation' of capacities and capabilities in this testing situation. The artificiality of the whole thing may well tell against it. Again, philosophically it is based on the premise that the situation can provide the opportunity to test the candidates, and this is debatable.

These activities flourish in the environment of **assessment centres**.[19] Although they are useful for developmental purposes, there is some debate as to their value in selection. Again, the 'test' mentality is here, artificiality occurs, and a battery of tests, led or leaderless discussions, case studies or in-tray problem-solving exercises is used to grade the candidates.

We will take an example from a typical assessment centre using behavioural analysis. The candidates are asked to sit at the front facing a team of assessors. A controversial item is selected, from abortion to Irish politics. The four or five candidates have to express a view, defend their position, make contributions and relate to the rest of the group.

The assessors are examining both the contribution of the candidates and their social qualities and skill in social contacts. On contributions, the type of remark, the nature of criticism or agreement, the comments, the repetition, the jokes, the summaries, etc., are all analysed. One assessor tends to focus on one candidate. The characteristics of the contributors are then examined. The suggestions and their defence, the elocution, the clarity of expression and the references to previous arguments are all noted on a pro forma. The candidates' behaviour towards the group and the group's behaviour towards each candidate are also analysed. The role of leader, the attempt to influence, the type of authority, the degree of friendship or aggression, the level of opposition or acceptance by the group and each candidate's 'prestige' are all classified. A profile of each candidate is then collated.

So reliable and valid methods of selection do exist. The psychometric test and the selection interview as well as assessment centres can sift the candidates out. A professional approach to the content and format of those processes will help the manager overcome some of the many pitfalls. If there is a key, though, it is the systematic procedure. Solid job analysis is the foundation stone, assuming a vacancy exists via the manpower plan. It is the job and person specifications that should maintain us throughout the whole recruitment and selection procedure. Without this systematic process, the candidate is faced with 'appearance' and 'social acceptability' as criteria of entry, which is not acceptable. Able candidates will be missed and the organization becomes poorer as a result.

So far we have concentrated on the organization's viewpoint on recruitment and selection. In line with the focus of the book, we will now briefly cover the individual's perspective as well.[20]

The Individual and Recruitment or Selection

We cannot give rigid guidelines for everyone. The needs and wants of the new entrant to the labour market and the experienced executive are clearly diverse. Themes to facilitate self-analysis can be given, though, and these can be related to the job market. Unfortunately we do not start off our working lives with clean sheets, and once we go down one route, there may be few opportunities to change direction. Consequently we need to be able to build ourselves an 'investment portfolio' on an ongoing basis.

Let us focus on this 'investment portfolio'. The theme here is that the individual has assets and resources (like the firm). It is the core responsibility of the individual to analyse this source of talent, energies, personality, motivation, aptitude, etc., and continually update and develop this investment through education, course attendance, guided reading and other self-developmental activities.[21] The collective experiences, knowledge, skills and appreciation of aptitudes will make intrinsic and extrinsic benefits accrue to the individual over the years if the portfolio is well organized. Of course, organizational and domestic realities can constrain a free-ranging portfolio. (See Activity PM2.5.)

The personal portfolio allows you to take a realistic view of what you can do and what you want to do. This needs to be translated into a resumé or c.v. (see Appendix 2: A curriculum vitae). Good scanning of the press and professional journals as well as joining 'contingency' registers with agencies can be critical. A high profile will help you with head hunters. Jobs are product led, so innovation in the marketplace, from new projects to construction sites, can mean opportunity. It is critical to match the job opportunity with your personal strengths, derived from your personal portfolio.

To conclude this unit: we have advocated a systematic process throughout. From manpower planning to job analysis, from recruitment to selection, and from an employer's perspective to self-analysis, a 'scientific' approach is critical. From the perspective of the firm, we have now the

ACTIVITY PM2.5

INDIVIDUAL PORTFOLIO SELF-ANALYSIS

Activity code
✓ Self-development
☐ Teamwork
☐ Communications
☐ Numeracy/IT
✓ Decisions

Physical:
What impression do I make when first meeting people?
Am I well turned out?
Do people see me as socially poised?
Do I have a polished speech?
Is my manner pleasant?
Am I physically fit?

Education and training:
What is the highest educational qualification that I have?
Have I a trade, professional or technician's qualification?
What training have I undertaken?

Work:
(If you have no work experience, see 'aptitudes' below.)
What functional experience do I have (e.g. sales) and for how long?
What companies have I worked for?
What expert knowledge do I possess, e.g. products, services, equipment, machinery?
What geographical experience and knowledge do I possess?
What successes or achievements have I had?
What failures and underachievements have I had?
What opportunities existed in my actions?
What constraints existed in my actions?

Aptitudes:
Do I have an administrative ability (collecting, dealing with figures, attention to detail, following policy, etc.)?
How flexible am I? Can I cope with the unexpected?
Is my speech fluent and precise?
Do I like making things, from equipment to machinery?
Am I good with people?

Do I have a strong grasp of ideas?
How creative am I?
Do I like spending lots of time out of doors or on my feet?
Do I like ideas?
Am I a problem solver?
Do I like working with words?

Personal:
Do I feel that I am acceptable to most people?
How flexible am I?
Do people see me as stable?
How independent am I?
How perceptive am I?
Do I apply myself?
Do I take the initiative?
How persistent is my drive?
How broad is my outlook?
Do I withstand pressure?
Can I fit in to most places?
What domestic factors should I take into account, e.g. family, money, mortgage, pension, travel, geographical limits, etc.?

suitable candidates recruited and selected. One key element of this selection in the open market will be payment and reward. Further, once in post, incentives will be critical, so we will turn to this area of reward management in the next unit.

Appendix 1: Effective interviewing

This appendix gives a summary for all formats – single, group, etc. Interviewing is an evidence-gathering process that should not be intimidating. Here are some guidelines:

- Establish rapport, being warm but businesslike.
- Outline the purpose of the interview and ensure that the candidate is clear on the particular stage of the process.
- Describe the company (literature) and outline the job (profile to be available for the candidate).
- Have a plan of key areas.
- Be systematic.
- Encourage the candidate to talk (use open questions).
- Listen.
- Maintain the tempo of the meeting.
- Give the candidate an opportunity to discuss and ask questions.
- Make a firm conclusion and tell the candidate about the administrative arrangements and time scales in coming back to him or her. Make no promises – you have not met the next candidate. Even if this is the last candidate, reflect.
- Write up your notes and comments immediately after the event, relating them to your profile of the job and person.
- Later, consider all the candidates and then select the most suitable (not necessarily the best) for the particular job.

Appendix 2: A curriculum vitae (c.v.)

Summary	e.g. marketing manager with multinational experience in communication, television and radio
Personal	Name Address for correspondence Telephone/fax Marital status (ages of children if applicable) Age/date of birth Nationality
Education/training	Schools with dates and summary of Colleges qualifications – not naming each of University your 10 O-levels or GCSEs Courses Professional associations
Work experience	Job title, company, core duties (brief) with achievements (give dates) – it is normal to work backwards from the present.
Other information	e.g. fluency in languages, written a book on marketing for multinationals (job-related, not flights of fancy)

Notes

1 Porter, 'Takes personality tests to task'.

2 See Anderson and Barker, *Effective Business Policy*, and Anderson and Kyprianou, *Effective Organizational Behaviour*.

3 See Bramham, *Practical Manpower Planning*, for a refinement of the definition and the concept. The core definition comes from Department of Employment, *Company Manpower Planning*.

4 See Bell, *Planning Corporate Planning*, and Bartholomew (ed.), *Manpower Planning*.

5 An example of the supply side of events and the demand not reconciling is seen in Pearson and Pike, 'The graduate labour market in the 1990s'. The post-1992 European market was supposed to bring graduate supply problems, but economic downturn has complicated the picture as the demand has also decreased, resulting in rising graduate unemployment – particularly in the UK in the early 1990s.

6 Cowling cites an example from the clothing sector, with the cost of recruiting and training skilled employees being up to £1200 per head. For managerial and professional employees it would be even higher. See Cowling, 'Manpower planning, information and control'.

7 Atkinson, 'Four stages of adjustment to the demographic downturn'.

8 French, *The Personnel Management Process*, provides a good example of this format, which is critical for the cost control of the whole process.

9 The guidelines from the Management Charter Institute can be cited in this context.

10 Boydell, 'A guide to job analysis', is a good starting point.

11 See the readable account of the whole process in Plumbley, *Recruitment and Selection*.

12 See Ray, *Practical Job Advertising*, for the actual design of an effective job advertisement.

13 Makin and Robertson, 'Selecting the best selection techniques'.

14 See Miller, *Psychological Testing*.

15 A useful review of the sometimes contradictory research in selection interviewing can be found in Mayfield, 'The selection interview'.

16 See Munro Fraser, *Handbook of Employment Interviewing*, for an alternative plan of campaign.

17 See Sidney and Brown, *The Skills of Interviewing,* which is a classic text, and see also the people skills of Argyle, *The Psychology of Interpersonal Behaviour*.

18 Variations on the theme exist but Bass some time ago encapsulated the concept in 'The leaderless group discussion'.

19 Stevens gives an analysis in 'Assessment centres: the British experience'.

20 Although we go down the route of the individual's approach to work, the Professional and Managerial Position Questionnaire (PMPQ) of Mitchell and McCormick tackles the job aspect, rather than the person aspect, to give a very detailed breakdown of current work, from 'planning/scheduling' to 'technical activities'. It goes to the heart of the job of most professionals, and supplements the personal analysis.

21 See Burgoyne, Boydell and Pedler, *Self Development*.

Unit Three

Money and Rewards

Learning Objectives

After completing this unit you should be able to:

- place pay in the context of a motivator of employees;
- construct a payment scheme and use a range of payment methods;
- examine the role of employee services as incentives to work;
- conduct a job evaluation exercise;
- apply the generic skills.

Contents

Overview

The Importance of Money, or 'For Bread or Beans Alone?'

Pay: Levels and Structures

▶ The general environment (external)

▶ The specific environment (external)

▶ The internal environment

Payment Methods

▶ Intrinsic incentives

▶ Job rates

▶ Wages and salaries

▶ Indirect incentives and employee services

▶ Unionization

▶ Performance incentives

Job Evaluation and Equity

Flexibility

Unit Three

❝ And the key explanatory action to which we have referred is not that of the enterprise as a production system, but that of the definition of work and of the work situation, dominant among the [vehicle] assemblers we studied, that is, as we have shown, a definition of work as an essentially instrumental activity – as a means to ends external to the work situation which is not itself regarded as a milieu in which any worthwhile satisfactions of an immediate kind are likely to be experienced. ❞

J.H. Goldthorpe[1]

Overview

This unit is concerned with 'compensation'. It involves money and non-wage benefits, and concerns employee services, from welfare to counselling, as part of the benefits in kind.

Various ideas are put forward:

- Payment is important.
- Payment needs to be planned taking account of the external labour market as well as internal realities.
- While a range of payment methods is available, pay needs a baseline to meet core security needs and an incentive element.
- 'Employee services' are prevalent in industry but a mixed view is taken of some of them.
- Equity is critical in payment systems.
- A flexible payment scheme is necessary to take account of flexi-working, with group or individual incentives depending upon the needs and wishes of the participants.

The unit content follows these ideas and propositions. Pay and motivation are discussed. Pay levels and structures are designed. Methods of pay follow on and employee services are considered. Flexible pay and recent innovations on incentives conclude the unit.

The Importance of Money, or 'For Bread or Beans Alone?'

Wages, salaries and fringe benefits are part of the overall compensation package for employees. The term **reward** is preferred to 'compensation',

ACTIVITY PM3.1

MONEY AND MOTIVATION

Activity code
✓ Self-development
✓ Teamwork
✓ Communications
✓ Numeracy/IT
✓ Decisions

You have been asked to give a speech on 'money is not as an incentive' to your local management association.

Outline your main arguments.

as the latter smacks of a bribe to get people to work, while reward emphasizes incentives. (See Activity PM3.1.)

To the employer, these benefits often represent a major cost to the whole operation, yet if the payment system, the levels of pay and the overall makeup of the package are not adequate or not seen as fair, the motivation and retention of labour will be very difficult. An interesting departure in an employer's approach to pay is shown in the case of the beans (see Box PM3.1).

BOX PM3.1

Paid in beans

A firm at Witton, Birmingham, involved in plastics has decided to pay its employees in beans. High-flying executives can be paid in gold, so the workers can be paid in beans. Cocoa beans were chosen as a commodity as the price is reasonably stable.

Seemingly the workers earn £54 per week plus cocoa beans on top. A bonus is paid every quarter depending on the price of beans, and in the interim period the company gives the employees cash depending upon what the beans are worth on the commodities market.

The government loses out as National Insurance for both employees and employers is considerably reduced owing to the operation of a lower basic rate plus payment in beans.

Source: Adapted from the *Guardian,* 11 January 1993

Money systems and the nature of payment are part of the *raison d'être* of trade unions.[2] To the individual employee, money can be a key motivator or merely a 'maintenance' factor. Money can stimulate effort, give freedom of choice between increased leisure and an increased pay packet, and provide a snapshot of the individual's status in the community – if not a picture of his or her self-worth (see Box PM3.2). To government, manipulation of pay through prices and incomes policies, or through incomes policies alone, can give a tool of intervention and arguably some short-term impact on inflation, consumption and overall fiscal policy. However we look at it, money is important for all concerned.

BOX PM3.2

Money and motivation

Does money motivate people? The simple answer is 'Of course', but the evidence from researchers into motivational needs is more mixed.

Researcher	Views
Maslow	The basic needs at the physiological and security level require money as protection from deprivation and to ensure that the physiological needs are met. As we go higher, through the social ego and self-fulfilment phases, money may enhance status but it becomes less important.[1]

Researcher	Views
Alderfer	Pay and fringe benefits apply to the existence needs but far less so to the relation- and growth-oriented needs.[2]
Herzberg	Money tends to be more of a maintenance need which awards dissatisfaction rather than creating satisfaction. Pay can be an incentive, as part of the 'satisfiers' such as recognition, and may reinforce achievement and responsibility, but overall it is not a critical component of creating satisfaction.[3]
Vroom	The whole effort–outcome equation does include pay, but other factors are evident as well. It may relate to Goldthorpe's concept of instrumentality, whereby pay is seen to be the means to an end.[4]
Adams	Equity and comparison with others lie behind motivation. A sense of inequity and unfairness can devastate a payment system, while a comparative analysis with the external going rate and an internal fairness based on job evaluation go to the core of any payment system. Equity theory is critical for an understanding of payment.[5]

Sources
1   Maslow, *Towards a Psychology of Being*
2   Alderfer, 'Existence, relatedness and growth'
3   Herzberg et al., *The Motivation to Work*
4   Vroom, *Work and Motivation*
5   Adams, 'Towards an understanding of inequity'

From our perspective of effective personnel management, money and payment systems must be one of the most critical issues that we will have to deal with.

While the administration of these schemes tends to fall to management even in heavily unionized environments (although the unions may 'police' them as well), the key aspect concerns *agreement* not administration per se. In non-union organizations, such agreement occurs particularly at the time

---

BOX PM3.3

Managerial approaches to people and pay

Theory X
People dislike work and evade it if they can.

Force or bribery is required for people to put effort in. People must be directed, as they evade responsibility. They are motivated mainly by money, concerned about security, and use little creativity.

The implications for payment are that 'economic people' need control and pay becomes a bribe to get these lazy people to work. Carrot-based incentives and punitive reductions, fines, etc., can be employed to maximize effort.

Theory Y
Work is necessary to people's psychological growth. They want to be interested in work and can enjoy it. They direct themselves to a target, and will accept responsibility. Self-discipline is important and is more severe than imposed (external) discipline. People are motivated to realize potential; creativity and ingenuity exist, but are grossly underused.

The implications for payment are that 'complex people' are more self-directed and disciplined. They need money, but money is only part of the motivational mix. Less punitive incentives and rewards more linked to responsibility can be used.

Source: Adapted from McGregor, *The Human Side of Enterprise*

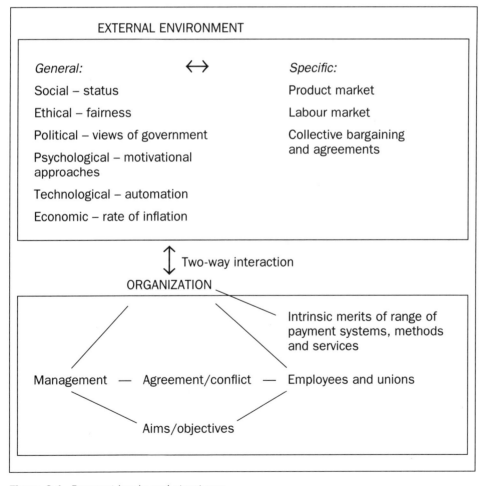

EXTERNAL ENVIRONMENT

General: ↔ *Specific:*

Social – status

Ethical – fairness

Political – views of government

Psychological – motivational approaches

Technological – automation

Economic – rate of inflation

Product market

Labour market

Collective bargaining and agreements

Two-way interaction

ORGANIZATION

Intrinsic merits of range of payment systems, methods and services

Management — Agreement/conflict — Employees and unions

Aims/objectives

Figure 3.1 Payment levels and structures.

of entry to the firm and there is some (limited?) scope for renegotiation on an annual basis. Variation of terms and conditions tends to rest with the employer, and voting with your feet is often the only route. In unionized organizations, ongoing negotiation and potential collective conflict surround the whole issue of pay and benefits. In both types of environment, the managerial philosophy towards its people can be reflected in its approach to pay – control versus motivation, the punitive carrot and stick compared to genuine freedom and real incentive. The caricature provided in Box PM3.3 is illustrative.

Pay: Levels and Structures

The checklist in figure 3.1 gives a useful way forward in the design of pay structures, taking into account a range of variables within and outside of the organization.

Pay levels can be determined by conventional market forces of supply and demand and/or by collective bargaining. The aims and aspirations of the parties, the general and specific environments as well as the intrinsic merits of different types of payment will have an impact on both this level of pay and the structure of a payment system. The content, nature and responsibility of the job, as well as the desire to compensate or to reward incentive, all contribute to the level and structure of pay. The structure and to some extent the level of pay are very much the preserve of the effective personnel manager. (See Activity PM3.2 and Box PM3.4.)

ACTIVITY PM3.2

MANAGERIAL AIMS AND PAYMENT SYSTEMS

Activity code

☐ Self-development
☐ Teamwork
✓ Communications
✓ Numeracy/IT
✓ Decisions

As a manager of salaries and payment systems in a non-unionized organization, outline the managerial aims in establishing any given pay system.

To what extent do you think that these aims would be different in a unionized environment?

BOX PM3.4

Pay-level determination: collective bargaining or market forces?

The determinants of pay levels are complex. On the one hand, there are market forces, and on the other, power and institutional forces through collective bargaining and their knock-on effect on the labour market. Both determinants raise the issue of the relationship between bargaining and the laws of supply and demand.

If an economic vision is assumed, pay is the price of labour and, without some control mechanism, it is determined by supply and demand like any other price. The supply side has such dimensions as population size, the percentage of people gainfully employed, the number of hours worked and the quality of the productivity level. Several factors have an impact on the demand side of the equation, including the quantity and quality of the other factors of production, the organization of work, the methods of payment, education and training and, above all else, the product market.

The **classical economists** felt that a given share of the national income would accrue to labour. This rate was determined by both the supply of labour and the 'wage fund' which employers decided to spend on labour.

The **neoclassicists**, with their theory of perfect competition, looked at wage rates as equivalent to the value of the product which labour produced. The marginal productivity theory of wages was born, with rational employers, homogeneous groups of labour and a free operating market predominating, without institutional controls. The demand for labour is seen as a derived demand, dependent on the price of and demand for the product.

The **social theorists**, taking a Keynesian view, torpedoed the concept of aggregate wages, as increases in the general level wages can cure as well as cause unemployment. Rises in levels of money wages will not inevitably result from contraction in employment. The institutional aspects of trade unions were also developed to suggest that trade union wage policy was based not necessarily on supply and demand, but on equity and fairness.

Trade unions are generally seen as organizations that restrict the 'free' labour supply, as bargaining institutions concerned with pay and as organizations which attempt to shift upwards the demand for labour. On pay bargaining, the concern of unions is **real wages**, as these determine living standards.

In times of depression, unions resist money cuts, and in favourable times they aim to raise real wages. Unions are no monopoly, of course, and often 'compete' with one another, perhaps being more concerned with differentials *vis-à-vis* other unions than with increasing their own real wages. Their objectives are complex – if not conflicting – and collective bargaining is only partly concerned with increasing monies. The range of options in collective bargaining may also be restricted, as the 'zone of settlement' may be narrow. Other parties to the wage bargain from the state, employers' associations and management will restrict the trade union freedom in collective bargaining as well. Most importantly, the precise location of the final settlement will be within the limits laid down by the parties to the agreement, so some scope exists for a powerful union to push the employer to the limits.

Clearly there is no perfect competition and no perfect supply and demand curve. Collective bargaining exists in a world of imperfect competition and there seems to be some scope to push employers to given limits. At the end of the day, though, the area of the sports field seems to be decided by the state, with 'cash limits' for its employees and by other employers, with their 'available monies' from the product demand. Collective bargaining can move the ball around and, if aligned to hard-hitting industrial action at sensitive times for the employer, the field itself may become larger, but it is not infinitive. The market seems to dictate the availability of the funds while the actors (management, unions and employees) can jostle for the allocation of monies.

The general environment (external)

The organization is in constant interaction with its environment, so a two-way 'open systems' view is taken.

Socially, the pay level is inevitably linked to status, and indeed pay itself is one key aspect of determining status. Exceptions exist, of course, and the 'caring professions' such as teaching, nursing and the church may have relatively high status but low pay. These impoverished middle classes still retain some salaried status, though, *vis-à-vis* the rest of the community. *Ethically*, the concept of equity, however judged, is paramount in the minds of many. The wage:effort equation of output ($£$) related to input and effort can use a comparison with others. For example, if all in the shop are being paid the same monies, why should one person do the ordering and balance the daily books for the same money as his or her colleagues? *Politically*, the environment outside of the enterprise is also relevant. In strictly power terms, for example, the trade unions are far weaker across much of western Europe than in the late 1960s. This relative weakness must impinge in their negotiating ability. *Psychologically*, we have been bombarded with many theories of 'what makes people tick'. One example is that of Hackman and Oldham (see below),[3] according to which a meaningful job with responsibility and clear results may lead to the employee's internal motivation, hence reducing the impact of external and money motivation at work.

The degree of automation in *technology* and the prevalence of capital-intensive industries, as opposed to labour-intensive ones, can have an impact on pay levels. Chemicals, oil and gas, with their high capital investment, may pay more to labour, as labour costs are less significant to the whole cost than in labour-intensive retail stores. Economic conditions are clearly critical to this melting pot. For example, full(er) employment may push up pay levels as employers compete for scarcer labour, while wage or salary freezes and cuts may occur in harsher economic times.

The specific environment (external)

We have covered both collective bargaining and general market forces, so a brief word on the product and labour markets is all that is required. In an interesting article, Professor T. Husband examined payment structures and formulated a model which included both product and labour markets.[4] Indeed, he went so far as to classify organizations by their pay orientation towards trade unions, the marketplace and the product market. Whether we accept his classification scheme or not, it does show the significance of both the product and labour markets for payment. Clearly the state of the product market will have an impact on the organization's ability (not necessarily willingness) to pay, while the abundance or shortage of skill in an occupational or geographical market will affect pay levels and structures as well.

The internal environment

Internally, within the organization, the objectives and aspirations of employees and unions, if present, must be taken into account in this payment scheme. The job content and its contributions to the objectives of the organization are important. The nature of the employees' individual performance – whether it is above average or not – is also relevant. The age structure and seniority of the labour mix can be significant, as, given an ageing profile within a company, compensation may be sought for 'loyalty'. Against this, job satisfaction at work, an inability to move elsewhere and pension ties, etc., may give more 'loyalty' from such an age profile. Other aspects of job satisfaction may be present, from team spirit to self-esteem, and money will be less important. Equally 'instrumentalism' may dominate at the expense of other potential satisfiers.[5] It was Jaques who suggested that we intuitively know whether our pay is equitable.[6] External comparisons may make equity more of an issue. Employees' aims and aspirations over pay and reward systems are equally complex. Whether we believe that people are wanting animals, never satisfied with money, or take a more altruistic vision based on motivational theories, perceived fairness and adequacy of payment are objectives and aspirations for most employees.

Trade unions
As trade unions are collective bodies, it is easier to determine their aims and activities concerning money and reward than those of the multitude of individuals. Trade unions and their overall aims in money and other socio-

political matters are covered in depth in another volume in this series,[7] so this discussion will be brief. Unions have both defensive and offensive strategies over payment – in crude terms, to hold on to what they already have and to seek 'betterment' on their existing position.

Union arguments to advance their position are the more fruitful discussion point. The main arguments put forward by unions in seeking pay advances are:

- cost of living
- productivity
- profitability
- supply/demand
- betterment
- comparability[8]

The cost of living is based on the retail price index, and so takes account of inflation. In many ways it could also be inflationary, as it is not necessarily based on the ability to pay or on productivity increases. This is particularly so in times of high inflation, when claims for 25–30 per cent increases clearly add fuel to the fire. Equally, in less inflationary times, it gives a marginal increase to the labour force. In both situations, of rampant or negligible inflation, this type of claim in many ways is geared to the status quo and the perpetuation of the existing customs and practices of a hierarchy of payment to different sections of the labour force. It tends to form a 'going rate' which may not be negotiated at all, but becomes the industry norm.

Productivity agreements seek to improve labour efficiency and its utilization at work in return for some increased reward to labour. In *The Realities of Productivity Bargaining*,[9] several interesting case studies were examined at a time of almost frantic effort to achieve a productivity bargain. Times have moved on and flexibility agreements encompassing productivity deals have taken over from these 'pure' productivity bargains. Their definition, though, has stood the test of time and it gives a flavour of the whole productivity vision:

> *Exponents of productivity bargaining see it as a means of achieving better labour utilization as a result of positive management initiative and planning. This is translated into action through co-operation on the part of labour in order to achieve higher efficiency, a reduction (or stabilization at least) of unit, labour costs and higher earnings.*

Profitability, assuming some surplus made by an organization, is a good basis on which unions can advance their financial arguments. Assuming that the surplus exists without creative accounting negating such monies, the ability to pay is a healthy basis for both management and unions to work upon.

The *supply/demand* argument is more opportunistic. Essentially this means exploiting labour supply difficulties by pushing for higher rates and 'consolidating' in times of demand difficulties. Such tactics are not particularly conducive to harmonious relationships between unions and management.

'*Betterment*' seems to focus on either low pay, a general improvement or some plan for 'catching up' with other employees. It is used particularly in the public or state sectors. The unions' justification of pure improvement may be more difficult here, unless based on productivity or profitability. On the low pay dimension, such arguments reiterate the strong hold of custom on the payment hierarchies, with the rich getting richer and the poor, if not getting babies, certainly remaining poor.

Parity bargaining, or seeking a similar going rate with another sector or work group, is a weak form of justification for unions in the private sector unless the jobs and the companies are transferable. In reality, the jobs may be similar, but ability and willingness to pay will differ. In the state or public sector, some mechanism is needed to review the pay of state 'servants' and *comparability* has been used to this effect. For example, in the UK police pay has been 'indexed', top civil servants and the judiciary have had special review bodies, there has been job-for-job analysis by the Pay Research Unit of the Civil Service, and there was an attempt at job evaluation using factor analysis by Professor Clegg and his small staff in the late 1970s.[10] In the absence of a genuine review, indexation or job evaluation, salaries in the public sector seem doomed to lag behind those of private industry. In this case, the state and management have a key role to play in stimulating and maintaining a 'healthy' payment scheme. The concept of 'health' is important to payment, and we will return to this point when we consider criteria.

Management

Management, of course, has an important role – if not the most critical one – to play in payment at the level of the firm or employer federation or association. The management of the organization will have a variety of payment aims and aspirations. It may be useful to categorize these objectives.

One objective is the attraction and retention of labour. Obviously, there must be parity with the going rate to attract people into the organization. This parity ought to be established once the individual joins in order for the organization to retain his or her services. Perhaps some firms also like to be perceived as 'good' employers, and a 'progressive' payment policy may help to give a competitive edge, while other firms use such policies to inhibit unionization among their own employees.

Management has an economic role of co-ordinating scarce resources within the organization.[11] Cost control is clearly in this category. If minimizing costs is not an objective (it tends to be, from anecdotal experience in many firms), then value for money is an aim.

The payment system should relate to the planning cycle as well. For example, a management development programme based on MbO (management by objectives) or some target-setting scheme must dovetail into the salary and career planning schemes. (See Unit Five.)

Depending upon the managerial style, flexibility or control can be furthered by an appropriate approach to money. People's motivation can be enhanced or discouraged by payment policies. (See Box PM3.5.)

BOX PM3.5

Not for bread alone: restrictive practices and output limitations

---

The carrot and stick approach to money management may not be sufficient to motivate the employee. A lot of management thinking is still based on a diluted form of Taylorism, whereby motivating workers means getting more effort by increasing income. However, soon **output limitations** exist.

Various explanations are put forward for such limits or restrictive practices:

1 'Work is the curse of the drinking classes.' The working masses avoid too much effort at work by what Taylor described as 'systematic soldiering'.[1] Dodging or 'skiving' is the norm unless controlled by management.

2 A more sophisticated rationale is provided by the likes of Roy.[2] Group norms predominate on 'what is required around here'. Group consolidation and harmony exist through a binding by this informal organization and shared norms. Rate-busters are deviants, and sanctions, from ignoring the rate buster to physical violence, may exist.

3 There is an implicit if not explicit relationship between the amount of effort we put into work and the reward that we expect. The work of Vroom can be cited in this context.[3] There is an expectancy that a given level of effort will result in a given outcome. The value of the outcome is important to the individual and this is termed a **valence** by Vroom. Expectancy and valence are then related to several levels of outcome.

Sources:

1   F.W. Taylor, *Scientific Management*
2   Roy, 'Banana time'
3   Vroom, *Work and Motivation*

Organization by management can be enhanced by joint agreement on pay levels and structures, as participation may inhibit conflict. Leadership style, as we have seen, can be exercised through such payment. Yet management must do the following:

■ *Reward the employee.* Organizations need to take account of the needs of the employee and service pay-cum-'loyalty' bonuses may be in order as well as 'security' device.

■ *Reward talent.* Merit, individual talent, experience and professional or technical abilities can all be rewarded through payment, and progressive payment schemes can stimulate the most important resource within the firm to even higher levels of achievement.

■ *Stimulate efficiency.* Results-oriented schemes and productivity packages can enhance the productive capacity within the organization. These will be dealt with later.

The administration of pay levels and of the payment system has been left on one side. As we mentioned earlier, it is the responsibility of the effective personnel manager (line and staff) in most organizations. Armstrong provides an excellent text on how to administer such schemes, from routine administration to conducting salary surveys.[12] We will therefore concentrate on methods of payment. First, though, it is worth examining a model of payment. (See Box PM3.6, which is more prescriptive than the coverage of the complexity of levels and structures of pay in this section.)

BOX PM3.6

Selecting a wage payment system: towards a model?

The writers verge on a contingency type of approach to payment systems. It is not 'pure' contingency dependent upon the situation, but linked to a profiling technique which, although standardized for all organizations, gives an insight into the priorities and objectives of the firm.

The first action is to construct a situational profile using twenty-three dimensions, classified under the four main influences of technology, the labour market, disputes and disputes procedures, and structural dimensions. They are as follows:

Technological dimensions
1 type of effort
2 unit of accountability
3 length of the job cycle
4 number of job modifications per job
5 degree of automation
6 rate of product change
7 recorded job stoppages
8 average length of job stoppages
9 percentage of job elements specified by management for operator
10 percentage of material scrapped
11 percentage of product or components declared defective

Labour market dimensions
12 number of days required to fill vacancy, including training time
13 labour stability index
14 annual labour turnover

Disputes and disputes procedures dimensions
15 number of stoppages due to pay disputes
16 average length of such stoppages

Structural dimensions
17 percentage of total pay settled outside firm
18 number of trade unions carrying on separate negotiations in firm
19 number of job grades × number of work units × number of shifts
20 recorded absence as proportion of normal time
21 average age of working force
22 percentage of labour cost in total cost
23 percentage of males in working force

The type of effort (1) is further classified into competence-, energy- or time-based effort. The unit of accountability (2) is also divided into individual, group or plant elements. The remaining dimensions are quantified on a scale (1–9). A quantified profile can thus be scored for the organization.

A grid is used to demonstrate that rewards can be broken down into reciprocal or non-reciprocal categories. Then effort is classified into time, energy and competence.

The next phase is to classify tried and tested payment systems according to time, energy and competence.

The grid and classification schemes are now merged. The types of reward from the grid are related to each of the twenty-one dimensions. By superimposing the profile over the grid, payment systems can be derived which are appropriate to the particular situation. This is perhaps a little mechanistic for some, but the principles of knowing our objectives and our situation and relating them to the most suitable payment system are still very sound indeed.

Source: Adapted from Lupton and Gowler, 'Selecting a wage payment system'

Payment Methods

The approach to methods of payment that we will follow is shown in figure 3.2.

Intrinsic incentives

We will not dwell on this area, as we have touched upon it earlier and return to it in depth in Unit Six. Suffice it to say that responsibility,

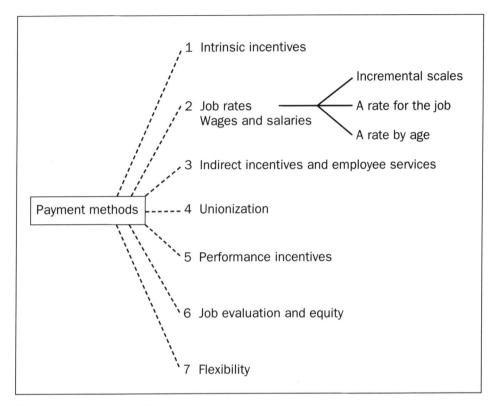

Figure 3.2 Payment methods.

meaningfulness in work and constant feedback can give us 'inner benefits' from our job.[13]

Job rates

Flexibility requirements, if not a desire for quality, have blurred the traditional distinctions between salaries and wages. Yet the division still remains, so we can analyse job rates from this perspective. The make-up of indirect incentives compared to job rate provides another classification, as does the degree of unionization and co-determination of job rates compared to unilateral (managerial) rates. Moreover, payment by time or by performance and output seems to be the issue of the 1990s in the UK[14] and this gives yet another analytical division. So we have:

- wages and salaries
- indirect incentives and employee services
- degree of unionization
- performance incentives

The concept of equity, particularly through job evaluation, will conclude this section.

Wages and salaries

A wage is an amount of money paid at periodical intervals, usually weekly, to an employee. In turn, wages can be divided into main categories: payment by time; payment related to effort, output or results; and payment for inconvenience. The wage packet may well be divided up into these categories of time payment, bonus and inconvenience monies, but we shall tackle each item as a separate analytical entity, ignoring items like geographical weightings and allowances.

Payment by time is usually at a flat hourly rate for a given period (40 hours per week, for instance). An example of lorry drivers with guaranteed overtime as part of their basic week can be cited, but such overtime was still only paid at flat rates in this distribution sector. The rate is paid irrespective of output. Traditional for unskilled, semi-skilled and skilled blue-collar workers, this hourly rate is spreading into temporary jobs, particularly as labour seems to be being casualized.[15]

The hourly rate is not attendance money per se but a payment for the perceived level of skill and the degree of union power over wage negotiations. Philosophically its bases are as follows:

■ It assumes that the employee desires some stability of earnings, as does the employer, since wild fluctuations in payment can engender insecurity if not industrial conflict.

■ It assumes that the employee desires security and does not desire a competitive pay structure of neighbour vying with neighbour.

■ It perhaps assumes that employees are basically conscientious, so the basic rate provides some form of non-carrot incentive.

■ It perhaps facilitates low(er) pay, as the flat rate is depressed in the full knowledge that overtime at premium rates will probably apply.

So a flat rate on its own may not motivate the harder worker, whose share will be the same as that of the slacker. The flat rate on its own will not reflect the mixed abilities of the work group, either.

Time rates seem to be most commonly used where:

■ the amount or effort at work is difficult to measure;

■ quality is more important than quantity;

■ output can be maintained at a given level almost independent of the employee (e.g. machine-paced);

■ delays to supplies or raw materials are frequent;

■ setting up alternative 'measured' schemes may be uneconomic.

There are three main types of time rate:

■ a proper minimum rate perhaps negotiated centrally with the facility of a top-up at local level;

■ a fall-back rate which gives some minimum payment in a results-oriented scheme;

■ a guaranteed payment, irrespective of effort.

Time rates may give more security of income, but they fail to reward the diligent or those giving greater output. Time rates are open to abuse, with potential 'go-slows' to stack up overtime payment. Interestingly, in the salaried work group overtime is usually worked but payment is not generally made. With no incentive in pure time rates, we cannot expect much excitement among the labour force. Indeed, when they are based on low base rates (as they seem to be in the UK), we can hardly expect great effort – quite the reverse, actually: to get decent earnings many have to work excessive overtime.

To some extent, salaried status may overcome some of these low pay/overtime difficulties – provided that the salary is pitched at a socially acceptable level. Salaries are often seen as financial 'compensation', traditionally paid to white-collar employees. Salaries tend to be an annual amount paid monthly, and longer terms of notice apply than for those paid in wages. Unions do negotiate in this area, particularly in the public sector, for example, and at technical or supervisory levels in the private sector, but there is – on paper at least – greater scope for individual negotiation of salary. Anecdotal evidence does not support this scope, however, as distinct salary scales with levels and hidden or actual increments tend to inhibit negotiation in most larger organizations.

Market surveys and job evaluation may facilitate the 'correct' pay for a given job. Salary structures can include a performance element but they tend to be based on time, covering the following:

- incremental scales
- a rate for the job
- a rate by age

Incremental scales

This can be based on a 'hidden' salary scale with management monopolizing the knowledge of the bands and the 'set' increments without the full knowledge of employees. In the public or state sector, scales and increments are published and known to all – for example, there may be a range of some eight increments of £600 each. Sometimes barriers or ceilings have to be crossed, with criteria such as changed job context or levels of experience being sought. Increments may not be even, with greater increases at the top of the scale to reflect seniority and/or expertise.

Problems exist, though, with a pure incremental/time-based structure. Although there will be anniversary increases in line with inflation under normal circumstances, 'bunching' at the top increment will occur as the years go on, and a rate for the job will be established rather than an incremental structure. For example, over 50 per cent of lecturers in the UK outside the traditional university system are seen to be at the top of the scale. Mediocrity can be subsidized by ability, with the only escape through limited opportunity for promotion to another scale (whereby the procedure is repeated at a higher level) or by leaving this type of organization to one that genuinely considers and rewards merit.

Tinkering with these scales through 'accelerated increments' or the withholding of increments is possible, but flexibility in a 'pure' incremental scale is limited.

A rate for the job

Some jobs may have a specific salary tag attached to them, with the only increase being a cost of living allowance. These jobs are exceptional in most firms, but in a 'decayed incremental system', as in lecturers' scales in the UK, this mechanism is widespread. There is little opportunity for progression and no real incentive inherent in the structure. It presupposes a low basic level of performance.

A rate by age

In some organizations there is a 'run-in' scale for younger personnel (aged under, say, twenty-one), and the full 'adult' rate is given after that. The idea behind this structure is that the young person is learning and has not reached 'experienced work standard'. It is a most frustrating period for a young person, with little or no incentive and definitely no reward for effort.

Other variants on pay can be seen in Box PM3.7. (See also Activity PM3.3.)

BOX PM3.7

Variants on pay: some examples

High day rates	Basic job rate is augmented with an additional payment often a bonus. The additional bonus has 'decayed' over time and becomes consolidated into the basic rate – at least in the minds of the employee. Not recommended.
Job rate evaluation plus job top-up	An unwieldy scheme whereby the basic job rate is used as an overtime calculator, etc., but there is a top-up based not on merit or productivity but on a superimposed job ranking scheme (see below). This type of scheme can bring chaos. Not recommended.
Overtime	The UK is increasingly becoming a low pay/long hours economy. Wholesale overtime working to eke out a poor basic wage cannot be productive for either party. Excessive overtime is not recommended and the basic rates, productivity and efficiency need to be examined.

Abnormal hours	Split shift working, call-out monies and standby 'plus-sages' are used particularly with maintenance crews. These payments are untidy and difficult to adminis-ter. Consolidation into the basic wage or salary should be examined to encourage flexibility.
Abnormal conditions	Payment for noise, dirt, heat, cold, etc., are often made. Again, these conditions are part of the job and these adverse conditions can be legislated for in proper basic rates. Such consolidation into a wage or salary does not have to have a knock-on effect on overtime, as a lower overtime calculator can be used.
Timekeeping, etc.	Deductions for bad and 'plussages' for good time-keeping are outdated. Good timekeeping should be part of the job unless flexible hours have been agreed.

'Plussages' tend to be linked to wage payment systems while salaries attract greater fringe benefits.

ACTIVITY PM3.3

THE LONDON BREWING COMPANY

Activity code
- ✔ Self-development
- ☐ Teamwork
- ☐ Communications
- ✔ Numeracy/IT
- ✔ Decisions

The London Brewing Company has some 7,500 employees and sales of almost £800 million per annum. As the name suggests, it was founded in London, and the head office remains there. Times have moved on, though, and given its national and increasing international market, it should perhaps be renamed 'The UK Brewing Company'.

The company moved out of London into geographical 'divisions' after the Second World War. With acquisition and the removal of some of the fiercest local competition through a policy of attrition, the six geographical divisions became regional companies responsible for their own costs and profitability. Increasingly each of the regional companies has been given fuller autonomy. Apart from the corporate plan, capital/investment projects and the overall marketing plan, each company is virtually independent.

The focal point of each regional company is a brewery, so there are six breweries altogether making over forty-five different beers and lagers. On the retail side there are 4,221 tenanted public houses, thirty-two shops specializing in selling wines, beers and spirits, and eight 'inherited' inns-cum-restaurants, all in East Anglia. The pubs and inns are controlled by the regional companies while the shop side is controlled by a specialist company based in Stevenage, Hertfordshire. Each of the companies has a regional board of directors, whose chairperson is on the main board in London.

The brewery company had a payments problem. Union pressures, management concessions and years of drifting along had put the whole payment system for manual workers out of control. Low basic rates, 'plussages' on top for other duties, overtime working on a wholesale basis, and excessive bonuses which had long since decayed all meant that the scheme was a cost accountant's nightmare, and that there was little positive correlation between payment and effort. Indeed, the unskilled operatives were earning far more than the experienced craft technicians, who in turn earned more than the majority of junior and middle management. The problems were compounded by a system of job and finish, or 'job and knock', as the workers preferred to call it. Once the quotas (already slack through negotiation and decay overtime) were met, the workers were allowed to go home (i.e. knock out). One director had noted years previously that in spite of this incentive to the 'under' operatives (it applied to no one else, and this became a great aggravation to the skilled indoor personnel and to the drivers), the volume of work was not being met – or the operatives were working too hard and completing their tasks in $4\frac{1}{2}$ hours instead of the scheduled $7\frac{1}{2}$. More capacity would be required, so Len Dayne, the director, decided to go for overtime, as he did not wish for more indoor employees. The overtime would be worked in the shift, so that the men now worked the $7\frac{1}{2}$ hours but got some 3 hours overtime at time and a half. The others did their overtime after their shifts. The rates still looked slack, and the indoor staff now voluntarily gave up their teabreaks. They were now completing the basic shift and the overtime in $6\frac{1}{2}$ hours and going home. Discontent was rife among the other workers, while the indoor operatives watched their pay packets spiral to the equivalent of £32,000 p.a.

After many hours of discussion, the personnel specialists and the senior line managers agreed some criteria for a new wage payment scheme. They also agreed to employ external specialists in incentives and payment schemes. The criteria of the company for a fair wage scheme are given below, and the consultants' interim report follows.

The company's criteria

The criteria are these:

■ There has to be a sense of equity about the whole scheme, and a fair relationship between individuals and between groups.

■ Incentives should be there to gain improvements in working methods, if not greater efficiency.

■ Incentives should build the common interest of the (regional) company as a whole, and divisive schemes between groups should not be accepted.

■ Simplicity should prevail.

■ So far as is practical, there should be stability of payment with no wide weekly fluctuations.

■ So far as is practical, the expectations of the workers should be met.

■ Cost control and company performance are critical criteria, and costs should be minimized while performance at least remains as at present.

■ The company is willing to pay for greater company performance, but not to specific groups.

The consultants' interim report dealt with principles rather than specific payment and went on for some twenty-five pages. The essence of the findings is summarized below (some average figures are included for context).

Consultants' report

The average earnings for a 'typical operative' (some earn more, others less) are as follows:

Basic	£11,000	
Shift	£4,000	
Supplement to basic	£520	
Bonus	£3,500	(£1,000 in group and £2,500 personal)
Overtime	£11,500	(includes shift, weekend and Bank
	£30,520	Holiday monies)

The 'inside' service staff average two-thirds of their operatives' basic, shift and supplements, with overtime of an average of £3,000.

The drivers have an average as follows:

Basic	£12,000	
Guaranteed overtime	£2,500	(Not necessarily worked)
Shift	£4,000	(If applicable)
Supplement to basic	£500	(Meal allowance c. £20 a week)
Bonus	£3,500	(£2,000 group and £1,500 personal)
	£22,500	(+ £200 'safety' allowance in theory –
	£22,700	discretionary)

The drivers' 'mates' have an average of two-thirds of all the drivers' payments.

The maintenance staff (motor and maintenance engineering for the brewery) earn similar amounts:

Basic	£15,000 (£16,000 for the non-motor engineer)
Shift	£3,300
Supplement	£100
Bonus	£1,000 (individual)
Overtime	£2,000
	£20,400

The first-level management do not receive overtime, shift or bonus, but are on a 'salary' type arrangement – although paid weekly. Their average salary is £22,000.

The guiding principles are as follows:

■ Reliability: conflict exists over the reliability of money as the basic monies are the only ones fully guaranteed (apart from the drivers' guaranteed overtime). There is a lack of stability of earnings: people outside of the operatives will not meet sudden changes in demand. The group payment scheme does little for reliability and is seen as unfair. There is considerable dissatisfaction with the scheme.

■ Costs: there is a lack of motivation to a high performance; 'drift' occurs; budgetary control is problematic; the bonus is not results-oriented; and the administrative costs look to be high.

■ Cost reduction: this looks difficult to achieve.

■ Managing change: the firm has paid significantly above the odds (and the labour market rates) for little material gain, while the employees have gained much material gain and will not change readily.

Using the criteria and taking into account the constraints of the consultant's report, design a payment scheme for the jobs outlined in the report.

Indirect incentives and employee services

We will now examine non-financial incentives. Perks are more than a mere tax dodge. They seem to reinforce status and self-esteem needs, fulfil our consumption needs and, perhaps more importantly, advertise our success for others to note. Some perks are not strictly meant to be 'rewards' at all but seem more linked to a welfarist tradition. It is not the purpose to give an exhaustive commentary on the detail of perks, but a brief overview and rationale will suffice before we look at the trade union dimension that we started with.

A useful summary of fringe benefits from a trade unionist perspective is given by Cunningham.[16] If we take the liberty of revamping his themes, we get the following classification:

Time off work	Holidays, sick leave, for family sickness, bereavement leave, public affairs and duties, court attendance, time to study, and to further mother/fatherhood
Welfare/health	Subsistence, subsidized meals, sports and social clubs, childcare and crèche facilities, loans, company discount on goods, and private health insurance
Travel/transport	Travel to and from work, using your own transport, travelling by public transport, and company vehicles
Accommodation	Tied houses or cottages, holidays, holiday homes and relocation assistance, from legal fees to bridging loans

These indirect wages or salaries or fringe benefits are a mix of social security provisions and top-ups to the payment schemes. They can be a useful tax avoidance strategy and can make life more tolerable in times of government-enforced pay restraint, as they are easily manipulated to compensate for a pay freeze or limit. Again, at times of high inflation such fringe benefits are a useful hedge.

There is a differential issue between blue- and white-collar employees, with the latter traditionally being favoured by better fringe benefits. This covers clocking on and off, holidays, sick pay, hours of work and notice periods. Over the years, though, the British trend has been to follow North America, with a closing of the differential and fringe benefit gaps between staff and manual workers. There may be a trade-off between the salary plus fringe benefits and the loss of overtime for those previously on wages.

There is also the issue of who should pay. Unions do have some friendly society role; the individual has a responsibility to look after him or herself; the state can give (and has given, up until the late 1970s in the UK) universal coverage; and the employer can give as well.

The philosophy of the firm giving out these benefits seems to be a combination of meeting the expectations of employees and potential employees, compensation for low(er) wages, security for employees, a welfare orientation by management, and securing loyalty, if not some form of commitment.

The 'time off work' seems not to be in dispute, and the need to relocate employees is an important accommodation item. A company vehicle for a sales representative is crucial, while childcare provisions can make socio-economic sense in getting female returners back to work. The other benefits have a clear welfare tag to them. We can go down this welfare route, or we can argue that the money would be better directed into real wages and salaries for the individual to dispense with as he or she sees fit.

This concept and application of welfare must be developed, as it was one of the original philosophies of personnel management and it has a hangover in many organizations under such guises as employee services and counselling. Welfarist policies as part of the overall benefits package

---

BOX PM3.8

Welfare and employee services

Altruistic minded people	Holders see themselves as custodians of the organizational conscience. They tend to be staff specialists. If seen as such by line management, it would reinforce the role.
Social responsibility pundits	These managers look to the good of the wider society. Since work organizations are part of that society, they have a responsibility to their fellow citizens.
Efficiency merchants	If we remove 'distractions' and offer palliatives, it should give greater security. Tensions and stresses can be relieved, so welfare gives a safety valve.
Union bashers	These managers take a unitarist vision. The trade union is an interloper. The union must be either reduced in power or eliminated by enhancing working benefits and by welfarist policies.
Participators	A two-way dialogue is sought between management and labour. The contract is a psychological one and the individual expects and should get humane treatment and involvement, with organizational objectives being met by such treatment.

---

can be problematic. Box PM3.8 gives a summary of some welfarist orientations.

Although the starting points of welfare may differ, the journey's end is similar. Some people find the whole thing repulsive. A former lecturer of mine, Jim Jocelyn, termed welfare 'industrial feudalism'. T.P. Kenney summarizes the anti-welfare movement as follows:

■ An atmosphere of charity and patronage is repugnant to the self-reliant.

■ Unions look on welfarism as a device to keep the workers down.

■ State provisions have replaced the voluntary need for welfare.

■ The behavioural sciences have provided another phase of managerial thought.[17]

Kenney's last two points may have been overtaken by events in the UK and the USA in the late 1980s and 1990s, but the first two have some validity. His theme was the 'rediscovery of welfare'. My feeling is that it has not been rediscovered across the board; it was a phase, a stage of development of which there are still traces in some organizations, but not in most. Having said this, Thomason argues for treating people with respect and with dignity at the place of work.[18] If this is welfare, so be it. But concern for human dignity is not really welfare; we may be moving on to the 'quality of working life', and to leadership styles and philosophies of people at work. These factors are pursued in Unit Six.

We cannot ignore welfare, though, as it has many existing manifestations, from canteens to saving schemes, from long-service awards to recreational facilities, and from transport to housing. Given this 'industrial feudalism', we should develop a more personal manifestation of welfarist issues which seems to be blooming: the area is counselling. Absence, inefficiency, low morale, etc., can be put down to personal or work problems, so there may be some pay-off in counselling even for the most hardened manager.

Originating in America in the 1930s, **counselling** has increased significantly in many non-American organizations. Now we find structured voluntary assistance programmes for workers involving a wide range of problems from financial management to marital difficulties. External consultants have been involved in providing such programmes and in-house variations of these **employee assistance programmes (EAPs)** seem to be an expanding area. Perhaps we need to differentiate between such a wholesale programme as the EAP and the skills of counselling. Indeed, many companies have not (yet) gone down the EAP road, but the skills of counselling should be at a premium for all people managers, and are transferable to other interpersonal sessions. (See Activity PM3.4.)

ACTIVITY PM3.4

COUNSELLING

Activity code
- ✔ Self-development
- ✔ Teamwork
- ✔ Communications
- ☐ Numeracy/IT
- ✔ Decisions

The personnel manager was at the head of department's meeting. Her budget was coming under scrutiny from the financial manager, who was not only suggesting an overspend but was demonstrating a significant variance on each budget head. The personnel manager noted that these figures were not consistent with her numbers. Finally the chief executive said, 'Settle this out of the room'.

Mary Pearce was quite new to the company as personnel manager and she could have well done without this. Later, Bernard Smith, the engineering manager, confided in her that Joe Marshall, the financial manager, was often up to such 'mischief' and delighted in showing up colleagues in front of the chief executive. She noted this meeting and the advice, but time passed and she put the incident to the back of her mind.

Months later a problem occurred in the finance department. A clerk, Molly Higgins, refused to 'honour' her job description, according to Joe Marshall. He phoned Mary and said, 'I've spoken to her on many occasions. She recently got regraded and her duties changed. She's taken the money but not the job. I'm going to discipline her and I need your support.' Mary, a cautious woman, tried to calm Joe. She did not want to launch into discipline, and said 'I'll have a word with Molly on my own.' Subsequently she pulled out her personal file and checked up the background details on Mary. She was the wife of a driver at the company. As it happened they were having great labour relations difficulties with the drivers and the disputes-cum-negotiations had reached a critical point.

Mary managed to fit Molly into her busy schedule. The meeting went as follows:

Mary: I'm pleased to meet you, Molly. I believe that there is a slight problem with your duties.

Molly: There is no problem – I'm not doing it. Joe Marshall's a crook – he keeps altering jobs and schedules. I've got an important job for the operation of customer contact paperwork and he has loaded me up with another job that he does not want to do.

Mary: I object to the term 'crook'.

Molly: You don't work with that conniving swine. I do. You ask the rest of the girls – he says one thing and does another.

Mary: Fine. About this job.

Molly: What about it? What job? I'm doing two at the moment.

[Clearly the meeting was going nowhere at the moment and Mary needed to check out the facts, so she decided to calm Molly down and leave it at that.]

Mary: OK Molly, we'll pick this up later. How are things going generally? I believe that your husband works here as well as a driver.

Molly: Don't bring him into it. Don't you threaten me by threatening him. You lot are all the same.

Mary: No, I was only making conversation.

Molly: No you weren't – you're trying to get to me through my Sam. I'll tell him at dinner break. He won't like that and he'll get onto his shop steward.

[The meeting ended with Mary trying to undo this damage, but to no effect.]

1 Analyse the dynamics of this situation.
2 Did the meeting go wrong? If so, where?
3 What script would you have written for Mary in preparing this meeting?
4 What script would you write for Mary in preparing for another joint meeting with Molly and Joe Marshall?

Unionization

Deliberately, the role of unions has not been placed centre stage in this book, as it is covered in depth elsewhere in the series.[19] However, unions have a clear view of money and reward, and play an important role in the formulation and acceptance of the financial package for members. Indeed, there can be a spin-off to non-union firms as well, as the unionized 'going rates' spill over to the local labour market. The degree of unionization is an important variable in the make-up of the influences on pay and on the selection of payment methods.

Performance incentives

Relating pay to effort and not just time has run through this unit as a guiding principle. However, safeguards must be provided as well, for the core money must still be time-based and there is a case for incentives for all employees.

Wright and Brading see the issue of performance related pay as 'one of the most dynamic issues of human resource management and arguably the most topical component of reward policy today'.[20] It may be topical, but it has a history and there are lessons to be gained from history – although no two epochs are identical. With sufficient safeguards to protect the wage-earners, unions accepted slowly the move from flat time rate to **payments by results (PBR)** as a means of rewarding good or industrious workers. The reduction in the labour force in the UK after the Second World War, the drive for productivity and an awareness of being paid what you are actually worth all helped stimulate PBR.

The processes of introducing and maintaining PBR schemes are in themselves classic examples of joint consultation and bargaining between managed and managers. Guaranteed basic (fall-back) rates were established, allied to the quality or volume produced in a given time minus due (agreed) allowances. The carrot philosophy behind the scheme is that workers want more money and are prepared to work harder to get it.

Some general points can be made about PBR:

- It is best where work is easily measurable.
- The work should be capable of being paced (not necessarily controlled) by the employee.
- It suits conditions where there is a steady flow of work and where the work is consistent (i.e. without constant changes).
- Work should be easily attributable to a group or individual.
- Bottlenecks need to be abolished or at least minimized to give a constant workflow.
- There needs to be some quality control or inspection to ensure that payment is given only for work that reaches a certain standard. This point is critical, for many schemes fall or fell into disrepute as management accepted 'slippage'.

Clearly, PBR schemes are not really appropriate for, say, maintenance workers, diagnostic technicians or designers. They are very much geared to a continuous flow operation with standardized outputs and an ongoing flow of uniform work which can be measured and monitored.

PBR can mean a costly exercise on work measurement and rate fixing as well. Loose rates will destroy the scheme very quickly while work-group controls, as we have seen, are still present and groups tend to set their own standards. It can lead to a cost explosion for management and an expectation among employees that it is an automatic payment. A lot of time is spent on ongoing negotiation even once the scheme is up and running. So the benefits seem mixed, particularly for management, while variable earnings can mean insecurity and heightened tensions for the workers. Of course, variation on the theme exist, from simple piecework systems, with or without fall-back and payment proportional to output, to more sophisticated versions of premium bonus schemes, with pay either less than proportional to output but with a premium payment, or increasing more proportionally to effort, with no guarantees and no fall-back in incentive piece-rate schemes.

Measured day work (MDW) was seen as a lifeboat for many PBR schemes. The wage-earner is asked to maintain a specified level of performance. Pay, however, does not fluctuate if the performance does not meet this specified level – at least in the short term. Some schemes adopt a stepped approach with, say, performance levels one to four, each of which is measured with specified levels of performance. Payment is geared and differentiated according to each step, so movement between the steps is possible.

There are clear similarities with some PBR schemes, but the underlying philosophy of MDW looks different: the employee is required not to work harder or faster as in PBR, but to work constantly at a predetermined and agreed performance level. Again, earnings should be more stable under the MDW approach. Conditions appropriate for MDW include the following:

- 'Standard times' must be available for each job.

- Operators must meet the specified level of performance.

- Management must avoid 'drift' in time standards and maintain control over performance levels.

- The labour relations climate must be good enough to facilitate changes to the scheme, particularly over revamping standards if necessary.

Another variation on the theme is the **premium payment plan**. Here performance is computed monthly, not daily as in MDW, and performance scales tend to be more in operation. A safeguard for management is that the employee is not moved up the scale until he or she has hit the performance level, and the safeguard for employees is that performance downgrading is less likely.

These schemes (MDW and premium payment) may have some merit, but the potential for wage-drift and work-group controls, and the need for constant monitoring by management, illustrate their drawbacks.

These group schemes and their variations, often geared mainly to manual workers, have had mixed results. The current trend among white-collar workers in particular is to move away from such collective schemes and to emphasize either individual merit or organizational performance through some profit-sharing experiment.

Merit payments can cover both wage- and salary-earners. Merit rating is a form of performance appraisal which is covered in depth in Unit Five. The key factors reflecting work performance are assessed – for example, quality, quantity, reliability, etc. These 'desired behaviours' are obviously crucial in such a scheme, as indeed is an objective assessment of performance. The 'blue-eyed syndrome' – subjectivity and favouritism – can dog the merit system and, as we would expect, it tends to be unpopular with trade unions. Many salaried employees are non-unionized, and such merit schemes operate in conjunction with performance appraisal. This often degenerates into box ticking or, worse still, into some amateur psychological discourse on the 'qualities' of the individual rather than on the job performance of the appraisee. If objectively based and carried out, merit rating has much to its credit, but it can easily fall prey to subjective manipulation, and I have seen many examples of outright nepotism through such schemes.

Arguably, a more objective format is the **share of 'production' schemes**. These can be company- or plant-wide. Many examples exist: Priestman-Atkinson, Rucker, F.R. Bentley and the Scanlon Plan, to name a few.[21] We are now moving into the area of a collective incentive which can apply to all within the organization. In simple terms (the plans are quite complex), a certain percentage of the revenue is allocated for wages and salaries. This figure should be linked to some added value within the firm. The wage and salary costs are deducted from this overall added value and a surplus is left to be distributed to the employees. Such schemes necessitate:

- excellent financial records to discern the added value;
- salary and wage entitlement being monitored on an ongoing basis, as the pay bill may not be a fixed percentage of the added value (many schemes assume that it is);
- the good times (bonus allocation) being related to the bad times (no bonus);
- an open management style which is prepared to disclose financial information.

In many ways these schemes are a half-way house to profit sharing, which has become more popular in the UK in the 1980s and 1990s. Other variations of these plant- or company-wide bonuses have included and include efficiency, quality, scrap reduction and general cost reduction.

When the climate of labour relations is quite sound, where the plant is smaller and more containable, or where a crisis occurs, these **cost-reduction schemes** can be useful mechanisms of survival. Arguably they are less of an ongoing system, and although they can be linked to incentives, they tend to be expedients of survival rather than growth.

The **profit-share concept** has been the preserve of senior management for some time and an incentive (albeit remote in some cases) can be seen, as it is linked to growth and any financial surplus the company makes. These schemes have great potential from management's perspective but are a mixed blessing from the employees' viewpoint (see Box PM3.9). Rewards are allocated when the firm is in profit, and in practice look to be quite marginal. The hard-working employee may be remote from the other factors involved in the return on capital employed. When allied to other incentives, there is considerable scope for such schemes provided that the 'payment' is not marginal and that the 'share' is more real than imagined.

Equity is important to these incentive schemes – indeed, it is important to all payment schemes. We will conclude this review by looking at job evaluation as a basis of equity within payment schemes.

BOX PM3.9

Performance pay: share ownership

Profit sharing through wider share ownership is one method of rewarding employees for increased company performance. A range of schemes operate and include:

Bonus	A proportion of company profit is allocated to its employees as a form of bonus. If paid in cash it becomes an extension of the wage or salary; if it is paid in shares the cash bonus is deferred.
Save as you earn	The employer nominates a number of shares which will be available for purchase. 'Options' are given to buy these shares, often at a 'fixed' (lower) price.
Deferred share trust	Unlike the bonus above, the rewards are not immediate as the shares are held in trust for about two years, but they are exempted from state deductions in pay as you earn (PAYE).
Executive share options (ESOs)	A discretionary share scheme for selected senior employees.
Employee share ownership plans (ESOPs)	An increasingly popular method of employee shareholding.

Is there any merit in these employee share schemes? Some greater identity with company aims may occur; people can become more aware of costs and company performance overall; 'poor performers' may feel peer pressure to work harder; and some may think twice about embarking on strike action, as it could disrupt the pay-out. Yet the schemes can be expensive and the pay-out is not usually immediate, and in many schemes is marginal. The concept of employee participation through shareholding is at best remote. As it is performance linked, poor trading results will mean low(er) pay-out. By definition there is no real link between individual effort and individual incentive in this collective performance scheme.

Do these schemes work? It depends what we are trying to do. The financial rewards are not great, so they must be seen as part of the overall benefits package. Perhaps better communication comes from these schemes, with all the relevant details being passed on to the employees, and this can only be good.

They are not, however, active employee participation schemes, but indirect schemes of involvement. The link to greater productivity looks to be tenuous, but it seems to bind the employees together and lead to a more 'supportive' climate. If this is generally the case, such schemes can be termed as 'unitarist' in their philosophy and, if this is the company aim, then perhaps they work after all. For the employees (and unions) the limits of such schemes as presently operated should be kept in mind – although there may be a limited pay-off to the employees.

Job Evaluation and Equity

The success of any payment system will be based not on the technical purity or the intrinsic merits of its component parts, but on its acceptability to the employees. The concept of **equity** – that is, fairness and equality of treatment – goes to the heart of any payment system. This is where **job evaluation** becomes important, for it is concerned with the relative worth of jobs and underpins any balanced payment structure.

Job evaluation rates the job not the person. The primary issue is: 'What is the job?'. Another issue is 'How much is the job worth financially?'. The two evaluations are related, but they are separate exercises. It helps form the job hierarchy of any pay structure, but first comes the job ranking, then the allocation of money.

There is a strong case for job evaluation, as the alternative seems to be impressionistic views of the market value of jobs and a casual opinion of what is 'right', or a power-oriented job hierarchy determined purely by custom via years of collective bargaining. Job evaluation is not a scientific process, but it is a useful and logical tool that gives a systematic approach to job content, a feeling of fairness and a rational approach to differentials in the organization. It gives:

- reliable data for working out wage and salary scales;
- fair treatment for jobs, hence limiting favouritism;

- a logic to pay differentials;
- a precise description of the job;
- an opportunity for job regrading when changes in job content occur;
- the opportunity for equal pay for equal work;
- a logical, unfragmented pay structure.

Although there are many types of job evaluation scheme and different methods of approaching the analysis, there are some fundamental features which are common to most schemes. These broad principles contain the following elements:

- A thorough investigation of the job is made.
- A job description is prepared in conjunction with the job holder and his or her manager.
- The job is analysed, and broad elements or factors of the job are noted.
- The jobs are compared with one another or with a 'benchmark' – a job selected as being representative of a particular level of work.
- The jobs are put into some classification or hierarchy according to this comparison.
- The jobs and hierarchy are translated into some monetary value.

Experience of job evaluation in a nationalized industry showed that the scheme should be not only logical and equitable, which it was, but acceptable and negotiable, which it was not: the unions and management had not agreed the system, and the unions' involvement seemed to be to appeal against the findings of the management job evaluation panel.

The International Labour Organization some time ago in a study of job evaluation summarized the main factors commonly used in a range of job evaluation systems.[22] There are four main factors and thirteen sub-factors:

Factor	Sub-factor
Mental	Reasoning ability
	Co-operation with others
	Initiative and observation
Physical	Muscular strength
	Dexterity and motor accuracy
	Stamina and agility
Acquired skills and knowledge	Education
	Training required
	Experience required
Working conditions	Physical/mental disagreeableness
	Hazards and risks
	Responsibility (equipment and materials)
	Responsibility (safety and work)

The range of factors being considered will vary according to the type of scheme in operation. For example, for blue-collar workers criteria such as skill (experience to training), responsibility (for material to the safety of others) and effort (from physical to visual) may be adequate. For white-collar staff, criteria based on knowledge, experience, problem solving and 'answerability' may be adequate. The work of Brian Livy provides one of the most comprehensive and readable accounts of the whole process of job evaluation.[23] Box PM3.10 gives a summary of the main approaches.

BOX PM3.10

Job evaluation: methods (pluses and minuses)

Ranking
Jobs are judged as entities and ranked against one another. The method is not analytical.
+ Simple for a small(er) firm for example
+ Cheap
+ Easy to explain
− Results can be superficial
− May perpetuate the existing job hierarchy
− Cannot cope with larger number of jobs in a big organization

Classification
Grade and monetary levels are determined before the ranking exercise is done. Grades have a common narrative for each grade category. For example, Grade 1 = 'simple and procedural work, routines well established, no judgement and no resources administered'. Jobs are allocated to the categories.
+ Cheap, quick and easy to understand
− Subjectivity of evaluators
− Jobs overlap into different categories

Factor comparison
Jobs are assessed in terms of factors, not of the whole job. For example, the jobs could be broken down into 'skill, responsibility, effort and conditions'. Each job is graded by these categories, so the labourer ranks lower in skill and responsibility but higher in effort and conditions, and so on. A 'price' is given to the factor or to the hierarchy as a whole.
+ Discriminates better than the previous two types of scheme
+ Not too complex
− May be inflexible
− Apportioning monetary values to the factors and their weightings of importance given to the factors can cause problems.

Points rating
An analytical and popular method. Factors are chosen, but there are a number of degrees or levels within each, reflected by points. The factors are then weighted – for example, we may give education 20 per cent, experience

20 per cent, judgement 30 per cent and responsibility 30 per cent. Take education: the ability to read and write and do simple arithmetic may be worth 15 points while a degree may be worth 180 points.
+ Looks 'scientific' (but beware!)
+ Logical and objective
+ New jobs can be slotted in
− Weighting difficulties between the factors can be a problem
− Can be expensive
Altogether this seems to be the most acceptable method.

Yet there are also limitations inherent within the job evaluation:

■ The factors, their weighting and point rating all contain a subjective element.
■ It may give a numerical expression of relativity – but it is not mathematically precise.
■ It takes time and money for the system to get going and to operate.
■ Specialist job analysts may be required to report back to a committee.
■ It requires some form of consensus at committee stage, where all the grades are considered.
■ Employee involvement looks to be critical and this may not tally with the predominant management style.

See Activity PM3.5.

ACTIVITY PM3.5

JOB EVALUATION

Activity code
✔ Self-development
☐ Teamwork
☐ Communications
✔ Numeracy/IT
✔ Decisions

You have to conduct a job evaluation of a senior payroll accountant for a large organization. First of all, comprehensive job details will be given and then you must relate these tasks to the job evaluation scheme that follows. The job should be graded in terms of the factors of the scheme. No payment is necessary, as we are coming to terms with the mechanics of job evaluation.

Obviously it presupposes that job analysis has occurred and that a scheme is up and running. Equally, the transfer to money terms and grades would have to occur after this event.

Job details

Job: senior payroll accountant in the finance section reporting to the director of finance.

Job outline: co-ordinates the work of fifty staff responsible for the preparation of wages, salaries and pensions to some 15,000 staff and 3,000 pensioners.

Core specification: an experienced accountant and manager with about five years' payroll knowledge within a large firm. Probably a qualified accountant with good social skills, as he or she deals with queries from staff at all levels and from external auditors, bank managers, tax people, etc.

The job holder is under the general 'supervision' of the finance director but considerable latitude exists in the job. He or she directly controls two managers (salaries/pensions and wages/pensions). Indirectly he or she controls forty-eight other subordinates.

He or she will have responsibility for complex computing equipment, money (£25 million at a time) and associated materials of a confidential nature. Security is an important aspect of the job.

The conditions of work are essentially those linked to an office in central London, although he or she may have to work weekends and visit sites as necessary.

Duties (outline): The job holder is responsible for managing the whole section. The work involves weekly and monthly remuneration, monthly pensions, and expenses (*c.* £5,000 per month). Ancillary work involves such items as deduction of union monies, company savings scheme, tax and insurance, court orders (for deducting monies) and the calculation of bonus, etc. The job holder has membership of the pension trustees' fund, and administration of it. The job holder authorizes all monies for salary, wage and pension payment. He or she manages the staff, from selection to discipline, and is responsible for maintenance and innovation in procedures and training.

Job evaluation scheme

Experience: this includes the amount and type, given a certain educational background, necessary to fulfil the duties of the job. It may include general and specific experience.

		Points
A	Under 1 year	5
B	1– under 2 years	10
C	2– under 3 years	20
D	3– under 4 years	30
E	4– under 5 years	40
F	5– under 7 years	60
G	7– under 9 years	80
H	9– under 11 years	100
I	11 plus years	140

Education: basic requirements are:

		Points
A	Basic secondary school	5
B	GCSE/SCE O	10
C	GCSE/SCE A/H-level	15
D	Higher National	20
E	Degree	25
F	Professional qualification	30
G	Honours degree	35
H	Postgraduate degree	40

Job content:

		Points
A	Simple repetitive task	5
B	Detailed instructions applied (given)	10
C	Memorizing and application of more diverse instructions	15
D	Skill necessitated by application of managerial techniques or study	20
E	Complex tasks	25
F	Conceptual tasks	30
G	Strategic tasks	40

Job scope: This covers independent action without constant recourse to a boss, and the level or degree of established procedures.

		Points
A	Procedures well established/work checked	10
B	Well-defined procedures/some deviation allowed/work spot-checked	20
C	Established policies but choice of work method; no real daily check (weekly only)	30
D	Assignments given and told to meet deadline	40
E	Administrative/functional supervision restricted to 'end results' being monitored on a larger time scale	60

Responsibilities: this can cover money, people, machines, accuracy, risk, etc.

Money/machines:

		Points
A	Responsible for money on machines or plant under £500,000	20
B	Responsible for money on machines or plant from £500,000 to under £1,000,000	40
C	Responsible for money on machines or plant from £1,000,000 to under £2,000,000	60
D	Responsible for money on machines or plant from £2,000,000 plus	100

(Risk of loss should be included in this calculation.)

People/contacts:

		Points
A	Responsible for routine contacts with internal staff only	10
B	Responsible for less routine contacts with internal staff only	20
C	Responsible for routine contacts with internal staff plus contacts with external agencies	30
D	Responsible for less routine contacts with internal staff plus external liaison, which may be difficult with external agencies	40

Conditions:

		Points
A	Office work	5
B	Office work with some physical effort and/or hazards	10
C	Manual work	30
D	Manual work with exposure to hazards	50

Total:

	Grade	Points
Experience		
Education		
Job content		
Job scope		
Responsibilities		
People/contacts		
Conditions		

However, there are important spin-offs from job evaluation as well:

- Apart from the more rational and logical pay structures, there is greater equity over pay.

- More information will exist on jobs, which will facilitate initiatives in selection, organizing structuring and training.

- A better mutual understanding between management and labour may prevail after such an exercise is started and for the lifespan of the scheme.

Job evaluation by definition concerns jobs, not the performance of people in the jobs, so separate mechanisms are needed to reward merit and performance. Equally, the economic forces outside of the organization, from inflation to income distribution, must be considered alongside the influence of collective bargaining, both outside and inside of the organization. The internal (organizational) market for labour may also be seen to dictate market rates. These factors may constrain the impact of job evaluation.

Flexibility

Finally, we will look not only at evaluating jobs but at moving towards job **flexibility** as well.[24] This skill fluidity must be represented in the pay package. The turbulence of the external environment has increased in the 1980s and 1990s and it seems destined to continue. The labour force must be adaptable and versatile in order to meet this turbulence.

Numerical flexibility involves options such as part-time and temporary workers as well as flexible working hours. This can lead to a steady core of workers and to a peripheral poorly paid sector with little or no job security. **Functional** flexibility means more activities and stepping over traditional demarcation zones. **Multi-skilling** and **job enlargement** can only benefit all parties concerned. 'Distancing' strategies of using the self-employed and contracting out or franchising may give some flexibility but the core–peripheral theme is still here. **Pay flexibility** must follow on from job flexibility with changing structures. Excessive breaching of structures is not recommended, as the system itself would need to be revamped to accommodate such change, and the breaching would lead to the fickleness and subjectivity we have been arguing against.

Pay flexibility must take account of flexible working practices, and in turn these practices are dependent on skill acquisition and retention. We turn to training in the next unit.

Notes

1 Goldthorpe, 'Attitudes and behaviour of car assembly workers'.
2 See Anderson, *Effective Labour Relations*.
3 Hackman and Oldham, 'Motivation through the design of work'.
4 Husband, 'Payment structures made to measure'.
5 Goldthorpe, 'Attitudes and behaviour of car assembly workers'.
6 Jaques, *Equitable Payment*.
7 Anderson, *Effective Labour Relations*.
8 These views are based on the discussions with Professor S. Kessler while undertaking an MBA at the City University Business School in London.
9 Harris, *The Realities of Productivity Bargaining*.
10 Clegg, 'General Report No. 9 (Clegg Commission)'.
11 See Anderson, *Effective General Management*.
12 Armstrong, *Principles and Practice of Salary Administration*.
13 Hackman, Oldham, Janson and Purdy, 'A new strategy for job enrichment'.
14 Without subscribing to the conspiracy theory of history, we have a clear plot going on in the UK at the moment. In the public or state sector, the present Conservative government is determined to introduce payment for performance irrespective of the merits of the scheme. The format chosen tends to be individualized (not group-based), so it becomes a device not to improve the student pass rate in education or the quality of patient care at a hospital, but to break the nationalized bargaining of the unionized sector.
15 Atkinson, 'Four stages of adjustment to the demographic downturn'.
16 Cunningham, *Non Wage Benefits*.
17 T.P. Kenney, 'Stating the case for welfare'.
18 G. Thomason, *Textbook of Personnel Management*.
19 Anderson, *Effective Labour Relations*.
20 Wright and Brading, 'Performance related pay'.
21 See, for example, McKersie, 'Changing wage payment systems'.
22 International Labour Organization, *Job Evaluation*.
23 Livy, *Job Evaluation – a critical review*.
24 Flexibility is covered in depth in Anderson, *Effective Labour Relations*.

Unit Four

Training

Learning Objectives

After completing this unit you should be able to:

- demonstrate the potential value of training and use techniques to evaluate the training;

- conduct a needs analysis;

- design a programme;

- implement a programme;

- apply the generic skills.

Contents

Overview

The Context of Training

Why Bother with Training?

The Trainer: Towards Competency

Training and Learning

The Training Cycle

▶ Needs
▶ Programme design and development
▶ Implementation
▶ Evaluation

Unit Four

> " Training is work-based learning and can be seen as the systematic development of the attitude, knowledge and skill behaviour pattern required by an individual to perform adequately a given task or job. "
>
> *Department of Employment*[1]

Overview

There is a tripartite vision in this unit of training as the responsibility not only of the training specialist, but of all managers who are in charge of people. Further, the motivated trainee or learner is critical to the process, so we need to take full account of his or her role as well. A simple model of the training cycle will be used (see figure 4.1), although a more complex contextual model will be discussed.

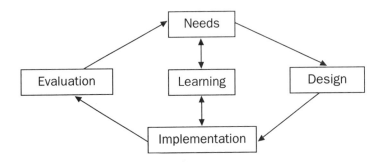

Figure 4.1 The training cycle.

The Context of Training

There are many approaches to and models of training. Many focus on the internal process of needs, design, implementation and evaluation, while others have a greater focus on the learner as the hub of the system. Others again take a more pragmatic view and look to specific 'interventions' rather than a holistic system.

Clearly training does not operate in a vacuum, so we need to be aware of the *external environment*: the wider political, economic, social and technological factors that have an impact on the firm also have an impact

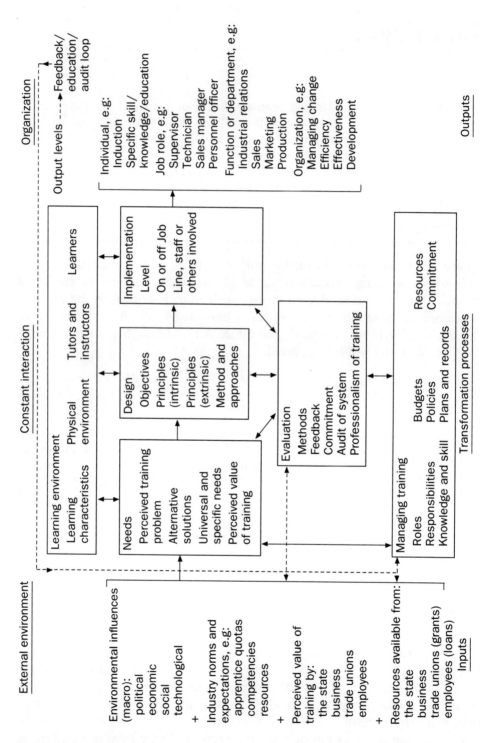

Figure 4.2 The training system.

Source: Anderson, *Successful Training Practice.*

on training. Government policy, for example, on training the unemployed through a grant-assisted scheme can be cited. The industry norms and expectations are also relevant. Apprentices, for example, as in engineering, have been (in the past at least) a key feature shared by most firms in the sector. The perceived value of training and the associated resources made available for training are important as well. The government may provide funding, or a levy system could provide reinvestment by business, or trade unions could make grants (rather than obscure investments in oil paintings) and loans to employees.

The external environment may provide the 'input' but the *organization* itself provides the 'transformation process' and the 'output'. In a sense the 'outputs' are easier to deal with, as these are the results of training, so we will take these first. They can be seen at various levels:

- individual
- job
- function
- organization

The **individual** level can be illustrated by a specific induction session geared to a new starter; the **job** role can be seen in training for, say, a technician in electronics; the **functional** level can be seen in a sales seminar for all 'customer care' employees within sales on 'how to close the sale'; and the **organizational** level can be seen in training strategies to further change.

The 'transformation process' is permeated by learning, the oil of the training machinery. This transformation is best seen as a series of interlapping processes whereby specific problems are examined, a programme is designed to meet the programme, it is put into effect, and then the results are checked. The whole transformation process involves behavioural change or learning. Of course this transformation of problem to solution must be managed and roles, budgets, responsibilities and competencies must be co-ordinated. This context of training is illustrated in figure 4.2. As stated, the focus will be on the inner aspects of the transformation process – the training cycle. This focus is for analysis only. It simplifies the picture for the busy manager but the fuller model is a more genuine reflection of reality.

Why Bother with Training?

Training is big business, so the rationale must be clear and there has to be a pay-off. First let us consider the business of training. We will use the UK as an example to get a feel for the scope of training. This is not to hold the UK up as a model of good practice, for it can be seen that other developed countries seem to have greater commitment to the cause of training.[2] Fortunately we have access to a fund of data on training trends which are reasonably recent.[3] Some keynote points from this 1986/87 survey showed the following:

- There were approximately 350 million 'training days' in the year (1986/87).
- The approximate cost was £33 billion.
- Employees sponsored c. 145 million training days; government sponsored the rest.
- Fewer than 50 per cent of employees received any training in that year;
- Almost 50 per cent of employed adults with no formal qualifications have not been trained since leaving school.
- Smaller companies were less likely to train employees.

Organizations benefit from training in the following ways:

- Employees become more conscious of the aims, goals and specific targets of the organization and their own jobs.
- The newcomer becomes fully operational more quickly as learning times are reduced.
- More effective working methods and techniques further a better way of working.
- A greater application of skill to a task can improve output and quality.
- Accidents, waste and scrap can be reduced by better job knowledge.
- Attitudes towards customers or clients and other liaison departments can be made more constructive.
- Job and task flexibility can be encouraged.
- Resources, such as computing facilities, can be put to better use.
- Relationships between managed and managers can be enhanced through training in leadership and labour relations skills.
- Widespread product knowledge can create a better external image to actual and potential customers.
- Financial systems and training in management information and intelligence can stimulate shrewder financial decisions in, say, investment analysis.
- Better induction and skills training may reduce labour turnover.
- Operational areas can be made more efficient by more programmed decisions for certain tasks.
- Above all, the organization can become more profitable and growth-oriented.

As we are aware, training is only one of the disciplines of personnel management, so other areas from selection to remuneration may be appropriate in an attempt to improve performance. Equally, machines, methods, tools, equipment, plant, etc., may be manipulated to improve performance. However, there is an 'acid test' to determine whether training is *the* issue at stake: does the problem involve any of the following – skill, knowledge, attitudes, techniques (knowledge plus skills) or judgement?[4] If so, it is a training issue.

Certain benefits can be derived from training by the individual as well:

- Increased job knowledge should make the job easier to handle.
- Pride in doing a good job can be enhanced by a skilled performance stimulated by training.
- Greater awareness of self, group and the organization in its environment can be challenging for many.
- Learning new techniques may make the individual's skills more transferable.
- 'Learning how to learn' is in itself a very important output of training; apart from leading to self-discovery and self-fulfilment, such learning makes transferability to new ideas, concepts, practices and techniques more accessible to the learner.

The state has a vested interest in a well-trained, highly qualified, thoroughly competent workforce. Such a workforce is a prerequisite for economic take-off and for recovery in times of depression, and is a crucial factor in the maintenance of long-term growth. However, the *raison d'être* of training must be to meet organizational goals. Personal needs are important, of course, for without individual commitment to training it will degenerate into a fruitless and costly exercise. So training must cater for the needs of both the managed and the managers. Before we look at the training cycle and learning, we must touch upon the skills of the trainer, which are critical to the success of the whole venture.

The Trainer: Towards Competency

The staff specialist and the line manager must work together in a partnership, and this is particularly so in training, as transferability of learning will be inhibited if this partnership does not exist.

It has been suggested that some form of 'congruence' is required between the person doing the job, the actual role of the job and the culture or personality of the organization.[5] Others have argued that trainers have 'predominant orientations'.[6] On the one hand, a traditional 'educational' approach is contrasted with a more dynamic 'interventionist' strategy; on the other, a maintenance-cum-steady-state approach is compared to a more dynamic change orientation. Our approach will be to examine the core competencies required by all trainers – although weightings will alter according to organizational reality, culture, the professionalism of training and how it is interpreted by the organization and job holders in the maintenance–change spectrum.

BOX PM4.1

Proposed strategic and operational roles and responsibilities in training

---

These roles and responsibilities assume a line–staff format.

Strategic activity:	Responsibility:
Corporate plan	Senior management with specialist corporate planners' assistance (unlikely to have training input unless the director of personnel is lobbying)
HR/manpower plan	Senior management with HR involvement at senior level (possibly a manpower planner involved; training implications from plan for *all* managers)
Training policy	Statement (action?) of training position, usually written by the chief executive or at least signed by him or her (should be used as the 'guidelines' for all managers)
Training plan	Possibly an annual event, derived from overall policies and corporate/human plans; senior training person to draw this up in conjunction with senior line management (priorities decided by senior management line and staff)

Operational activity:	Responsibility:
Needs analysis	Essentially a *line* task, as manager has in-depth knowledge of his or her people; technical back-up and standardization from staff – collated information by staff given to senior management for priority and action
Design	Traditionally a staff role, but learning must percolate through to line; hence it is proposed that this is a *joint* initiative
Implementation	Again a *joint* initiative; the *line* manager or trainer has a focus on training 'on the job', and 'off-the-job' focus is given to *staff* trainers
Evaluation	A *joint* initiative; the shorter time scale tends to be *line*, while the organizational view and longer time-scale tend to be *staff*

First we need to discern the distinctions between line and staff and to allocate responsibilities to both. (See Box PM4.1.)

The focus here is on the **operational activity**, although some of the competencies may be transferable to the strategic overview. Trainers fall into the following categories:

- consultant/problem solver
- designer/learning expert
- implementer/instructor/teacher
- administrator/manager/arranger of training

These classifications are self-explanatory, so we will turn to the skills required by such trainers. A comprehensive analysis of skills was conducted by Jones (see Box PM4.2).[7]

> **BOX PM4.2**
>
> ## Training intervention: skills taxonomy
>
> ■ *Diagnosing*: this is research-based and involves data collection, developing constructs and approaches, and gaining agreement.
> ■ *Translating*: understanding the personality of the organization and its ability and willingness to change forms this theme. Organizational needs should be converted into learning objectives.
> ■ *Designing*: this is the creative phase, involving model building and making learning experiences.
> ■ *Resourcing*: maintaining a capability to train throughout the organization is involved in this theme.
> ■ *Implementing*: putting training into practice is this main category, from workshops to handling real relationships at work.
> ■ *Enabling*: this category covers processes from coaching to counselling, from applying learning to influencing people and events.
> ■ *Catalysing*: making things happen and getting support are the key factors.
> ■ *Evaluating*: review and results orientation complete the taxonomy.
>
> *Source:* Adapted from J.A.G. Jones, 'Training intervention strategies'

So there are four main elements to the trainer's job:[8]

■ a direct training/instructing role;
■ an organizing/administering role, including needs analysis;
■ a managing element;
■ an advisory service to management.

The line trainer/manager would obviously focus on the first element to some extent, and the second and third aspects only in the context of his or her other non-training managerial role. (See Activity PM4.1.)

Training and Learning

To understand training and development fully (see Unit Five on development), we must grasp the concept of learning and its characteristics. Learning, a relatively permanent change in behaviour which is not attributable to maturation, growth or illness, goes to the heart of the 'design' and the 'implementation' phases of the training cycle.

We are not going to take an academic approach and examine theories of learning. Instead we will look at the principles or characteristics of learning which may be present to a greater or lesser extent in a training environment. The weighting on these characteristics is affected by the initial frame of reference or school of thought, be it behaviourist, social learning, phenomenological, humanist, cognitive or gestalt.[9]

ACTIVITY PM4.1

KNOWLEDGE AND SKILLS REQUIRED BY TRAINERS

Activity code
- ✓ Self-development
- ✓ Teamwork
- ✓ Communications
- ✓ Numeracy/IT
- ✓ Decisions

Determine a range of knowledge and skills for each of the four main roles shown below.

Role: **Knowledge:**   **Skill:**

Direct training

Organizing

Determining

Consulting

Box PM4.3 gives a summary view of the main factors of learning which one would expect to see in a training (and developmental) situation.

BOX PM4.3

Learning characteristics

- *Motivation:* the individual commitment to learn is important and is reward-oriented.
- *Knowledge of results:* this is a form of reinforcement and should stimulate refreshed and renewed activity.
- *Reward and punishment:* the reward, rather than punishment, stimulates and motivates a fresh response.
- *Trial and error:* this is not particularly recommended, but it illustrates the experience and the activity of learning. Association and structured repetition are preferable.
- *Insight:* the individual is not a machine and creativity needs room for growth. The individual's 'mental map' is important in this context.
- *Practice/doing:* action and practice run through most of these approaches. Again, repetition is important in ongoing learning.
- *Scale:* there is a constant interaction between the individual and his or her environment, so the scope and scale of the subject matter needs to be considered in relation to the capacity of the learner.
- *Individual differences:* individual orientation and relating to 'own' mental map are evident.
- *Period of learning:* this should be noted as another variable for training or applied learning.
- *Structured repetition:* this is very important for association and relating x to y.
- *'Interference':* as this is a communications exercise, 'blockages' must be overcome, so this should be noted. This is not evident in the various approaches but is self-evident given the earlier learning 'blockages'.
- *Transfer:* this is critical to the line and staff trainer for the carry-over of learning to the place of work. It emphasizes the applied nature of training.

Source: Anderson, *Successful Training Practice*

It is possible to have 'rules' of learning, though the characteristics are more usefully seen as guidelines, particularly for design. The International Labour Organization (ILO) has formulated some 'rules' or guidelines to assist the trainer, especially in implementation (see Box PM4.4).

BOX PM4.4

Guidelines on learning and implementation

- The trainees' learning capacities determine what can be learned (and for how long).
- Presentation order is important, e.g. the first and last items are remembered best.

- Repetition reduces the rate of forgetting.
- Varied repetition is better than repeating exactly the same thing over and over, e.g. use video to make points.
- Feedback to trainees helps to increase learning.
- Practice makes perfect.
- Learning should have a sequence and factors need to be related, e.g. use a training model.
- There are learning plateaux, when new learning levels off, so plenty of breaks are required.
- It is preferable to build on experience.

Source: Adapted from International Labour Organization, *Teaching and Training Methods for Management Development*

The point on experience from the ILO checklist is worth pursuing even further. Training (and development) mean a lot more than sending someone on a course or seminar. Real training and development mean structuring a situation where the individual will maximize his or her learning. One useful approach to training and development that you can adapt is based on experience as being the best way of learning (see figure 4.3).[10] The idea here is that training and development are essentially based on some experience, from which we build up some 'rules' or 'themes', which we then test in everyday working life. So much of learning has a focus on real, concrete experiences at work.

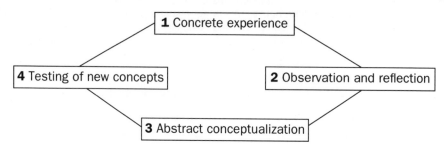

Figure 4.3 Experiential learning.

The role of the learner is important, if not critical, to the whole training process. Much work can be concentrated on the style of the learner, examining the activities from which he or she learns best.[11]

Whether we should accept this learner orientation and the value of experience to the detriment of other variables in the training system is debatable, but whether we are using a systems vision or the experiential (experience led) approach, we must have some **training objectives** to facilitate any programme of training. These training objectives are geared to what should be being learned, and are gleaned from the analysis of training need. However, as we are dealing with learning, it may be appropriate to look at objectives before tackling the training cycle.

These learning objectives should contain:

- an action which can be observed;
- criteria which you can measure;
- the context in which you are operating.

The **action** tends to be a verb such as 'select', 'provide', etc. The **criteria** are the quantifications of this action: 'how well?', 'how many?', 'how often?', 'how much?', etc. The conditions are the immediate **context** in which we operate:

Action:	Criteria:	Conditions:
Identifying the training needs of the group	All the group to be covered	Use an inventory or questionnaire and feed back results

The Training Cycle

To be of real benefit, training must be:
- based on sound learning principles;
- geared to real performance issues at work;
- based on training need;
- systematic.[12]

(See also the checklist in the appendix.)

We have covered learning, and it goes almost without saying that training must be related to the job and to increased performance. The responsibility for training ultimately must rest with management, and the cycle will ensure that real need is being met. Before we go on to that we will briefly note the importance of a systematic approach. A planned, non-random approach to training will help to make sure that real needs are being met. The **systematic process** allows:

- the correct standards to be reached;
- the minimum effort to reach them;
- fewer errors on the road there;
- the most economic use of resources, particularly time and money;
- more likelihood that the right training will have been identified, implemented and evaluated.

Needs

Training needs analysis involves looking at performance. Essentially, a training need is a shortfall in performance caused by a deficiency in knowledge, skills, techniques (the application of knowledge and skills), attitudes or judgement.

The early approach to training needs had a focus on two levels, the **organization** and the **job**. Laird, for example, usefully classifies the training need, or gap, into 'macro' and 'micro' factors.[13] The 'macro' is more concerned with the larger picture derived from the manpower or human resource plan, with implications for staffing from induction of new personnel to changing methods of work to cope with the introduction of, say, new technology. The 'micro' factors are more job-oriented. The example of personnel systems can be used:

- *Promotion:* gaps in the new knowledge required for the promoted post can easily appear.
- *Transfer:* the new 'culture' and job can mean a temporary mismatch.
- *Career planning:* fast, medium and slow routes for careers may mean distinct job competencies to be mastered for each route.
- *Appraisals* (see Unit Five): the 'suggestions for improvement' may involve some training implication.
- *Performance targets:* flashing warning lights on the failure to meet targets may have some training implication.

Another level worth considering is that of skill. It may not involve the whole job, so a **task analysis** or **specific skill analysis** may be useful if a comprehensive survey is not required.

One of the themes of this book is the integration of task needs with people needs. We find this in training needs analysis: needs can be examined almost from a development or individual perspective to give us a third level of gap analysis. This can be task related, of course, but it also looks to the career and individual aspirations as well. As this is developed in Unit Five, we will move to the next level of training need, that of competency.

There is a strong move afoot in training and education within the UK to move towards a competency-based approach. If care is exercised to ensure that competency is not mediocrity and that the unique culture of organizations is taken into account,[14] the competency approach, a fusion of knowledge and skill which underpins this series, has much to offer. (See Box PM4.5.)

BOX PM4.5

Competency and excellence: training standards

Example: identifying learning needs
- Determine learner competence (individual and group).
- Assess competence.
- Clarify development needs.
- Take account of changes in work role etc. which impact on performance.

■ Clarify individual's long-term aspirations.

■ Agree priorities.

■ Agree prioritized objectives and learning needs.

An example illustrates the 'standard':

Title:	Identify and agree learning strategies that meet client requirements.
Element:	Identify/assess significant learning experience and personal characteristics which influence choice of learning strategy.
Criteria	– Special needs/circumstances of individuals stated.
	– Prior learning identified.
	– Criteria for strategy options created, etc.
Range indicators:	– Prior learning
	– Personal characteristics
	– Methods of assessment.

Source: Adapted from Training and Development Lead Body, *How Do You Spot Good Trainers?*, and Anderson, *Successful Training Practice*

BOX PM4.6

Triggers for training

The top ten external and internal factors that were seen to trigger training were:

Overall ranking
(sample total 499):

External factors:

The anticipated demand for products or services	1
Forecast profitability (allowing for environment)	5
Local labour market (existing)	6
National labour market (existing)	8
Expected labour market (local)	10

Internal factors:

Plans to change method, technology, etc.	2
Views of line manager	3
Views of training department	4
Recent company profitability	7
Loss of a key employee (unforeseen)	9

(*Note:* differences occurred owing to the sizes of firms)

As an aside, trade union policies, shop-floor views, local educational facilities and government grants trailed in at the bottom of the league table.

Source: Adapted from RBL, 'Research on external and internal influences in training report'

A useful way of examining training needs in practice is to look at 'secondary sources', such as accident rates and scrap or wastage, as well as to design a primary source, such as an applied research questionnaire or interviews. First, though, Box PM4.6 gives a brief checklist of the 'triggers' that can spark the whole training initiative.

Once the training has been triggered, we need to use appropriate methods of needs analysis to deepen the investigation and to derive the performance shortfall, which will be the basis for the next phases of the training cycle. Other sources fuse the levels of training need (organization, job, skills, individual and core competency) with the methods in Box PM4.7.[15]

BOX PM4.7

Training needs: examples of sources

Secondary sources

The information in these is already available in some format or another within the organization. Care must be exercised, though, to extrapolate the training implication. These secondary sources can be allied to the triggers shown in Box PM4.6 to zoom in on a problem, but they are not sufficient in themselves to give a full training needs analysis.

Source	Comment
Materials, workflows	Look for blockages and bottlenecks
Assessment centre	Often used to examine developmental needs. Care needs to be exercised to divide 'promotion'-type centres from developmental-cum-training sessions, as the latter will suffer at the expense of the 'selection mentality'.
Appraisal	Money, promotion and post mortems must be distinct from the training and developmental aspects.
Career plan meetings	Training implications can be derived.
Audit of personnel data	The 'skill mix' or the 'qualifications mix' can be derived from a personnel stock-take, and trends and shortfalls can be noted.
Manpower plan	Clear training plans and priorities can be established.
Grievances, disputes and discipline	Perhaps there are more manifestations of conflict (see *Effective Labour Relations* in this series), but cumulative problems may indicate training problems in managerial style, and in the understanding of rules and procedures.
Targets, MbO (management by objectives), etc.	Again, this is a clear performance issue, but watch that it is an actual training need.
Accidents	Causation is widespread but repeated problems with or lack of awareness of health and safety may be a training problem.

R & D projects	Innovation may stimulate new skills to meet new products, etc.
Quality control	Recurring scrap or quality issues may have a training undercurrent.
New job holders	Chatting to them will focus on their training problems, which can be built into a programme.
Corporate plan	New directions and strategies will have manpower and training implications.
Termination interviews	These can throw up moans and grumbles but also constructive criticism which may have some training implication.
Counselling	Job counselling may indicate an actual need for training in the person being counselled.
Attitude surveys	These can be very revealing, showing attitudes which may require redeveloping or restructuring.

Primary sources

The secondary sources may highlight trends and manifestations of need; the primary sources go to the heart of the matter.

Source	Comment
Evaluation of past training	This should be the first port of call.
'Do it yourself'	Individuals know themselves and an 'open' managerial style will encourage insight into their training need.
'Diaries'	Keeping a daily log of contacts, tasks, crises, etc. can help time management and focus on any training need..
Questionnaire	The anonymity will help form a realistic picture and trends can be seen.
Interviews (formal, unstructured)	The unstructured 'chat' may be more revealing for our immediate purpose.
Self-assessment	The do-it-yourself technique may not be linked to a system of training, while the self-assessment aspect can form part of the interview, with management sharing the assessment as well.
Activity sampling and observation	A snapshot of various jobs can give a perspective (not necessarily a full one) on training problems.
Reference to experts	Discussion on the quirks of a job with a skilled employee can show the key areas to be mastered and the pitfalls to be avoided.
Case	Writing up a narrative of events (with outside help?) can be illustrative of need.
Survey	A tailor-made organizational or departmental survey (depending on scale) is difficult to beat for breadth.
Group discussion	A day away from work can be an excellent mechanism to determine group needs.
Testing	Assuming the norms of expectation are known and understood by the tester, testing can highlight issues.

Here we will classify main methods into secondary and primary sources only. (See Activity PM4.2.)

ACTIVITY PM4.2

THE PAPER MILL

Activity code
- ☐ Self-development
- ☐ Teamwork
- ✓ Communications
- ☐ Numeracy/IT
- ✓ Decisions

The company

The company in question is an independent manufacturer of paper and board, based in Donside, Aberdeenshire. The paper is not high quality and is used for the packaging industry. The board, or chipboard, is predominantly used for the building industry. The firm employs some 400 people on a continuous shift system (6a.m.–2p.m., 2p.m.–10p.m. and 10p.m.–6a.m.) and works all year round, apart from three weeks' maintenance closure in July which coincides with the main vacation of the nearby town. It is an old plant, founded in the late eighteenth century, but with considerable modern machinery recently imported from Germany. There are two board machines and two paper machines with approximately 100 employees to each. In addition, there is a staff white-collar administrative and commercial group of ninety-two.

The market

Although it is well established, the board market is quite fickle, as it is dependent primarily on the building industry – itself a good indicator of the economic wellbeing of the country. The packaging industry is less fickle and is expanding, although there is competition from the plastics industry. However, from milk cartons to chocolate eggs, the company has a growing presence in this market sphere.

Production

Production is a continuous flow process, with the raw materials (which are increasing in cost) being mixed at the wet end of the machine and appearing at the dry end as almost the finished product. Printing and coating as necessary are done in the finishing department. Breakages of paper flow through the machine are quite frequent.

Finance

The company is still family owned but increasingly it has opened up to take professional managers in to run the firm. It is highly profitable and much of the money has been ploughed back over the last ten years (at least) to buy more modern machinery. This has trebled the potential output, although the plant is running at only 68 per cent capacity. There are no cash-flow problems, although an over-reliance on the building industry in the past has caused difficulties, particularly over the winter months owing to the construction slump then. Reserves and borrowing power are strong.

Organization structure and personnel

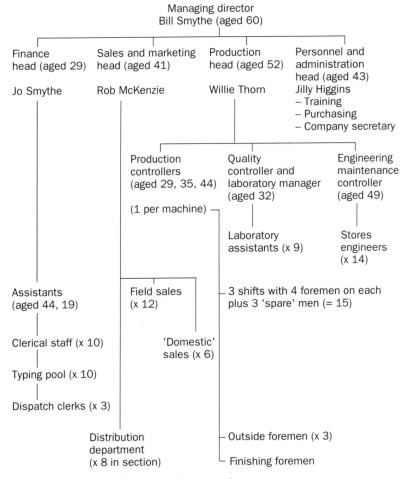

Figure 4.4 Organization structure and personnel.

Figure 4.4 shows the structure. The rest of the employees are employed in production, catering, finishing and as 'outside' staff. There is an external security firm (400 people).

The training officer, Jim McDonald, has recently been appointed to the mill. He reports to Jilly Higgins, who is always busy. His mandate was to conduct a training needs analysis. Time was not on his side, though, and top management wanted a needs analysis to cost the training as part of their longer-term budgets for that year. Jim was an experienced trainer with a background in paint, manufacturing and publishing. He decided to use problem analysis. 'Training by exception', not dissimilar to management by exception, would allow him to focus on the real issues of concern to management. A functional or departmental analysis would give some structure to the proceedings. The method of work would be to discern the problems with a likely training implication and extrapolate the training need.

Management and organization

Although the span of control is quite small, there is a wide gap between top management and the first-level line managers. The shift system does little to help communications between the production and maintenance functions and the day workers of sales and administration. The senior managers have a tremendous knowledge of the sector and of the processes, but the next tier of managers, although competent, is not ready for succession. The organization itself leads to specialization by function, with few general managers being groomed for the future.

Finance and administration

The financial people worry about cost control, particularly as the costs of raw material – imports from Scandinavia in particular – have spiralled over the last few years. Finance staff spend their time cutting costs and making themselves very unpopular with the others in the plant. So there is an image difficulty here. They have a partially qualified accountant, Jo Smythe, the two assistants and the clerks. Their level of financial knowledge is seen by them and by others to be 'light'.

The common complaint about administration is that there are too many of them and that they do little in return for nice, safe jobs in comfortable surroundings. It is difficult to distinguish myth from reality here, but these perceptions clearly exist. There is duplication of effort by the personnel people and the payroll people over the administration of sick pay and bonus calculations, which are often wrong. The laboratory (for testing quality) has an administration person who works 9–5, but in essence, the work is more geared to that of the shift-working production department. There is a dispatch clerk in each of the shifts for checking the goods out on contractors' lorries. Most are older workers from a production background, but they have lost considerable earnings by moving to this job (no shiftwork and little overtime opportunity), and there is a general attitude problem among these six men. The personnel manager is in charge of the social club, but she seems to spend too much time socializing, particularly with a young employee named Andreas Glycophilus. Gossip predominates on these two issues of drink and relationships.

The administration people co-ordinate health and safety, and, as in many such mills, the record is not good. There have been some serious accidents over the last few years, with people being maimed and two fatalities occurring. There are no specialist safety officers, and the function tends to rest with the busy foremen.

Production

The company is dominated by this function. Most of the management come up through this route including the current managing director, Bill Smythe. Willie Thorn, well named according to most, has a grumpy approach and his style contrasts with that of the more benevolent managing director. This is unfortunate as Thorn is in essence the deputy – or believes himself to be the deputy. Rob McKenzie, a dashing 'young 40-something', also seems himself as the natural deputy and particularly so when the company edges towards more of a marketing orientation.

Problems exist in the production area. Labour turnover is high, other than in the finishing department, and the quality of the end product in three shifts across four different machines causes customer dissatisfaction. The operators tend to be young and resentful of the shift work, particularly at the weekend. Absence soars at this time and cover is difficult.

Last year, fifteen trainees were recruited into the function. For the first time these people were put on a local college course in paper technology and encouraged to train on the four machines and in the finishing department. There is one trainee left, as they have all moved on – the training failed. The more experienced workers were unsure of these trainees and their potential role. Two people with A-level equivalents (SCE H-level school leavers) have been recruited and placed one in the laboratory and one as a 'deputy' to a production controller. The foremen are resentful of this.

Sales and marketing

Rob is dynamic but his department is not. The distribution section is made up of transport people, not marketeers, while the rest of the team tend to be either sales people or sales administration types. Rob is the marketeer and he has trouble converting his own team, let alone the rest of the management, to a marketing concept.

The sales team is quite solid but a little set in its ways, seeking 'follow-ups' rather than pitching for new business. The marketplace, however, is becoming increasingly turbulent.

Engineering and laboratories

These are specialist areas. The engineers tend to be on their own. They recruit and train craft engineers quite well, but the stock-taking unit is a long way from using 'just-in-time' techniques.

The laboratory supports the production side and recruits young technicians who stay there for a while, get a local scientific qualification and then move away. They are very slack during the late shift and the evening shift, apart from the hourly samples which need to be tested (a five-minute task). Thereafter the keen study, while others read books and magazines, which are in plentiful supply from the outside staff who are in charge of pulp and raw materials. Turnover of staff is very high.

1 By function, highlight the difficulties which may have a training implication.
2 Note training priorities for top management to act upon.

Programme design and development

Programmes tend to be 'on the job' or 'off the job', although there are some half-way houses, such as vestibule training in major engineering with a mock garage and pits, etc., or cockpit training for a pilot, in a simulated environment. Whatever the format, the design has to be based on real priority need. Learning, as we have seen, permeates this part of the cycle, and we can never escape resource constraints. As discussed earlier, a key aspect of this phase which we will use to evaluate the programme is the **terminal** or **learning/training objectives**, which mirror the behavioural outcomes of training. So the aims and objectives are clarified at the outset, on the basis of real need which cements the systematic training cycle together.

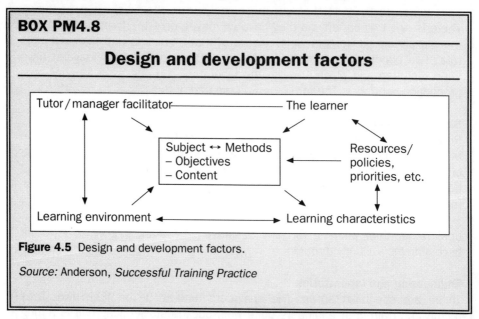

BOX PM4.8

Design and development factors

Figure 4.5 Design and development factors.

Source: Anderson, *Successful Training Practice*

Box PM4.8 shows the key factors in any programme that have an impact on the design and development phase. We have covered most of these points in this unit, so we will now concentrate on the subject and methods, and in particular on any relationship between the programme objectives and the methods available to meet these aims.

First we should scan some of the main methods (see Activity PM4.3). The list is not exhaustive but it is quite comprehensive. The range of methods should be self-explanatory, but some of the more obscure methods are clarified briefly.

ACTIVITY PM4.3

TRAINING DESIGN AND DEVELOPMENT: METHODS

Activity code
- ✓ Self-development
- ✓ Teamwork
- ☐ Communications
- ☐ Numeracy/IT
- ✓ Decisions

Various methods of training are noted below. For each one, make a brief comment on its advantages and disadvantages.

Method	Comment
Lecture (one-way, formal)	
Talk (one-way, some feedback)	
Discussion (two-way)	
Case	
Role play	
In tray ('Problems' given in a basket to work through)	

Method	Comment
Business game (e.g. computer simulation exercise)	
Open learning	
Group training (e.g. group effectiveness and team building)	
Outdoor training (e.g. hillwalking, leaderless groups)	
Coaching, counselling and monitoring	
Project (work-oriented)	
Planned experience (rotated over a period of time)	

Various attempts have been made to link methods and learning objectives. For example, Carroll looked at knowledge (acquisition and retention), attitudes, problem solving, interpersonal skills and acceptance of the methods by the learner.[16] In brief, case studies, discussions and business games had a high rating for meeting these aims. Long looked at a learning hierarchy from knowledge at the base to self-awareness at the apex and not only related the methods to these aims, but added the dimension of feedback and involvement.[17] Anderson proposed a link between the learning characteristics that had to be met and a range of methods.[18]

One of the most comprehensive approaches combining objectives and methods is the work of the Cambridge-based industrial training research unit and its innovative vision of CRAMP.[19] The CRAMP approach specifies the learning type, and an algorithm is used to trace the method which is applicable. Other prevailing variables are also included. It is very much skill based but it can be usefully adapted elsewhere. The C-type of learning is concerned with comprehension; R means reflex learning involving a skilled movement; A-type learning involves attitude development; M is more memory-oriented, so we know what to do in a given situation; and P is procedural learning, such as following instructions in a handbook without commitment to memory. (See Box PM4.9.)

BOX PM4.9

CRAMP

Learning type	Some variables to consider	Examples of methods
C Understanding/comprehending	Transfer to many situations Key principles Related past knowledge	Textbooks Lectures 'Discovery' Basic concepts
R Skilled (physical)	Simplify job Planning skills (level) Sequence of tasks	Simplify tasks Breakdown into progressive steps Discrimination
A Attitude development	Replacement attitudes New attitudes Build on existing attitudes	'Discovery' Role playing Sensitivity/T groups, etc.
M Knowing what to do (memory)	Relevant job details Length of material Memory 'load'	Rules Structured material Deductive and cumulative parts
P Knowing what to do (relying on relevant information at hand)	Procedural complexity/ simplicity Availability of material	Checklists Instructions Algorithms

Source: Adapted from Industrial Training Research Unit, *Research Paper TRI*

All the methods are self-explanatory apart from 'Discovery'. This is an important method which, to some extent, tells against the systematic approach which has been advocated. At the same time, a systematic planned approach lies behind the denouement of the discovery plot. Box PM4.10 gives some insight into the main principles of discovery learning.

As a method it is particularly useful for mature adults who have considerable background experience to call upon, but beware of the method being perceived as a 'game', and particularly as a manipulative game being played by the trainer.

BOX PM4.10

Discovery learning

- The instructor, tutor or manager must have a plan of action related to the overall learning objectives.
- This is best achieved by planned questions (open-ended). Some flexibility should be built in to counter obstacles.
- The questioning is progressive and guided.
- The learner must trust the tutor.
- The learner needs to be aware of the concept discovery approach.
- The learner sets his or her own pace.
- This approach is seen useful to comprehension-type learning, e.g. being able to understand a mathematical formula.
- The individual learner is given scope to discover the techniques, principles, etc., which will lead to understanding of the whole concept or process.
- Unobtrusive stimulation of the learner should occur and questions from the learner should be met with questions.
- Silent observation of the learner is encouraged and demonstrations by the tutor or manager should be discouraged.

Through discovery or not, we have now reached the implementation stage.

Implementation

This stage concerns the routine but important administrative arrangement, from booking programmes, rooms, accommodation, meals and equipment to record maintenance after the event and to physically carrying out the training. The focus here is on the last of these.

The priorities of the training plan (usually an annual event derived from the manpower plan), the needs analysis, the design and development stages as well as resources all play an important part in physically doing the training. So, not forgetting these constraints and opportunities, we will examine some useful approaches to implementation – *particularly from the perspective of the line trainer or manager*. These include:

- mentoring
- coaching
- action learning

This phase will end with an activity – an implementation within a consultancy.

Mentoring

The process of mentoring can be a bridge between training and development. In essence, it consists of using an experienced tutor-cum-coach who can guide a protégé through a series of planned experiences. The mentor–protégé relationship may have the stamp of nepotism unless a whole range of relationships is established across an organization.

The protégé can benefit by being under the guidance of a committed mentor. Self-confidence can rise, access to more senior meetings, etc., can occur, a more thorough appreciation of the mores of the organization is possible and potential career routes (vertical and lateral) can be seen more clearly. The mentor can benefit by 'bouncing off' new ideas, undertaking a new learning experience and getting a fresh perspective on old problems. Mature or smaller organizations can benefit by creating openings, if not a full job, through mentoring, which can assist new people to reach experienced standards of work more quickly than by being left to their own devices.

Perhaps it is better if the mentor is slightly removed from the protégé in the line structure, as the boss–subordinate relationship may inhibit full mentoring. Clearly, line and mentoring relationships have to be compatible. The mentor must have a mature outlook and be prepared to initiate a programme of events for the protégé to share.

Mentoring has often been restricted to perceived high flyers, so that they move on and up more quickly. Arguably it should apply to all professionals and managers who have a career structure. It could be taken further and perhaps it should apply to all employees. However, job constraints, the

---

BOX PM4.11

Mentoring: a training and development process

Organization	Examples
Major brewing company	Young employees who are seeking master brewing qualifications are mentored by technical specialists.
Major leisure and hotel group	Under the direction of senior managers, middle managers are assisted in their development via an MBA programme.
Multinational computing firm	Experienced branch systems engineers give guidance to trainees in their induction process and their training programmes.
Health care multinational	Senior managers are guided by corporate directors on their development programme, which includes a 'live' project.

lack of any career structure for the majority of employees, and jobs designed on Taylorite principles would inhibit such a democratic process.

Mentoring is open to abuse. It can perpetuate an elite; it may result in a cloning effect, with the protégé a mirror image of the mentor; and it may be difficult for those excluded from this magic circle to come to terms with this approach. The widening of the circle may break down some of these defects. (See Box PM4.11.)

Coaching

The sports analogy can be used to understand coaching at work. Preparation, guidance, counselling on weaker areas, a game plan, standard responses to situations, and the growing complexity of various strategies to meet the objectives of the game are all transferable to the coach or manager at work. However, the coach takes a backseat when the sportsperson actually performs, and this is the case in the workplace as well.

The coach can be **non-directive** and non-judgemental, assuming an empathy with the learner and helping him or her to provide his or her own solutions. In this way, the learning remains the full property of the learner. Yet such an approach may be too vague at the outset of a relationship between coach and trainee. Direction and goals may be required, and **behavioural modification** may be a more useful approach than that of a softer counselling style.[20] As the relationship develops and the expertise is heightened, the non-directive approach can be introduced to a greater extent while the target-oriented directives can be mollified. (The fine balance between giving the cure and developing the individual to cure him or herself will be recognized by academic staff who tutor students.)

The **outcome approach**, which emphasizes tangible results, gives a focus to the coaching and a target to achieve. However, the means by which it is achieved depends particularly on the sound coaching skills of the line manager. To this end the academic tutor–student relationship may help the line manager.

Several stages can be determined:

- *Establishing the roles.* The roles of both are clarified at the outset and responsibility for different areas outlined. This is very much a confidence-seeking relationship.

- *Issue(s) identification.* The tasks and goals to be met need discussion and any blockages to achievement or constraints, etc., should be noted by both parties. The ownership of the issue(s) needs to be clarified while the support facilities on offer can be illustrated.

- *Action approach.* This will be ongoing, and the targets (however defined) can have some timetable or regular feedback session in a 'safe' learning environment, first without exposure to the real job and then with staged exposure, if the issues warrant such an approach.

- *Review and close.* The coaching can go on in the action review stage for some time, with increasing complexity of issues or tasks so that the trainee hits peak performance. Feedback can become less formalized and more ad hoc as experience is gained, and the relationship may end once given targets are achieved. The manager can turn to other trainees at various stages of need, while not forgetting the more experienced members of the team.

Action learning

This process is identified with the work of Revans.[21] The core idea is that traditional interventions in training and development relate to programmed (P) knowledge while neglecting questioning insight (Q). It is very much a problem-solving technique and is at the apex of the learning hierarchy of training. As such, it has found favour particularly in management development schemes. Arguably, though, if the job involves some elements of problem solving, the concept (whole or part) ought to be transferable.

The problem has to be real, not imagined, and it has to be significant to both the learner and the trainer. The main learning vehicle is an action project, which in turn is geared to perceiving an often uncharted problem. Individual and group responses and mind sets may have to alter to accommodate the organizational reality of the issue in hand; so there is a considerable self-developmental aspect to the whole process. At the same time, the process lends itself to closer group working on specific problems.

There are disadvantages, though. It is not highly structured and so may not be suitable for all; it needs a lot of commitment from the learner and his or her associates; we need so-called P learning *as well* rather than Q learning *instead*; it lends itself to wandering from the point unless some initial direction is exercised; and it is time consuming and so can be quite costly.

On the plus side, greater insights are stimulated; greater awareness of how the organization works can result; learning transfer problems (back to work) are minimized; the programmes can be tailor-made to the organization and individual needs; and it consolidates the experience-based learning process (with its disadvantages as well) that we looked at earlier.

So action learning can be of some value both to the organization and to the learner. It allows the individual trainee to take command of his or her own learning, with the specialists becoming more of a resource or facilitator. Altogether, it is a useful weapon in the armoury of training and development. Please refer to Activity PM4.4 which consolidates the training processes to date.

ACTIVITY PM.4

CATIM

Activity code

☐ Self-development
☐ Teamwork
✓ Communications
☐ Numeracy/IT
✓ Decisions

CATIM stands for Consultancy and Training in Management. It is based at 49 Longton Grove, Sydenham, London SE26 6QQ. Its managing director is Abbas Baba BEng, MSc (Systems Analysis), MBIM and MIMC. Founded in 1980, the firm is a member of both the British Management Training Export Council and the Institute of Management Consultants (UK).

CATIM specializes in management consultancy for Europe and the Middle East. Prior to starting this business, Abbas Ridha Mohammad Baba had worked in a national centre for management development in the Middle East, with a specific remit on organization development, management development and performance and appraisal systems. Experience followed in London and Saudi Arabia in organization and methods, project management, systems, organization and performance management as both an in-house consultant and an external management consultant. Language and communication skills were in great demand when allied to this expertise, so lecturing and interpreting projects also followed. By December 1980 all of these skills and knowledge came together and CATIM was founded.

Since its inception, CATIM has followed a clear philosophy and specific objectives. It follows a strict code of ethics and fully adheres to the code of practice set by the Institute of Management Consultants. Indeed, Abbas Baba has been and is active in the institute and is both a fellow and a member of its committee on developing countries. He is also a member of the UK-based Institute of Training and Development, and the firm follows the good practice of that institute. The firm aims 'to provide the highest possible standard of consultancy and training services in Arabic and English to any organization at the lowest possible cost'.

The quality programmes are realistically costed and use is made of able sole practitioners and small specialist consultancy firms. Low overhead expenses result. The 'norm' of consultancy profit of some 10–15 per cent is easily met due to pricing policy and overhead cost control. The firm has links, both formal and informal, with a range of experts (some 3,000 in the Institute of Management Consultants alone) including leading business schools, management institutes and experts in training, development and consultancy.

The firm, unlike many, offers a free initial service for in-house research and consultancy. This problem-solving exercise allows a formal proposal to be drawn up. Apart from travel and accommodation charges (given the geographical spread of the firm), the service is free. Many projects have emanated from this policy.

In the early 1980s CATIM began running a series of open courses in London for international managers. A range of courses of one or two weeks' duration was established as a summer school at London University. By the mid-1980s, some seventy-five different courses had been prepared and ran for different organizations on an in-house basis. Other non-training initiatives, from manpower analysis to research, also occur.

With an expertise in the Middle East and many contact points in major corporations, the firm has come together with AApma (see Activity PM2.4) for a joint initiative on expatriate recruitment and selection for managers, engineers, etc., and to run a new series of twelve one-week courses (at this stage) based on this *Effective Management* series from Blackwell Publishers. Babas and Anderson of AApma had met years ago at a lunch at the British Management Training Export Council. A friendship had developed and they had kept in touch, although going their own ways. They met again in late 1992, and compared notes at length.

It was agreed that CATIM with its overseas connections, particularly in the Middle East, would help Maureen Anderson to further develop the overseas selection side of the business. Both firms also had an interest in management learning. CATIM was well served with its in-house work as indeed was AApma. The 'open courses' were proving to be more demanding, as they meant heavy advertising over a range of subjects. It was felt that the course range was too wide as well.

A new concept was discussed which you must evaluate from a learning perspective for developing managers, both in an educational context in a college and at a place of work. This is described below.

In higher education, the emphasis in management education still tends to be on lectures, seminars and guided reading. In training for managers, the stress tends to be on activities or skills, with little real understanding of the basic concepts and theories behind the techniques. This leads to a knowledge-orientation in education at post-experience or graduate level and a skills vision at the level of training. The goal-oriented student of management needs both knowledge and skills (as well as a flexible attitude, etc.).

Management tends to be functionally based, coming through the routes of the specialisms of marketing and sales, finance and accountancy, personnel and operations. Of course, other non-mainstream elements needs to be catered for, from purchasing to economics, from export to quantitative techniques and IT application. Again, there is a need for more generalist management and policy making above these functions and below them at the level of the new and developing enterprise. There are also associated skills. Broader skills have been identified as well: the ability to develop yourself and learn how to learn; the group and team interaction; the ability to communicate; the application of numeracy and information; and above all else the ability to make decisions. These are all common to managers, irrespective of their job specialism, level or organizational context.

The functions, the functional skills and the generic skills are blended together and fused to make a knowledge and skills base for management learning and development.

The functions are:

- people: (1) personnel management, (2) labour relations, (3) organizational behaviour;
- finance and marketing: (4) accountancy and (5) financial management, (6) marketing and (7) international marketing, (8) communications (sales, etc.);
- operations and enterprise: (9) entrepreneurship, (10) managing the enterprise.

The other areas of policy and general management complete the core. Other inputs, such as specialist ones on self-development and numeracy, etc., can follow in due course.

The learning need is seen to exist in education. Resource constraints, growing numbers of students of business and management from undergraduates to MBAs, a need for more rounded, skilled people, and an orientation towards activity learning with student participation all indicate the need for this type of concept.

In training both agreed that managers come to sessions (open or in-house) with mixed backgrounds. A common knowledge base and developed material from exercises to cases, not in isolation but related to the whole, would be welcomed by trainers everywhere.

The format of the concept would be books. A leading UK publisher with a worldwide distribution organization, Blackwell Publishers of Oxford, agreed to publish and market the concept as a series on Effective Management: An Action Approach. Books are a traditional format in education, and in training they provide a physical entity for specific courses.

To motivate the learner, the format is important. Clarity, knowledge of results (of exercises, etc.) and learning by doing are all important. Trial and error should be minimized unless discovery learning is being used. The learning is broken down into parts which form a coherent whole. Individual differences are catered for with a story line or narrative plus a series of discussion and research boxes which add depth for the learner who wants more 'meat'. Each book has six units, so self-pacing of learning is easier across the series. Some structured repetition occurs through the application of principles and techniques in the cases and in the outline at the outset.

The publisher is marketing the books to the educational world while CATIM agreed to assist in marketing the books as part of its course portfolio, which would be based on these functional areas. The courses would be designed as six-day units in twelve courses for both in-house work and open courses. The development needs of managers in the UK and internationally would be met through these courses allied to the physical entity of books which would be given as a reference to all course participants. Blackwell agreed to print a company's logo on special editions of the books, assuming the requisite numbers are used for in-company management training and development. CATIM is linking up its courses with that of major companies so that no duplication will occur and the new material will be dovetailed into company need.

1 Evaluate the learning aspects of this series from a training and development perspective.
2 Write a report on this issue. (You may wish to relate the concept to the learning characteristics in this unit.)

Evaluation

Evaluation literally means the assessment of value. In our terms it can be applied to the cycle itself, showing its value, and the whole of the training system, examined in figure 4.2.

The work of Morris provides an excellent example of how to evaluate the whole of a given training system.[22] Box PM4.12 illustrates his problem-solving approach to the issue and his wide frame of reference,

BOX PM4.12

Training evaluation: the whole system

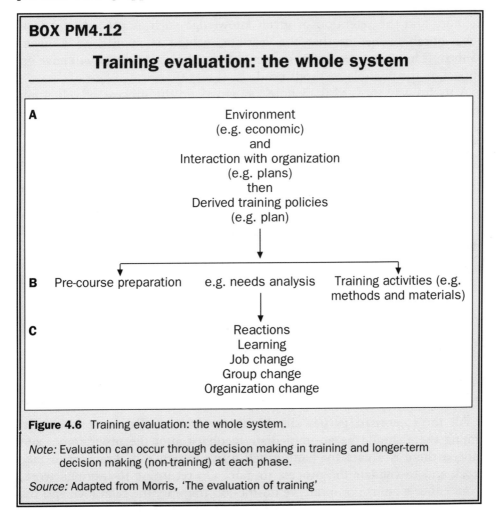

A   Environment
(e.g. economic)
and
Interaction with organization
(e.g. plans)
then
Derived training policies
(e.g. plan)

B   Pre-course preparation   e.g. needs analysis   Training activities (e.g. methods and materials)

C   Reactions
Learning
Job change
Group change
Organization change

Figure 4.6 Training evaluation: the whole system.

Note: Evaluation can occur through decision making in training and longer-term decision making (non-training) at each phase.

Source: Adapted from Morris, 'The evaluation of training'

which encompasses external environmental issues, business plans and the nitty-gritty of carrying out training. An audit of the training system based on figure 4.2 has been made elsewhere.[23] Here we will concentrate on the outputs and to some extent the cycle itself.

The achievement of the objectives laid down in the implementation phase is called **validation**, while an examination of the overall benefit of the programme, which can include the cycle, is termed **evaluation**. The validation and evaluation processes are inextricably linked. The initial achievement of aim (validation) feeds into the next level of wider measurement (evaluation), so validation is the first step in the evaluation process. The systematic approach comes into its own during these phases. An objective setting phase derived from analysed needs and put into effect has more chance of being 'measured' in the evaluation phase.

Although validation is a short-term approach to evaluation, it is more widely used than more esoteric, wider-ranging methods. In validation we need to determine what we are actually trying to gauge. Is it longer-term memory and the retention of given knowledge such as procedures? Is it behavioural change in that the learning gained is applied to a given context? The objectives differ, particularly on timing, and this will have an impact on the possible methods used.

A useful way forward is to note key issues on the process of validation which can be incorporated into the evaluation process. (See Box PM4.13.)

BOX PM4.13

Programme validation: on and off the job

Question/issue	Addressed to whom?
Were the perceived needs met, and if not, why not?	Trainees, tutors and managers involved in training
Outline the actual benefits gained from the training.	The individual trainee and perhaps the 'sponsor' who forwarded the trainee's name
Can the benefits be applied to the workplace?	The manager and the trainee
Programme details – comment on: objectives, content, methods, timing and duration, etc.	The trainee, but the tutor or manager should have an input as well

---

All the interested parties should be involved, including trainees. On timing there should be an immediate feedback after the programme, and indeed there is a case for halting half-way through a programme to take stock and to validate the process to date. On returning to 'normal' work, from either a course or intensive on-the-job training, the relevance and the immediate transferability of the training can be gauged. Longer-term transfer and an overview of how the benefits can be improved (if that is the case) by manipulating the programme details may be a useful way forward.

There are limits to validation, of course, and the longer after the event it is done, the more distortions may appear, and certainly the more work variables with an impact on performance will be present. Socially acceptable answers must be guarded against, for we must seek representative views from all concerned. Validation is limited, and we must not allow it to degenerate into 'happiness sheets' on which trainees complain about hard beds and mediocre food. The validation process feeds into the next phase of evaluation.

Evaluation needs a balance between objective measurement and testing and a qualitative response. The classic work of Hamblin still dominates many of the approaches to evaluation (see figure 4.7).[24]

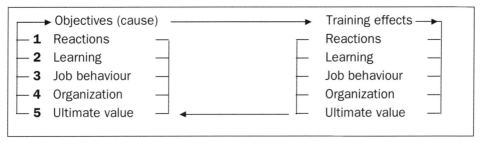

Figure 4.7 Training evaluation.

Source: Adapted from Hamblin, *Evaluation and Control of Training.*

The **reaction level** is, as its name suggests, an assessment of the trainees' reaction. Their opinions and attitudes to the usefulness, etc., of the programme is noted. This is akin to a validation phase. It occurs at the end of the programme or after a very brief return to 'normal' work. It has a short cycle for the benefit of current trainees and a longer cycle to incorporate these views for the benefit of future trainees. Questionnaires and discussions tend to predominate as the mechanism for this level of evaluation.

The **learning level** is the next stage. Changes in knowledge, skills or attitudes, a new approach to techniques or better judgement, etc., may be measured either during the training event or immediately afterwards. Written or practical tests are often incorporated into this level of evaluation, which can be used for remedial training of existing trainees or for the future benefit of others.

The **job behaviour** level seeks to examine work changes occurring as a result of learning. This has a longer time span, perhaps months after the event, and has the longer-term benefit of meeting the trainees' future needs and the next batch of trainees' aspirations as well. Observation, self-assessment, questionnaire, interview and appraisal methods are used. This tends to be a line manager's or trainer's role.

The next level is that of the **organization**, and clarifies whether training is helping to meet organizational objectives. There is a big jump between job behaviour and organizational effectiveness, but survey feedback measures, etc., may be used (see Unit Five).

The last level concerns **ultimate value**, which at best is verging on the metaphysical unless we look at the ultimate value from the individual trainee's perspective. (See Box PM4.14).

BOX PM4.14

Summary of evaluation: possible methods

This summary is extrapolated from Hamblin's approach.

Stage	Possible method and comment
Reaction	Questionnaire, formal interviews and group or one-to-one discussions
Learning	'Test' or exercise; individual can make some critique
Job Behaviour	Observation, self-assessment, questionnaire to manager and trainee, interview and performance appraisal
Organization	Some form of 'effective indicator' – but difficult
Ultimate value	Even more difficult

More quantified approaches include the following measures:

■ costs
■ opportunity costs
■ cost-effectiveness
■ cost benefit/profit
■ human investment

(See Box PM4.15.)

BOX PM4.15

Quantification: methods of training evaluation

Type	Method	Comment
Costs	As per learning/reaction but with 'price tag', costings and variance analysis	Some value

Type	Method	Comment
Opportunity costs	Cost of training compared with doing nothing or other interventions	Useful for back-up to rationale for training
Cost-effectiveness	Relate costs to objectives	Feasible, but 'pricing' of objectives = ?
Cost benefit/profit	Benefits outweigh costs?	Difficult
Human investment	Human asset accounting, value-added schemes, etc.	Sounds great, but . . .

The emphasis has been deliberately placed on the 'micro' aspects of evaluation. The 'macro' aspects must be reiterated and the innovative work of Morris, with his wide perspective, is worthy of note.[25]

Earlier we mentioned a training system and the concept of audit based on this system. As noted these are found in depth elsewhere (see figure 4.2). Instead of reiterating the mechanics of this system and its audit, we have instead asked a range of questions which will help the evaluation process of the training cycle. These questions appear in the appendix.

We will next move on to development.

Appendix: A checklist for the line trainer or manager

Suggested checklist Contribution of line trainers and management

Needs   Discovering a performance issue or problem.
Relating the performance issue to established performance standards or norms of achievement (e.g. the rest of the work group).
Placing the deficiency in a specific problem.
Relating the deficiency into learning and behavioural causes.

The training and development unit can give an overview of the problem (it may be occurring elsewhere or it may be emanating from the organization itself). They can help with relating the deficiency to learning 'causes' and 'consequences'.

Design and learning   Setting learning objectives and understanding the nature and contribution that planned learning can make.
Scanning the appropriate methods and techniques of design and relating them to the types of learning.
Selecting the trainees.
Assisting in the selection of trainers within and outside the department.

You need to get hold of the 'technology of learning'. You are probably not a psychologist and you do not have to be one either. You must know the principles of learning; the range of techniques open to the designer; the application of these techniques to the given problem; and how to construct learning objectives.

Implementation   Conducting 'on the job training' via a range of techniques and methods.
Recommending 'off the job' training via a range of techniques and methods.
Acting as the training communicator via counselling and tutoring, and as a catalyst to your own staff.
Tutoring or lecturing on a course in your own specialism or on an organizational input, e.g. planning.

You are not expected to be a specialist instructor who stands up and delivers a seminar or a lecture. The focus of your role is on training at the job itself. This covers induction for new people and skill and knowledge training on the job to enable the individual to reach a certain level of performance. It also has a developmental aspect, encouraging, listening and counselling more experienced people on their own career plans, and you need to be able to link these development plans to organizational reality.

A good working knowledge of the range, of the merits and limits, and of the relevance of implementation methods and techniques is required. This does not necessitate mastering the subject but it requires more than a passing familiarity. This working knowledge will enable you to manage on-the-job training effectively and to stimulate and recommend off-the-job initiatives.

| *Evaluation* | Establishing some benchmarks on pre-training performance (quantified if possible). |

Evaluation Establishing some benchmarks on pre-training performance (quantified if possible).
Establishing specific learning needs and objectives (quantified if possible) prior to training.
Monitoring past training and work performance.
Marrying up the performance gap and the knowledge/skill/attitude gap after the training to the pre-training situation.
Feedback and reporting on same for the next needs analysis.

Notes

1 Department of Employment, *Glossary of Training Terms*.
2 NEDO and MSC, *Competence and Competition*.
3 Training Agency, *Training in Britain*.
4 Traditionally training is seen to cover knowledge, skills and attitudes. A useful analysis by the International Labour Organization (ILO) adds techniques (i.e. knowledge plus skills) and also judgement, which is at the top of the training hierarchy of skills and knowledge. See International Labour Organization, *Teaching and Training Methods for Management Development*.
5 See Pettigrew and Reason, *Alternative Interpretations of the Training Officer Role*.
6 See Leduchowicz and Bennett, *What Makes an Effective Trainer?*
7 J.A.G. Jones, 'Training intervention strategies'.
8 Training Services Agency, 'An approach to the training of staff with training officer roles'.
9 See M. Jones for these theories, in 'Training practices and learning theories', and Anderson for the thematic approach, in *Successful Training Practice*.
10 Kolb, 'Towards an applied theory of experiential learning'.
11 Honey and Mumford, *Manual of Learning Styles*.
12 There is a case for unstructured 'discovery' learning which is not strictly systematic but has some pattern to the whole 'unstructured' process.
13 Laird, *Approaches to Training and Development*.
14 Fairbairns makes this point in her analysis of training needs, 'Plugging the gap in training needs analysis'.
15 Anderson, *Successful Training Practice*.
16 Carroll et al., 'The relative effectiveness of training methods'.
17 Long, 'A theoretical model for method selection'.
18 Anderson, *Successful Training Practice*.
19 Industrial Training Research Unit, *CRAMP*.
20 Grant, 'A better way of learning from Nellie'.
21 Revans, *The ABC of Action Learning*.
22 Morris, 'The evaluation of training'.
23 Anderson, *Successful Training Practice*.
24 Hamblin, *Evaluation and Control of Training*.
25 Morris, 'The evaluation of training'.

Unit Five

Development

Learning Objectives

After completing this unit you should be able to:

- understand the concept and principles of self-development;
- design a management development scheme;
- conduct a performance appraisal session;
- introduce change through an understanding of the issues and difficulties involved;
- apply the generic skills.

Contents

Unit Five

“ The responsibility for making development happen is shared. Manager and man have each a part to play. Management is responsible for maintaining a climate in the organisation that fosters the development of personal initiative and responsibility. Management is also responsible for sustaining a concern for high standards, for recognising ability and potential, and for devoting time and trouble to delegation. But given all this, the drive and effort must come from the man himself.”

M.L. Haider, then chairman of Standard Oil, NJ[1]

Overview

Like training, development is based on behavioural change, or learning; but the time scale is far longer and the needs of the individual are probably more important. This unit looks at development from three perspectives:

- individual or self
- management
- organization

A common theme of development in the three perspectives is **change**, and we will pursue this theme in each of these categories. Another common denominator is **consensus**. Change is traumatic and if it is to be relatively permanent it must be based on discussion, negotiation and agreement.

Self-development

To a great extent the route to any development must come from within the individual. All the systems, programmes and organizational resources come to no avail unless the individual wishes to develop him or herself. Several themes exist in self-development. First, there is a self-help vision in the view that the world does not owe us a living and we need to help ourselves. Then there is an anti-institutionalized thread, whereby the experts and their colleges, etc., are seen to be out of touch with individual needs. There is a financial theme as well, for self-development is cheap! There is a humanistic vision of the individual taking control of his or her life and of autonomy in the environment. In this school of thought, the individual's own learning style and past experiences are seen as very important. These self-developmental images all come together in a personal growth view akin to that of the self-actualized person in Maslow's hierarchy of needs.[2]

For my money, self-help is important and an onus does lie on a mature adult to push him or herself. However, this should not be confused with seeing self-development as a cheap alternative with the organization abdicating its responsibility. The anti-expert and anti-institutional strain may be understandable, but it would be an error to turn away from such

---

BOX PM5.1

Individual development

In the early section of *Career Dynamics* (see source), Schein looks at the development of the individual as he or she progresses through the major stages or cycles of life. Thereafter the work is concerned with the matching of individual and organizational need. The phases of development, not the matching process, will be discussed here.

To Schein, motives are complex and variable, so simplistic motivational themes are non-runners. In particular the relationship between work and non-work life needs to be understood in order to have a fuller picture of the individual and his or her needs. Self-development, career development and family development coexist throughout the life of an individual.

There are various life tasks which need to be determined in the development of the individual:

- *biological/ageing,* such as illness and patterns of behaviour identified with a certain age;
- *family,* such as potential conflicts between children and parents;
- *work/career,* such as the 'internal career' of the individual's aspirations and the 'external career' developed by the organization.

The damage of potential conflicts between these life tasks can be minimized by **constructive coping**. The essence of this coping mechanism is confronting and tackling the issue(s), which will result in self-growth and development.

The stages of this mechanism leading to self-growth and development can be summarized as:

- *problem diagnosis:* understanding the situation in which we find ourselves;
- *self-diagnosis:* gaining some insight into our feelings and needs;
- *selection:* a coping response – from doing nothing to seeking advice and guidance from others;
- *diagnosis of consequences:* a conclusion is needed to ensure that the real problems have been confronted and solved.

To conclude, such a process is necessary before we can adjust to any vision of self-development.

Source: Adapted from Schein, *Career Dynamics*

expertise and risk the process's degenerating into a navel-gazing experiment. Taking control of one's life may be easier said than done, and Box PM5.1 gives us interesting insights into 'life tasks' and coping mechanisms.

The experientially based learning approach is very much to the fore in self-development, and the learner style is particularly relevant. The concept of actualization is developed more in Unit Six. The critical thread is that of experience-based learning and learner style, for these underpin the whole process, while the core philosophy comes from a humanistic perspective. We will examine the philosophy first, then the process, then some techniques, and finally a perspective on the whole new trend, which seems to be sweeping all other approaches to training and development to one side.

The learning philosophy of what can now be termed the self-development movement or school of thought can be seen in the work of Rogers.[3] The environment of learning should be as free as possible to develop the individual. Themes from Rogers's work include the following:

- The subject matter to be learned must be perceived as relevant to the needs of the individual.
- Attempts to change the learner's self-perceptions will be seen as threatening, and may be resisted.
- To reduce such resistance, external threats should be minimized and steps taken to foster a safe environment.
- Learning by doing should be encouraged.
- Responsible participation by the student in the learning process should be encouraged, since this will facilitate learning.
- Self-evaluation is of primary importance: evaluation by others plays a secondary role.
- Self-initiated learning involving the whole person of the learner – feelings as well as intellect – is the most lasting and pervasive; hence self-development is centre stage.

This humanistic philosophy, while not being the whole picture and perhaps suffering from too much of an individual orientation at the expense of other variables in the learning environment (see figure 4.2 earlier), is far preferable to a behaviourist approach. (See Box PM5.2.)

In Unit Four (figure 4.3) we looked at Kolb's experiential learning, with its focus on:

- concrete experience
- observation and reflection
- abstract conceptualization
- testing of new concepts[4]

> ## BOX PM5.2
>
> # Individual development and performance
>
> The work of Connellan (see source) looks to improving organizational performance at the level of the individual. The theme is that behaviour technology can rectify inappropriate and ineffective working practices. This **'behaviour technology'** is a systems approach to the individual's development. It has certain key characteristics:
>
> - *Controllability:* we can change the conditions under which we operate to give a desired outcome.
> - *Predictability:* we can forecast what will happen when certain conditions are created.
> - *Measurability:* changes in results can be measured.
> - *Understandability:* we need to determine cause-and-effect relationships.
>
> The rationale behind behaviour technology is based on the view of an antecedent, a behaviour and a consequence. The **antecedent** is a realistic and clear performance standard; the **behaviour** is the desired action and any constraints which inhibit that action; and the **consequences** are the outcomes which necessitate some formal feedback measure. For example, we could do the following:
>
> - specify job behaviour;
> - establish performance standards;
> - acknowledge that the antecedents of the job behaviour are clear;
> - ensure that constraints are minimal;
> - give positive feedback.
>
> Connellan claims that behaviour technology helps not only the organization, but the individual. The process can be summarized as goal setting; the achievement of the goals through appropriate behaviours; and analysis of behaviour and results, with feedback and reinforcement. As a tool of management or as a mechanism of self-development, the goal of directed behaviour looks to be useful, although the mechanistic system that is in use may limit the impact in a real situation.
>
> *Source:* Adapted from Connellan, *How to Improve Human Performance*

This problem-solving approach to learning, based on past life experiences, has a clear self-developmental implication. The approach of Honey and Mumford's learning styles of individuals is also experience-based:

- having an experience;
- reviewing this experience;
- concluding from the experience;
- planning the next steps.[5]

Learner style can have an impact on these experiences. For example, some individuals may repeat old experiences and not try new ones; others may just observe other people and learn from these experiences rather than actually doing it themselves; while others still may conclude without having or reviewing the experience. A whole range of learner styles and the self-knowledge related to our way of learning can be derived from these concepts of learning, which can only help the individual in learning how he or she learns. In many ways this is the basis of self-development.[6]

We can split up the self-development theme further by looking at two aspects: self-managed learning and a range of appropriate techniques, and secondly a quality approach of 'What makes the individual effective?'. Burgoyne and others, for example, have merged the two themes in looking at self-development for managers.[7] We will mention this interesting work, of course, but we will concentrate on the techniques and also the self-analysis which can make for effectiveness in careers.

Self-managed learning: the methods

The list can be quite exhaustive, and exhausting, so we will isolate some of the main techniques, with a commentary. Before we do this we will reiterate the common principles:

- Learner-centred methods mean that control passes away from the trainer or co-ordinator to the learner.
- The trainer or co-ordinator may become more of an influencer.
- Tolerance of ambiguity is required by both trainee and trainer.
- The capacity for learning must be there.
- It requires commitment.

(See Box PM5.3.)

BOX PM5.3

Self-managed learning as part of self-development: some examples

Independent study	Either through some guided reading or through self-discovery, the individual plans and carries out a learning programme. This can be academic in the case of a vocational qualification, e.g. a Diploma in Business, or more short term in an area of interest, e.g. computer programming.
Action learning	See Unit Four.
Humanistic education/ 'learning community'	The basis of a liberal education with its 'learning community', as in a university, can be adopted. The aim is to put people together to meet their

	group and individual learning needs and to share their resources.
Group working	T groups or training groups, the autonomy laboratory and exercises on group dynamics can help the individual find greater self-awareness and realization of how he or she normally interacts within a group.
Discovery learning	See Unit Four.
Coaching and counselling	See Units Three and Four.
Learning from reality	Mumford[1] is particularly strong on supporting work-based initiatives. The opportunities to learn at work are immense, so the 'learning events', from attendance at a meeting to deputizing, should be maximized.

Source:
1 Mumford, 'Emphasis on the learner'

Self-managed learning has been manifested in a growing trend towards **continuous development**.[8] The concept is that learning is an ongoing activity throughout life at work and outside of it, provided that the learner is motivated to learn. Although many jobs inhibit such learning as they are designed to maximize 'scientific' output, many professional associations, such as the UK Institute of Personnel Management, seem to be committed to this cause.

Effectiveness and self-development

There has been a move to isolate key qualities of management which would give some harder direction to the self-development movement. For example, this list of attributes has been developed:[9]

■ command of basic information;
■ professional know-how;
■ sensitive perception;
■ problem solving;
■ interpersonal skills;
■ resilience, creativity and control of behaviour;
■ balanced approach to learning and adaptability to ongoing events;
■ self-knowledge.

Self-knowledge is important to the whole vision of self-development and it has been captured in the work of Schein, particularly with his 'career anchors'. (See Box PM5.4.)

BOX PM5.4

Career anchors: individual development and self-knowledge

Schein (see source) uses the expression 'career anchors' to explain an 'occupational self-concept' based on self-perceived talents and abilities, motives and needs linked to values and attitudes. The main types of career anchor derived from his specialist study are as follows:

- *Technical competence.* For people for whom this is the career anchor, the interest is in the work content and not in rising through the hierarchy. They like more challenging work and knowing that they are experts. They are technically competent.
- *Managerial competence.* The interest is in responsibility and authority and success is measured in rising through the hierarchy. These people like general management and large organizations. They are analytical and their interpersonal competence is allied to emotional control.
- *Security.* These people seek stability and benefits with the same organization. There is no real growth in their careers but they are very much 'organization people'. Success is linked mostly to a stable family and career.
- *Creativity.* The creation of their own product is important for these people. They like entrepreneurial projects and success is based on their own 'product'. They are unlikely to be in a large organization.
- *Autonomy.* These people are independent thinkers seeking maximum freedom from organizational constraints. Growth in career terms is less important than self-pacing of work, lifestyle and independent work habits. They are unlikely to be found in an organization.

I recognize myself here. Do you?

Source: Adapted from Schein, *Career Dynamics*

To conclude this section, note that self-development means looking to your goals and needs, implementing a plan of action, and monitoring and evaluating that plan. Yet the plan needs organizational backing, a learning opportunity, encouragement, resources and assistance, from coaching to counselling. However, often self-development, where it exists, is the preserve of management. There is a strong case for widening it out. One useful mechanism is to integrate the self-developmental plan (of managers and others) with the task objectives of the appraisal system. The next section turns to the appraisal system but before we go on we should take stock of our personal objectives. As a manager, you have a dual responsibility for forwarding your own development plan and that of your subordinates. Before you tackle Activity PM5.1, see Box PM5.5.

BOX PM5.5

Checklist for development

■ The potential for curiosity and interest needs to be encouraged as part of this training or learning.

■ The learning must be relevant to *organizational and individual need.*

■ Learning must be *non-threatening* and errors must be expected at the outset. (They can be minimized by carefully structuring the learning opportunity.)

■ *Action* needs to occur, so a developmental action plan will be drawn up.

■ The learner must be *encouraged to take the initiative* and some responsibility for his or her development plan and subsequent training.

■ You must help the learner by setting *realistic developmental goals* for the current job as well as looking to the longer term.

■ You must *stimulate staff* by example and commitment to continuous development and ongoing training.

■ Finally, *a supportive climate* stimulates development, and this support can be enhanced by your contribution and specific activities.

Gaining commitment

The aim is not a 'tell and sell' session but a joint agreement on development. Some principles of such a joint agreement are as follows:

■ *Preparing:* both you and your subordinates need to work through the main tasks and their developmental implications.

■ *Questioning:* a range of different types of questions can be used to increase the level of participation and involvement

■ *Discussing:* listening and debating points allied to 'ironing' out difficulties are important.

■ *Agreeing:* both need to agree the action points which will follow from this meeting.

Personnel and Management Development

Developmental schemes, processes or events are designed primarily to increase performance. Historically the emphasis has been on management-only development schemes, but there is a move towards 'performance management' and appraisal schemes for most white-collar staff, particularly in non-unionized organizations. Having said this, considerable research indicates that the UK does not take the development of its managers seriously, compared to its main competitors.[10] If this is still so, personnel (non-managerial) development will be very much at an embryonic phase, given the relative importance of management as a key resource to the organization and the absence of its development. The objectives, the prerequisites of success, the methods and techniques of both management and personnel developmental schemes are close to each other, so it may be useful to consider both together, highlighting significant

ACTIVITY PM5.1

SELF-DEVELOPMENT

Activity code
✓ Self-development
✓ Teamwork
✓ Communications
✓ Numeracy/IT
✓ Decisions

Core tasks
What are the key tasks of your current job? (Mention only about six main goals, and note outcomes if possible.)

1

2

3

4

5

6

Task plan
Now focus on the most important key task (a similar process can be used for the other key tasks later).

1 The key task is:

2 It is important because of (note resources, impact, if things went wrong, etc.):

3 The constraints inhibiting the task are:

■ professional/vocational education

■ competency – an application of the skill and knowledge

■ personal goals and ambitions (this can be geared both to the tasks in hand and the future)

This scheme can be used for you and your subordinates, and links individual need to task need. The task need still dominates and the self-developmental needs are constrained by the immediate task. In addition, a wider view of where you are going must be taken, for it may be removed from the immediate task. At the same time realism must be the order of the day.

4 The opportunities promoting the task are:

5 What further progress can I make to meet the task? (Note time scale and assistance if required.)

6 What evidence do I need to confirm that the task has been successfully carried out?

Self-development plan
This is divided up into a plan to meet the tasks above and a longer-term vision as well.

■ *Knowledge:* What knowledge is required to carry out the task above? Do I have it? If not, how do I get it?

Similar questions are asked for:

- *Skill*:

- *Technical and functional experience*:

differences as they arise. Of course, the literature is dominated by management development.

Tannehill suggests that there are three main perspectives on development:

- *No change is possible*. People do not change their fundamental behavioural patterns, so the mature person cannot alter his or her work patterns any more than he or she could change personality.

- *Self-appropriated learning is the key*. The only successful approach to change is self-initiated with the individual directing his or her worklife.

- *People are the key asset which can be developed*. The garden imagery of 'cultivating' people to maximize their usefulness is inherent in this approach.[11]

The first approach is a recipe for doing nothing; the second a formula for possibly passing the buck and for organizational abdication (although the truism is probably correct); while the third, when allied to real self-development, will ensure that people are fulfilled and meet the performance needs of the organization. We will pursue this approach.

There are three distinct routes of development.[12] One emerges **from the top** through the corporate plan, the manpower plan and the target-setting approach to MbO (management by objectives), KRA (key-result areas), or whatever. This is very much a structured task process. The other route has been a **bottom-up** approach with focus on the individual manager. This looked at the unique skills, knowledge and attitudes of personnel. A more recent approach is to look at **core competencies** across a range of jobs. The core competency approach is more generic. (Please refer to the 'Introduction to the Series'.) A group dimension can also be added to these stages of development. (See Box PM5.6.)

Top-down

This approach is derived very much from the organizational plan and is objective-based. Objective setting, target setting and planning, KRA and MbO are all variations on this goal-oriented theme. We will examine the MbO approach and target setting as they tend to dominate.

BOX PM5.6

The evolution of management development programmes

Stage I: *Common skills.* A common programme is given to all managers as their requirements are similar.

Stage II: *Individual.* Separate roles are analysed and underpinned by job analysis. Coaching, mentoring and off-the-job training follow on.

Stage III: *Team.* The management relationships are more complex. Team roles and development are emphasized.

Stage IV: *Change/organization.* The aim is to develop an enquiring attitude and a flexible approach to change within a dynamic organization.

Source: Adapted from J.P.J. Kenney et al., *Manpower Training and Development*

MbO

This has been seen as a process of:

- clarifying the 'mission' of the organization;
- streamlining planning, measuring and evaluation of goals;
- joint target setting;
- periodic performance appraisal.

Its beginnings seem to be with du Pont at General Motors in the 1920s, when, under reorganization, the firm initiated a cost-accounting goal type of system. Meanwhile, Watson at the IBM Corporation was stimulating leaders to help their subordinates accomplish their goals. At General Motors, the embryonic MbO began to develop with goals being divided into volume, costs, prices, and rates of return on capital. 'Standards' were introduced for performance at that time.

Peter Drucker, a consultant and writer, stimulated the rise of the objective-setting process in his consultancy work (at General Motors) and in his writings.[13] To Drucker, strategic planning and delegation of decision making were critical to the MbO programme. Concentration of effort on a 'few activities' would reap benefit. Top management should ask the following:

- What business are we in? (i.e. what are our objectives, goals and overall directions?)
- What are our 'points of excellence'? (i.e. what do we do best?)
- What are our unique resources?
- What are our priorities, derived from our points of excellence?

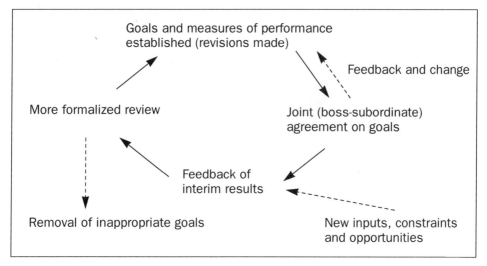

Figure 5.1 The MbO cycle.

The management team should thereafter be involved in the joint establishment of goals of all subordinates. The 'cycle' in figure 5.1 gives a feel of the process.

At the broader level of the organization, MbO can work, and its strength lies in its consensus. However, some objectives can be too broad-brush and are often concerned with activities not results, so we need some form of target setting or key result areas – hopefully with the same consensus type of approach as displayed in MbO.

Examples of MbO and KRAs are shown below and a checklist on KRAs is given in the appendix.

MbO

Profitability	Return on capital employed.
Market standing	By share or volume, by product, pricing or policies.
Productivity	Measure input and output.
Finance	Capital structure, etc.
Innovation	New, better products.
Management/development	Appraisal in operation? Level and type of training?
Employee attitude	Level and degree of consultation, etc.

KRAs

Key task	Performance standard	Control data	Suggestions
Manufacturer's orders to be completed on time	90 per cent	Weekly delivery reports	Do I get all the information?

See Activities PM5.2 and PM5.3.

ACTIVITY PM5.2

TARGETS AND PERFORMANCE

Activity code
- ✓ Self-development
- ✓ Teamwork
- ✓ Communications
- ✓ Numeracy/IT
- ✓ Decisions

Senior management felt that there was a need to introduce a target-setting programme based on key tasks or key result areas (KRAs). It was felt that it would make each individual accountable and an active participant in the objectives of the firm.

External help was sought to facilitate the process and a psychologist was recruited to introduce the scheme. The psychologist, a specialist in management by objectives (MbO), met the senior management, who enthused over the idea of MbO being introduced.

The psychologist, Ms Bird, was more careful in her approach and suggested that more 'experimental research' would be required before embarking on the MbO programme. She suggested that the marketing department be used as a 'control' while target setting was introduced into the production department. If or when it worked in production, it would be moved into the marketing area.

This was not acceptable, as both marketing and production directors wanted the target setting to start in 'their' departments. The psychologist argued that such activity would destroy the evaluation. The directors said that they wanted the scheme now. Ms Bird declined to go further until research was carried out.

It was agreed with the managing director that she would address all management and that the programme would be shelved until six months' research was carried out. However, during the very successful meeting, the director of marketing, Clarke, said that 'it was great and he was going to start setting specific goals from tomorrow.'

1 Do the managers realize what MbO is all about? Clarify their misconceptions.
2 Was Ms Bird correct in her approach?
3 How would you go about establishing a goal-setting, target-setting or MbO programme for:
   (a) an organization;
   (b) a department;
   (c) an individual job?

ACTIVITY PM5.3

GOAL OR TARGET SETTING

Activity code

✓ Self-development
✓ Teamwork
☐ Communications
☐ Numeracy/IT
✓ Decisions

Look at the checklist below.

		Yes				No
1	Do you know the boundaries of your job?	5	4	3	2	1
2	Is there any overlap of duties?	1	2	3	4	5
3	Do you have any uncertainty about your duties?	1	2	3	4	5
4	Are there any areas not covered?	1	2	3	4	5
5	Do you know the limits of your authority?	5	4	3	2	1
6	Are these limits understood?	5	4	3	2	1
7	Are many decisions left to your discretion?	5	4	3	2	1
8	Are the limits of your authority set too high?	1	2	3	4	5

Total _____

1 Answer the checklist questions 1–8, ringing the appropriate number on the scale on the right-hand side.
2 If possible, your manager should do the same – without consultation with you – regarding your job.
3 A discussion should occur between you and your manager on the perceptions shown by this checklist.

Bottom-up

There is a view that development should be based on increasing the proficiency of the individual (manager or employee) in three areas:

■ knowledge
■ skills
■ attitudes, values and behaviour[14]

This is a traditional 'K–S–A' approach.

Knowledge

This is the information aspect of the job. It necessitates some intellectual effort.

Skills

A range of skills can be determined for a given job type. In Unit Four, for example, we looked at a training skills taxonomy. Skills need to be integrated with knowledge to have enhanced meaning and transfer between situations.

Attitudes, Values and Behaviour

Developing the value systems of personnel which will meet both personal and organizational aims would be a laudable aim. Commitment and some acceptance of the value system and of the work norms are important aspects of any business operation. An awareness of attitudes and behavioural patterns of self and colleagues is an integral part of any development scheme.

Core skills and competency

Stewart[15] and more recently a study at ICI Organics Division[16] have come up with core areas of work for managers. The same approach could quite easily be used for less complex jobs as well. Shopping lists of such competencies are in vogue at the moment, but most would accept the following areas:

- *technical and administrative:* from specific professional knowledge to planning;
- *people:* from social and behavioural aspects to leadership style;
- *intellectual:* a judgemental and evaluative approach to logical analysis (including quantitative methods);
- *problem solving and decision making;*
- *attitudes and value systems.*

In this series we are using:

- *Functional knowledge:* from sales and marketing to finance and accounting, from enterprise and operational management to people management;
- *Generalist and policy knowledge:* cutting across the functional routes to give an overview of the subject;
- *Specific skills:* by function and generalist management;
- *Generic skills:* of self-development, teamwork, communications, numeracy/IT and decision making.

Disappointment

Problems occur with these developmental schemes. Perhaps great expectations do not help but other 'disappointments' have been noted.[17] Disappointing programmes were seen as:

- aiming at only one level;
- too short-term in their outlook, with too much emphasis on a given technique;
- having vague objectives;

- failing to consider incentives, group norms, organizational policy and the attitudes of the participants' managers;
- not having support from policies or from the immediate boss.

Methods

To a great extent we have dealt with the methods being used for developing people in the first section in this unit and in Unit Four. Reference to the work of Digman may give an appreciation of the methods being used by top companies.[18] (See Box PM5.7.)

BOX PM5.7

Methods of development

On-the-job experience ranked highest followed a long way behind by coaching by the boss. Assignments, in-house training and then university programmes followed on.

At top management level the following occurred:
- individual programmes
- conceptual skill and strategy emphasized
- environmental understanding to the fore
- interface of the organization and environment stressed

At middle level, the focus was on:
- human skills
- analytical abilities and decision making
- conceptual skills

At supervisory and junior level the emphasis was on:
- basic technical and human skills
- company procedures

Source: Adapted from Digman, 'How well-managed organisations develop their executives'

Prerequisites of success

The first thing to look for is commitment. Without top managers being actively involved, many development schemes fall by the wayside or degenerate into paper-filling exercises. Development needs to be both job- and people-oriented and placed in the context of the 'live' organization. There is a need for succession and career planning and the incentive link should never be far from the surface. The connection between organizational planning and self-development through a cycle (MbO) or target setting including developmental (not pure task) needs is important. Developmental needs differ according to your place in the hierarchy and your career anchor. At the same time, core competencies can be seen in managerial jobs, and these can pull together the whole developmental programme. Career development and formal vocational education can also be involved in this master plan. What we must never forget is that the whole rationale is to increase performance, and that the appraisal scheme, with its developmental vision, must therefore meet the task needs of the organization. We will now turn to appraisal.

Why Bother Doing Appraisals?

What is the purpose behind the appraisal process? What are the specific objectives behind an appraisal scheme? Assuming some ongoing feedback, various reasons for annual appraisal come to the fore. The weighting of these factors alters between organizations. See Box PM5.8.

BOX PM5.8

Appraisal: research findings

A UK business school in *c.*1980 surveyed the top 353 managers of 'one large organization' on the purpose of performance appraisal. No company details are given because of the need for confidentiality. The results are given below.

	%
To match rewards more closely to contributions	55
To reconcile individual needs and ambitions with the organization	54
To motivate individuals to greater achievement	51
To improve organization performance	33
To help people develop more satisfying jobs	31
To improve mutual understanding between boss and subordinate	27
To make better use of individual talent	25

More recently the Institute of Personnel Management has conducted another survey on why companies review performance:[1]

	%
To assess training and development needs	97
To help improve current performance	97
To review past performance	98
To assess future potential/promotability	71
To assist career planning decisions	75
To set performance objectives	81
To assess increases or new levels in salary	40
Others – e.g. updating personnel records	4

Source:
1 Derived from P. Long, *Performance Appraisal Revisited*

Improving current performance

This is related to the existing job. The emphasis is on *now*, the present, rather than *then* the past. Of course, a past review of progress will occur, but the major effort should be geared to the current job, its objectives and, if applicable, specific targets. The future should not be ignored, and planning is examined later.

To improve existing performance, certain processes apply to the boss and subordinate:

■ There must be some change in behaviour and a *willingness to change* based on an *objective*, not subjective, appraisal. Flexibility is important.

■ Perhaps there has to be a willingness to change *attitudes*, or at least a willingness to be open-minded about the job and, if possible, yourself. We need to be aware of the ethical issues in trying to alter people, and that changing the personality of mature individuals will be a difficult, if not an unwise, objective.

■ *Goals* need to be established and, whenever possible, a joint input by boss and subordinate is to be encouraged. Remember that impossible goals will not be achieved, and if the goals are set too high they will lead to discouragement and demotivation, as the subordinate can never attain the specific tasks. Equally, the organization is a place of work and its aims must be met, from survival and growth to profitability, through the highest possible targets and goals for each department, section, team and individual.

■ We need to be aware of the process of making *judgements about people at work*, as this goes to the core of performance evaluation.

■ *Standards* must be set for the future, based on past performance, existing objectives, and anticipated changes in objectives and priorities.

Identifying potential – *Rewards* –

Some organizations use appraisal as part of their assessment of 'promotability'. We need to be careful not to oversell this promotional aspect: a casual remark by the boss to the effect that 'you have a sound future here' may be interpreted, particularly later, by the subordinate as a hint that promotion is around the corner. If this does not occur, demotivation is almost inevitable.

An individual may be very good at his or her job, but the next job up the ladder may be completely different, with different skills and attitudes required by the organization. The move from a successful sales representative to a sales manager epitomizes this problem. In any case, the overall 'succession plans' may not be your responsibility. This is not to argue that there is no role for identifying potential for promotion, but this should be a separate phase of the interviewing process, if it is used at all.

Some organizations pay lip service to the idea of using the appraisal as a means of identifying potential, but actually abandon the system and canvass senior managers on an informal basis to trawl for potential. Such

---

BOX PM5.9

Appraisal: potential issues

You will need to reflect on some of the potential issues which may arise during the appraisal interview.

- Should you criticize? If we criticize too much, the session may be negative. Will this critique really produce a better performance? Is it better to give praise, or at least give both praise and criticism?
- The focus can be on the person or the task. If we combine the two, we may distort the image of both. Is it better to focus on the goals of the job?
- Should appraisals be an annual event or is there a case for ongoing feedback and/or mini-appraisals throughout the year? Should the goals be given, 'told/sold' or mutually agreed?
- Should we separate out the objectives of appraisal (money, performance, development) and have these sessions at different times?

---

subjective routes destroyed the credibility of the system in one major UK retail firm. Other organizations have a 'closed' approach to promotion and do not reveal such plans openly at appraisal interviews. So beware of the 'climate' in your organization, and do not oversell. If you become involved in this 'promotability' discussion, make sure that you can deliver. See Box PM5.9.

Rewarding the subordinate

The appraisal process gives an opportunity to reward the subordinate. This can be an **intrinsic** reward, in the sense that the subordinate can be given a feedback on his or her performance that is related to motivation, and/or an **extrinsic** reward – some organizations link the payment system to the appraisal system, which is thus used as a basis for rewarding effort and achievement. This is particularly evident in sales and marketing roles, where quantified targets can facilitate payment being linked to objectives.

We now turn to a series of activities based on objectives, appraisal and the problems of appraisal interviewing. See Activities PM5.4, 5.5 and 5.6.

Organizational Development

In the animal kingdom, organisms survive by their ability to adapt to their environment. A form of natural selection ensures that the strongest survive. Work organizations are similar in this, but the pressure for change may come from both the external and internal environments. The political, economic, social and technological pressures will have an impact on the

ACTIVITY PM5.4

OBJECTIVES AND THE PERFORMANCE REVIEW

Activity code

✔ Self-development
  Teamwork
✔ Communications
✔ Numeracy/IT
✔ Decisions

Clara worked in the busy consumer research department of a major advertising agency based in London.

She did not have a formal job title or schedule of responsibilities, as everyone 'mucked in' here to give colleagues a hand as necessary. Of course, Clara had some key tasks, such as the production of reports about sales revenue of the products and services advertised by her firm. She could turn her hand to statistics, compilation and collation, routine administration, liaison with the research consultants, and making the tea!

Sharma, her boss, was in the process of reviewing Clara's performance. Sharma decided to use a faults analysis which would highlight where Clara was going wrong.

1 The data on the Cosmopolitan Tour Company had been late and the appendices had been inaccurate. The company was a new client, and this had not impressed its managers.
2 Clara's team of four had been working hard on the projects, but they seemed to be a noisy, undisciplined gaggle who spent more time applying make-up than collating statistics.
3 The data had not been made available from the researchers. It was late, particularly for the annual report, and parts were often missing.
4 When Clara liaised with other sections such as key accounts or the computer unit, these service areas were often confused as to Clara's requirements, for she tended to talk in the jargon of the researcher.

Sharma was aware of these problems, and other sectional and unit managers in key accounts and computing had mentioned that Clara was causing them a problem owing to her poor liaison.

As the manager, you must be fair. Construct and write down key objectives for Clara and comment objectively on how she meets these tasks.

ACTIVITY PM5.5

THE APPRAISAL SCHEME

Activity code
☐ Self-development
✓ Teamwork
☐ Communications
☐ Numeracy/IT
✓ Decisions

Management from grade 3 to grade 10 are involved with appraisal (grades 1–3 are senior management). The top management see the value of appraisal, but are more concerned with the long-term business strategy of the organization. There is a management development manager, but he is new to the firm and he believes that the appraisal scheme is not integrated with the management planning system.

The new management development manager decides to canvass opinions on the existing appraisal scheme. Here is a sample of the comments:

'The boss always goes back two years when I made that dreadful error.'

'It's a waste of time.'

'It's OK if you have blue eyes.'

'What are the personnel department doing with our files?'

'Tick tick tick a few boxes, and my money depends on this!'

'Great.'

'The boss is never prepared.'

'As a manager, I don't like telling people bad news.'

'Why should I expose my inner self to the boss?'

'It lasts five minutes.'

'The personnel department gives us tons of paper but no help.'

'What's it all about?' [from the marketing co-ordinator]

'I'm a staff manager with two bosses, one staff and one line, and I don't know who is supposed to do it.'

'I've been ill for two months and all he talks about is his targets.'

'It's a shambles.'

1 Classify these problems.
2 Rank them in importance.

ACTIVITY PM5.6

INTERVIEWING FOR APPRAISAL

Activity code
- ✓ Self-development
- ✓ Teamwork
- ✓ Communications
- ☐ Numeracy/IT
- ✓ Decisions

How would you approach the following?

1 **Eager Eva**
   The interviewee agrees with everything you say, and does it far too quickly.
   Proposed action:

2 **Promotion Joe**
   Joe, a middle-aged manager, has still got his sights on that elusive top job. He has applied on various occasions for more senior jobs in the organization, but to no avail, as it was felt that he could not do the more senior job. Joe is seeking a more senior job, or a commitment to that, from his appraisal interview.
   Proposed action:

3 **Money Mad Mandy**
   Mandy sees the appraisal session purely in terms of money and is looking for an increase in salary, or some commitment to that, from the meeting.
   Proposed action:

4 **Timmy Temper**
Tim listens to your constructive comments, loses his temper for no apparent reason and starts a slanging match.
Proposed action:

4 **Passive Pat**
He is very downcast. His eyes look to the floor avoiding eye contact. He is very passive and unresponsive to what is going on.
Proposed action:

6 **Constructive Cynthia**
She disagrees with your points but in a very constructive fashion. She queries your assessment as it fails to take account of certain key factors.
Proposed action:

7 **Blameless Beryl**
Beryl listens to you. She blames others and the time pressures caused by excessive contact with consumers or clients.
Proposed action:

organization, while internal change can occur through a process of ageing – both of the product line and of the organization. Indeed, Greiner has suggested that there is a natural evolution and revolution of organizations,[19] while others would probably accept the evolutionary change more than the more radical element or 'crisis' suggested by Greiner.[20] Most commentators would tend to see this change as ad hoc and fickle. (See Box PM5.10.)

BOX PM5.10

Spontaneous growth

Starbuck suggested a range of motives for growth in organizations. Some examples are:

- *self-realization:* a justification for existence, e.g. to avoid decline and fall;
- *risk:* a sense of adventure and a bit of a gamble;
- *prestige:* status is enhanced;
- *salaries and rewards:* organizational size may (does) correlate to greater financial rewards to management (particularly at the top);
- *economies of scale:* unit costs decrease as size increases;
- *stability:* growth may give greater stability;
- *security:* this may be enhanced with size.

Source: Adapted from Starbuck, 'Organisations as action generators'

The basis for the **management of change** approach is that change needs to be flexible enough to anticipate and cope with pressures of change. The term 'management of change' has become overworn of late, and the original concept of **organizational development** will be used in this section.

The term 'organizational development' (OD) seems to defy an agreed definition. We hear talk of 'culture', 'group problem solving', 'agents or catalysts of change' and 'process' versus 'structure'. Bennis sees OD as: 'a response to change, a complex educational strategy intended to change the beliefs, attitudes, values and structure of organisations so that they can better adapt to new technologies markets and challenges and the dizzying rate of change itself'.[21] To Beckhard it is a planned strategy working at the level of the organization, with top management involved.[22] Its aim is to increase the organization's ability to adapt. Behavioural science knowledge facilitates this change towards greater organizational effectiveness.

Lewin's work provides a useful example of the behavioural science input into OD, but the whole concept of organizational culture or personality, the decision-making processes and the communication patterns all provide vehicles of change as well. The aim is not only planned change with the commitment of top management, but improving the 'health' of the organization as well. The concepts of sickness and malaise giving way to radiant health seem to underpin the whole philosophy.

This gives another philosophical linchpin to the whole of OD in the idea of adaptation to the environment. The healthy organization must survive and grow, so it needs mastery over its environment, and this is seen by most commentators as producing an **open socio-technical system**. The people–task element makes up the socio-technical aspects, while the enterprise is seen as a system interacting with its wider environment.

We need now to move to the mechanics of OD, to distinguish how we can go about this change to fruition and indeed the limits of this possible change.

Introducing change: the mechanics

A problem-solving approach is suggested, using Lewin's concept of unfreeze–change–refreeze. (See Box PM5.11.) The methods used in the change stage will be developed in the next section, but first we will give a little more detail on the process.

The diagnostic step is taken at the beginning. The perceived problem, its manifestations and views on its causes need to be discussed. A critical

---

BOX PM5.11

The change process

The theoretical underpinnings of the whole process owe much to the work of Lewin (see figure 5.2). Forces are seen to be exerting pressures on individu-

Unfreezing ⟶ Change ⟶ Refreezing

Figure 5.2 The change process.

als all the time and the basic philosophy of Lewin is that a **quasi-stationary equilibrium** exists. It is only 'quasi' as a dynamic, ever-changing balance of forces surrounds this steady social state of equilibrium. It is interesting to note that the basic theory of change has a core based on an idea of harmony – albeit a fluid one. Seemingly, there are **restraining forces** which inhibit change and **driving forces** which encourage an alteration in the status quo. The balance of these competing forces must be altered in the period of **unfreezing** to change the equilibrium. Driving forces can be increased, restraining forces manipulated or some combination can alter the status quo. Arguably it is easier to manipulate the restraining forces than merely to push with new driving forces. Once a vacuum has been created by these restraining forces being altered, **change** is possible. New driving forces can then be pushed harder to facilitate change. A range of tactics can be used, which we will develop later, and **refreezing** goes on to consolidate the gains and to re-emphasize a new equilibrium or steadier state.

Source: Adapted from Lewin, 'Group decision and social change'

BOX PM5.12

Introducing change: some methods

Process:
- developing an effective team;
- changing values or norms in a group;
- 'attitudinal structuring' programmes;
- goal discussion and goal-setting sessions;
- feedback on values and attitudes.

Techno-structural:
- job redesign initiatives;
- creating greater autonomy for work-groups;
- applying contingency models to structuring the organization.

Source: Adapted from Williams, 'Organisation development and change'

part of this early stage is to mobilize support for the project. A quick examination of the blocks and resistance to change, and the pressures for it, may be useful to give a feel for the capacity-cum-motivation to change. An independent **change agent** from outside the work group or organization may be a better facilitator of change than someone inside. The role allocated to this catalyst must be acceptable to both the organization and the change agent. This may range from a 'teacher' to an organizational or small group analyst reflecting needs rather than instructing 'trainees'.

The change element involves a range of techniques based on a careful weighting of the resistance points and the pressures for change. Objectives and targets are needed at this stage, and organizational reality must be addressed. A supportive ongoing relationship is needed between the 'client' and the catalyst, and opportunities must be created to practise the new, changed responses and behaviour. The change needs monitoring before the catalyst begins to pull back to allow the new situation to 'refreeze'.

Williams usefully summarizes some key methods of change.[23] He divides these into two: a process technique and a structural viewpoint, a dynamic group activity and more of a technical intervention concerning the nature of the job or organization (see Box PM5.12).

We will enlarge upon some of these key methods. **Teamwork** seems to be a common denominator. An attempt is made to develop teams from a group of people so that information is not distorted, positive norms apply and less negative stereotypes of individuals' functions and other groups can result.[24] **Changing attitudes** (group or individual) can be facilitated by

---

BOX PM5.13

Resistance to change

Likely resistance points, particularly to the mechanics and methods of change, include the following:

- Inertia exists.
- The status quo works.
- 'Better the devil we know ...'.
- There is no need for change, so why bother?
- Loss of job, status or power is possible.
- There is no involvement in the concept.
- Differences in personality, groups, and management–labour relations.
- There is no confidence in the idea or the proposer.
- The message, medium or timing is not right.
- There is uncertainty.
- The concept and process are too radical.
- The social group will be broken down.
- There is economic insecurity, e.g. redeployment and redundancy.
- The costs outweigh the benefits.

---

conducting surveys and objectively feeding back the results to both management and the participants.[25] **Job redesign** with enhanced responsibility and autonomy to individuals, and reconstructing jobs around people,[26] can be linked to moves to make the organizational structure more **flexible, adaptable and 'organic'**.[27]

Change is not easy and there is likely to be resistance to the philosophy, the mechanics and specific methods (see Box PM5.13). Resistance to the whole philosophy is more problematic, and we will address this point in the next section. At this stage, we can safely assume some resistance, so how do we tackle it?

The work of Kotter and Schlesinger provides some tactics for dealing with resistance:[28]

- *Communication and education:* this is really a propaganda-cum-public/employee relations tactic. It assumes that misinformation is causing the resistance, so discussions and one-to-one sessions can set the record straight.

- *Participation:* the idea behind this involvement approach is that people will have a stake in the ultimate decision, hence commitment should be greater and resistance should be lowered.

- *Support:* tension-reduction is the game here and support is used to reduce or eliminate fears and anxieties. This support could include counselling services.

- *Negotiation:* the give and take of a bargain to strike a deal between the parties emphasizes that the change is not just a unilateral imposition by management.

- *Coercion:* this is a unilateral imposition by management. Threats or actual sanctions can be applied. In the short term these may work but the change is left with a bitter taste and it may not become permanent.

- *Manipulation:* the distortion of some facts and the deliberate omission of others may give a short-term gain, but on discovery, credibility suffers and a bitter taste and lack of permanent change can again result. Coercion and manipulation damage the longer-term relationships.[29]

Problems of change

For Thakur, three key problems of change must be confronted:
- the introduction of change
- the flexibility of change technology
- its validity[30]

The **introduction** between 'client' and consultant or 'catalyst' has to be jargon free and based on a rigorous analysis of the perceived problem, and the competence of the external catalyst must meet the potential difficulties which will be encountered. The **technology** must be adaptable enough and diverse enough to deal with the problem. Evidence of change must be forthcoming to ensure the **validity** of the whole programme.

Greiner argues that prerequisites for success and overcoming problems include both internal and external pressures for change, top management

---

BOX PM5.14

OD: a big problem

Stephenson mounts a damaging assault on OD:[1]
- It is not OD at all but 'human development' a form of new human relations, as the emphasis is on people and not on the total system.
- It is based on an evangelical zeal for 'healthy' organizations and changing inappropriate (i.e. unhealthy) behaviour.
- Blame for the failings of OD is levelled at bureaucracy, but this is based on an over-rigid view of bureaucracy.
- The politics of the organization are ignored.
- It is an exercise in 'managerialism' as it negates the visions of conflict and pluralism (see Anderson,[2] where these perspectives are discussed more fully).
- The value system is oversimplistic.
- It is unethical, as the privacy of the individual is invaded.
- The techniques can be too self-consciously pursued at the expense of the whole.
- The client could be right.

Sources:
1 Adapted from Stephenson, 'OD: a critique'
2 Anderson, *Effective Labour Relations*

involvement, and shared decision making within the change process.[31] The whole philosophy of OD, its theory, its actions and its value system, are all called into question by the work of Stephenson.[32] (See Box PM5.14.)

Stephenson makes some critical points. The overemphasis on the human side of the enterprise must be balanced by the task and technology. The bogeyman of bureaucracy is not the only enemy. The value system is unitarist and it fails to take account of the legitimate interests of others. This can be broadened out to a more pluralist perspective, particularly if participation and negotiation occur. The accusation that it is a manipulative approach is also correct, but management is, finally, all about manipulation: the question really concerns the way that manipulation is handled and contained by unions and the individual employee. The managerial view can be limited by looking to the legitimate rights of individuals and groups.

Silverzweig and Allen tackle some of these issues.[33] The change programme must not only be results-oriented, but must involve people. The philosophy should be 'win:win' as opposed to a managerial imposition of 'win:lose'. It needs a commitment to change from all those involved, and this commitment must be ongoing. It takes time and effort, and people's behaviour may be difficult to change.

So OD has its problems; but it also has its potential benefits. The alternative seems to be a random, fickle approach to the organization. The techniques of OD can allow some mastery over the internal and external environments, but the processes need an ideology of agreement, a consensus, taking into account the pressures and politics of organizational

---

BOX PM5.15

The permanence of change?

How can we ensure that the change goes ahead?
- The main objectives of the objectors must be discussed and agreement reached.
- In particular, the objectors' insecurity must be dealt with.
- Involvement by 'objectors' may lead to greater commitment and joint acceptance.
- Rewards (bribery?) may be important.
- Information on expectations should be given.
- Top management sponsorship should help.
- The goals and methods must tally.
- Group and collective relationships need to be taken into account.
- The pacing of change must be right.
- Coercion and manipulation may work in the short term but resentment will fester.
- Negotiation, participation, communication, education and training can all help to cement the process of change.

life. The nature of change can be widened out from its narrow unitarist or managerialist vision to encompass a pluralistic perspective based on meeting the genuine needs, aspirations and interests of various groups within the organization. The processes of communication and education, linked to participation and negotiation and agreed goals, can mean that the available techniques of change can be used constructively. The role of manipulation and coercion linked to some unitarist vision of the organization is rejected. (See Box PM5.15.)

Change is a way of life and we need to adapt to it at the levels of the individual, the job (the unit gives a management example) and the organization. Behaviour can be changed, but it is difficult at whatever level we are attempting to deal with. Yet discussion, negotiation and agreement must be the hallmarks of any permanent behavioural change.

Unit Six consolidates this pluralistic vision.

Appendix: Target setting

The issues of performance and target setting come to the fore for they seem to be the key to successful KRA. The translation of 'macro' objectives into specific or 'micro' goals for the individual can be carried out by **target** or **goal setting**. The boss and subordinate should examine the job together. Both need to have agreed:

- what constitutes the job;
- what is expected of the job holder;
- whether it is possible to achieve a given performance.

Review should follow on irrespective of whether an 'improvement plan' has been made. The steps could include:

- comparing the individual's record to standards of performance;
- comparing his or her progress with improvement plans;
- readjusting standards if necessary;
- making a further improvement or action plan.

Finally, the specific **objectives of performance** must be:

- *complete* – a single end result (a goal), not an activity (how to achieve the goal);
- *measurable,* if possible;
- *precise,* usually written;
- *practical* and *important;*
- *challenging* but *possible to achieve.*

As a consequence of job boundary/authority issues we need some form of **job profile, outline or description**, covering:

- responsibility ⎫
- ⎬ to whom, for whom and what
- authority ⎭
- objectives and purposes
- relationships

Performance standards must be assessed. Most managerial jobs have responsibility in full or in part for costs, quality, people and time. Quantification should be used, wherever possible. Likely areas *may* include costs, service, training, communications and people management. **Action** and **review** may follow on from the standards being set.

When making **improvement plans**:

- Select the optimum number of priorities (four or five).
- Cover the period of review (six months to a year)
- Assess how easily the priorities can be achieved (be reasonable).
- Make priorities precise – do not over-constrain the individual, but avoid ambiguity.

Notes

1 M. L. Haider, quoted in *International Management*.
2 Maslow, *Towards a Psychology of Being*.
3 C. Rogers, *Freedom to Learn* and *Freedom to Learn for the 80s*. Themes based on Rogers's work are extrapolated in Anderson, 'Training and learning'.
4 Kolb, 'Towards an applied theory of experiential learning', and see Kolb et al. *Organisational Psychology – an experiential approach*.
5 Honey and Mumford, *Using Your Learning Styles*.
6 An applied activity on learner style can be seen in Anderson and Kyprianou, *Effective Organizational Behaviour*.
7 Burgoyne et al., *Self Development: theory and applications for practitioners*.
8 See Institute of Personnel Management, *Continuous Development: People and Work*, and also Barrington, 'Continuous development: theory and reality'.
9 Burgoyne et al., *Self Development*.
10 See, for example, Handy, *The Making of Managers*; Constable and McCormick, 'The making of British managers'; and Mangham and Silver, *Management Training*.
11 Tannehill, *Motivation and Management Development*.
12 Ashton and Easterby-Smith, *Management Development in the Organisation*.
13 Drucker, *Managing for Results*.
14 Anderson, *Successful Training Practice*.
15 Stewart, *Managers and their Jobs: a study of the similarities and differences in the ways managers spend their time*.
16 ICI Organics Division, *Management Training and Development*.
17 Anecdotal experience in several firms show these problems.
18 Digman, 'How well-managed organisations develop their executives'.
19 Greiner, 'Evolution and revolution as organisations grow'.
20 See also Anderson and Barker, *Effective Enterprise Management*, which adapts a growth model to a developing firm.
21 Bennis, *Organisation Development*.
22 Beckhard, *Organisational Development*.
23 Williams, 'Organisation development and change'.
24 Team development, for example, can be seen in the work of Belbin, *Management Teams*.
25 Survey feedback can be used, for example, in 'normative analysis'. See the work of Silverzweig and Allen, 'Changing the corporate culture'.
26 Hackman et al., 'A new strategy for job enrichment'.
27 Burns and Stalker, *The Management of Innovation*.
28 Kotter and Schlesinger, 'Choosing strategies for change'.
29 Anderson, *Effective Labour Relations*.
30 Thakur, *OD: The Search for Identity*.
31 Greiner, 'Evolution and revolution as organisations grow'.
32 Stephenson, 'OD: a critique'.
33 Silverzweig and Allen, 'Changing the corporate culture'.

Unit Six

Evaluation and Audit

Learning Objectives

After completing this unit you should be able to:

- relate employees' needs and aspirations to philosophies of work;
- relate organizational needs and aspirations to philosophies of work;
- conduct an audit of personnel management;
- conduct an evaluation of personnel management;
- apply the generic skills.

Contents

Overview

Organizational Needs

▶ Social responsibility and personnel management

▶ Personnel policies to meet the corporate plan

▶ People as the key resource

Employee Needs and Aspirations

People Philosophies at Work

▶ Welfare

▶ Quality of working life

▶ Justice and equity

▶ Participative management: a lesson from Japan

Evaluation and Audit of Personnel Management

▶ Ratio analysis

▶ Human asset accounting

▶ Strategic capacity analysis

▶ Key objectives

▶ Morale indices and surveys

▶ Quality management

▶ Functional approach

Unit Six

Then they just didn't want to give us promotion which was due us anyhow. They [management] just don't want to give you anything. The personnel man, all of them, they show you why you don't deserve a promotion.❞

Diane Wilson, quoted by Studs Terkel[1]

Overview

This final unit has a two-fold purpose: to reinforce the importance of personnel management to the organization and to the individual, and to evaluate and audit its contribution to both. On this basis, we will consider the organizational needs and how personnel management can dovetail into them, and then look in depth at individual aspirations and how personnel management can come to terms with these; for, after all, we are people managers.

Using part of these aspirations and how they can be met, we begin both to audit and to evaluate the contribution of personnel management. Other criteria are touched upon and a range of techniques is put forward for consideration.

The flowchart in figure 6.1 outlines this unit.

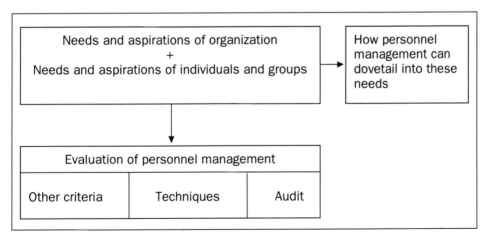

Figure 6.1 Unit outline.

Organizational Needs

The requirements of the organization, from its 'mission' to its objectives, are covered in considerable detail and from different perspectives elsewhere in the series[2] so a brief mention will do here. The significance of these task objectives is not being minimized *vis-à-vis* the people aims – quite the reverse: without the task there is no need for people.

Argenti argues that corporate objectives can be divided into three categories:

- aims and purpose
- aims and ethos
- the means to these aims[3]

Ethical objectives are usually translated into policies on social responsibility. Some overall guiding principles on social responsibility or wider business ethics can be seen in the work of Warren, Gorham and Lamont Inc.[4] A range of 'commandments' was put forward, including:

- taking a proactive approach;
- working with the 'constituents' of the organization;
- establishing and using codes of practice;
- the admission of error;
- social programmes in the community;
- environmental problem scanning, particularly over social issues, and taking a stand on these issues;
- employing a code of conduct within the organization.

These adopted themes are all linked to profitability as an objective as well.

The **corporate objectives** can be translated into more tactical or departmental objectives which together fulfil the total strategy. Operating plans, shorter-term budgets and individual objectives can all flow from these tactical aims. The operationalization of these objectives tends to be a resource-cum-commitment issue, where people are important.

The overall **financial objective** must be clarified and a target set; the ethical objective must be identified and clarified; and then the **aims** and the **means** must be noted. For example, the financial target is based on return of shareholders' capital or earnings share. Targets may be set for the division or unit which are not only financial but will involve resource implications, from physical premises to manpower levels. Clearly the personnel person can have an input at this level through some link between the corporate and manpower plans. (See Box PM6.1.)

Another approach where personnel management is more proactive is as follows:

- corporate philosophy and purpose;
- environmental scanning;

BOX PM6.1

Human resource planning and strategic planning

Corporate plan:

Strategic planning	Operational planning	Budgeting
Long-range perspective →	*Middle-range perspective* →	*Annual perspective*
Corporate philosophy	Planned programmes	Budgets
Environmental scan	Resources required	Unit, individual performance goals
Strengths and constraints	Organizational strategies	
Objectives and goals	Plans for entry into new businesses, acquisitions, divestitures	Programme scheduling and assignment
Strategies		Monitoring and control of results

Human resource plan:

Issue analysis →	*Forecasting requirements* →	*Action plans*
Business needs	Staffing levels	Staffing authorization
External factors	Staffing mix (qualitative)	Recruitment
Internal supply analysis	Organization and job design	Promotions and transfers
Management implications	Available and projected resources	Organizational changes
	Net requirements	Training and development
		Compensation and benefits
		Labour relations

Source: Adapted from Walker, 'Linking HR planning and strategic planning'

- marriage of strengths and weaknesses to environmental conditions;
- goal setting
- specific strategies.

This approach makes people management less demand-led and gives it an input at the outset of the overall planning of objectives. Of course, there are similarities as well to Argenti's approach.

We will briefly develop some key issues:
- social responsibility and personnel management;
- personnel policies to meet the corporate plan;
- people as the key resource to implement the objectives.

Social responsibility and personnel management

All managers have some responsibility to the wider community. There is a view that managers are there to maximize profit and this in turn will allow society to regulate its own affairs. This is not adequate. The examples of environmental pollution and disasters involving chemical and oil companies from India to the Shetlands reinforce the point that corporations must have a vision of social responsibility. Perhaps the issue is one of morality. (See Box PM6.2.)

BOX PM6.2

Social responsibility and morality

Velasquez classifies moral principles into three categories: utility, rights and justice.

Utilitarianism with its Benthamite philosophy is really an arithmetic sum of social costs and benefits: 'An action is right from an ethical point of view if and only if the sum total of utilities produced by that act is greater than the sum total of utilities produced by any other act the agent could have performed in its place.'

Moral rights are seen as a form of 'universal entitlement'. They are linked to duties towards others as well, as one person's rights have an impact on others. Such rights give 'autonomy and equality in the free pursuit of interest', and provide a basis for justifying actions and for 'invoking the protection or aid of others'. This morality comes from Kant: 'An action is morally right for a person in a certain situation if and only if the person's reason for carrying out the action is a reason that he or she would be willing to have every person act on, in any similar situation', and 'An action is morally right for a person if and only in performing the action, the person does not use others merely as a means for advancing his or her own interests, but also both respects and develops their capacity to choose freely for themselves.' So, a form of **justice** flows from this morality.

Source: Adapted from Velasquez, *Business Ethics: concepts and cases*

In terms of specialist personnel managers, this ethical consideration seems to be quite important. (See Box PM6.3.) A survey of UK personnel people (498 responses) showed the following ethical points:
- Personnel specialists (unlike company secretaries) scored highly on the ethical dimension.

- Widespread concern existed for environmental issues – but little real action seemed to result.

- Social and moral concerns within the organization were not to the forefront for the majority, who felt that business should be 'free' from such concerns.

- Women tended to be more principled than men and the older professionals of both sexes seemed less 'hard-nosed' than the young.[5]

An older, in-depth example of how a vision of social responsibility can actually work itself through is provided by Jones.[6] He gives a worthwhile study of the steel industry and its rundown, with a view of social responsibility that percolated through the whole rationalization process. Planning, consultation, counselling and developing new jobs were all part of this progressive policy conducted by the then management of British Steel.

BOX PM6.3

Social responsibility: health, safety, and accident prevention

Health and safety are both important aspects of employee services. However, given the international aims of this series, we cannot focus on the legislation, which will differ according to country. Instead, we will briefly examine management action to prevent needless suffering, from injury to death, through accidents at work.

Accident prevention is often given a low priority. The impact on morale, efficiency and productivity is not self-evident to many managers, while non-fatal accidents can easily become mere statistics. To many employees, safety is seen as dull and as with motorway pile-ups, we all believe it could never happen to us.

There are many variables in accidents, from unsafe working environments and buildings to power sources, from unsafe jobs with danger inherent in the work to unsafe people, from tiredness to faulty judgement and inexperience. Vant usefully gives us a perspective on accident causation and hopefully, by implication, prevention.

Individual:
- *Chance:* people are exposed to a risk and an accident just happens.
- *Proneness:* some people are more susceptible to accidents and this may have some psychological basis.
- *Burnt fingers syndrome:* if we have an accident once, we will take greater care to avoid a recurrence.
- *Stress:* some situations exert more stress and this will lead to maladjustment for some, and to possible accidents.
- *Job satisfaction:* alertness is reduced through monotony and accidents can occur.
- *Self-punishment:* some subconscious prompting may lead to self-punishment through accidents.

Systems:
- *Stages:* an accident has independent stages – the environment, some fault, an unsafe act, and an accident follows.
- *The situation:* breakdowns occur in the technology of work.
- *The union of events:* the victim, the object and the environment all merge to give an accident.

The causation may be complex and multi-factor, but its resolution and/or prevention are very much a managerial task, as well as an employee task, for this is a practical example of the social responsibility of management at work.

Source: Adapted from Vant, 'Reducing lost time accidents in North Sea drilling companies'

Personnel policies to meet the corporate plan

A code of conduct

Personnel managers (line and staff) should be guided by a code of conduct which in turn will permeate the policies and procedures of the organization. Such a code may include references to:

- people activities, the need for quality and the importance of standards;
- responsibilities to the employer and the special nature of people relationships;
- the need for integrity and high standards of behaviour;
- the importance of honesty in dealing with personally sensitive issues;
- the importance of promoting sound organizational policies on personnel management.

Policies

At the risk of even more bureaucratization of personnel management, there is a strong case for writing the policies down and distributing them across the organization. Clarity, uniformity, a widespread knowledge of 'the rules', a guide for management and a clear view of goal achievement can follow. But policies cannot legislate for every event and circumstances are ever-changing, so 'the rules' must not be rigid. Policies are guidelines and do not replace judgement. A code of conduct can place both the policy and the individual manager's judgement in context.

Typically the policy will include items such as:

- access to management
- job security
- payment
- training and promotion
- consultation (and negotiation)
- working conditions, health and safety

- discipline and grievance
- holiday and sick pay, etc.
- union membership

An anonymous example will give a 'feel' for the range of policies (see Box PM6.4).

BOX PM6.4

Personnel policies: an example

Checklist:

- *Code of practice:* integrity of employees is seen as critical. This involves high standards of business and compliance with the law, from securing business through honest means to financial transactions which can be independently audited.

- *Interests, gifts and the media:* to avoid conflicts of interest, personal involvement in the business of customers, competitors and suppliers is to be avoided, as is competitive businesses started by the employee while still involved with this firm.

  Gifts are not to be accepted and it is forbidden to make any agreements involving a bribe or kickback.

  Media relations must reflect the truth and be co-ordinated by senior management.

- *Employment policies statement:* this would cover recruitment and selection under the headings of 'employment', 'training and development' policies and principles, 'remuneration', 'labour relations' and 'welfare'.

- *Employment policies implementation:* employment – selection principles, placement of the disabled, retirement, promotion, dismissal and redundancy, etc.;

  training and development – induction, task training, education statement, development (self management etc.);

  remuneration – incentives, cost of living, salary scales, etc.;

  labour relations – disputes procedure, substantive and procedural;

  agreements and trade union – management relationships;

  welfare – pensions, sickness, medicals, counselling, etc.

Points of contact and a reaffirmation of access to management would follow.

People as the key resource

Capital, plant, equipment, office and factory availability, systems, techniques, etc., are all critical aspects of both contributing to the corporate plan via the strengths and constraints of internal organizational resources, and physically implementing the plan. A detailed analysis of internal organizational resources would be repetitive and should be self-evident: the organization, sales and marketing, operation and production, R & D-cum-innovation, finance and accounting, systems and IT, and general-cum-strategic management can all be examined.

Organizations, though, are essentially a collection of people hopefully striving towards some shared goals. Having covered these goals, let us now turn to the people side for its own sake, for both task and people need to be integrated.

Employee Needs and Aspirations

What do we want out of work? The meaning of work may be a very personal thing. Much research focuses on a manager's view of 'what makes people tick'. The aim is to manipulate the variables to increase productive efficiency. There is another strand to the research which is more hedonistic and is quite refreshing – looking at the needs of individuals on their own basis.

The interactionist work of Terkel may not be hedonistic but it gives invaluable insights into what real people actually seek and get out of work.[7] To Terkel work is mostly violence to the body and to the spirit. It is not about salvation, more about humiliation for the majority. He sees it as more than 'Orwellian acceptance' of 'making out' or than some coping mechanism, but as less than the machine-breaking antics of 'Luddite sabotage'. (See Box PM6.5.)

BOX PM 6.5

The meaning of work

Babe Secoli
With thirty years' experience in a supermarket she looked upon work as her life. She could not cope with a closed factory environment and takes pride in her lack of absence, her timekeeping and her commitment.

> I'm a couple of days away, I'm very lonesome for this place. When I'm on vacation, I can't wait to go, but two or three days away, I start to get fidgety. I can't stand around and do nothing, I have to be busy at all times. I look forward to comin' to work. It's a great feelin'. I enjoy it somethin' terrible.

Phil Stallings

A spot-welder in a large car plant, he was in his late twenties and quite recently married. His role is to clamp metal together and then fuse it. The work is so tedious that he fantasizes and daydreams much of the day.

> You got some guys that are uptight, and they're not sociable. It's too rough. You pretty much stay to yourself. You get involved with yourself. You dream, you think of things you've done. I drift back continuously to when I was a kid and what me and my brothers did. The things you love most are the things you drift back into.

Larry Ross

He was a business consultant who viewed the corporation as a jungle with the 'survival of the fittest' as the dominant force. He seems to survive in a fast-moving, 'no prisoners-taken' environment where fear is all pervasive.

> The danger starts as soon as you become a district manager. You have men working for you and you have a boss above. You're caught in a squeeze. The squeeze progresses from station to station. I'll tell you what a squeeze is. You have the guys working for you that are shooting for your job. They guy you're working for is scared stiff you're gonna shove him out of his job. Everybody goes around and says 'The test of the true executive is that you have men working for you that can replace you, so you can move up.' That's a lot of boloney. The manager is afraid of the bright young guy coming up.

Diane Wilson

She was a processing clerk in a section with initials whose meaning she could not recall. Her aim is 'making out' through a group counter-culture which is not necessarily in line with organizational aims.

> Then they just didn't want to give us the promotion which was due us anyhow. They just don't want to give you anything. The personnel man, all of them, they show you why you don't deserve a promotion. The boss, the one we converted – he came on board, as they call it, after we sweated to meet the deadline. So he didn't know what we did. But he told us we didn't deserve it. That stayed with me forever. I won't be bothered with him ever again.

Source: Adapted from Terkel, *Working: people talk about what they do all day and how they feel about what they do*

The common thread in Terkel's research is that of working people striving for more control over their working lives. We should take note of these aspirations and act upon them. However, this interactionist perspective does emphasize the diversity of individual orientations to work. Many of the psychological studies seem to seek common denominators which, in turn, can be manipulated by management. We looked briefly at motivation from this perspective when we considered payment as motivation (Unit Three). This unit is more concerned with looking at motivation in the needs and aspirations of individuals per se.

'Motivation' comes from the Latin verb 'movere' meaning to move. We are concerned with what drives or directs people. Motivation may be difficult to observe but its absence may be self-evident. If needs and aspirations are frustrated or blocked a range of behaviours may occur:

- *Aggression:* scapegoating, gossip and verbal slanging matches can be included in this category.

- *Regression:* this is a more childish response, such as kicking the car when the engine does not work.

- *Fixation:* actions are repeated irrespective of their value for the current problem.

- *Resignation:* this is a form of apathy or 'giving up', and the indifference of many employees is an example.

Where these behaviours abound in organizations, clearly the work motivational needs of people are not being met.

The problem with motivation is that it is an all-embracing concept and perhaps the people manager cannot hope to meet such diversity. The philosophies of motivation give a diversity which the people manager may have difficulty in reconciling. (See Box PM6.6.)

BOX PM6.6

Motivation: a range of philosophies

Types	Commentary
Pawn of fate	People are passive instruments of external forces. There is little free will, so needs and aspirations are neither here not there. Personnel management cannot help much.
Rational master	People shape the world to satisfy their desires. Rationality dominates in this ideal state. Personnel management can help.
Machine	People are complex physical machines, so motivation is superfluous. The key is stimulus response rather than needs and aspirations. The stimulants can be altered to motivate people.

Types	Commentary
Social product	The values, ideals and sanctions of society create our responses to work. As society's demands alter there is some room for non-deterministic motives. Personnel management may not change society but can take the mores into account.
Unconscious being	Our motives are deep-seated tendencies which may manifest themselves in some Freudian catharsis. Personnel management is not a help here unless counselling is to the fore.
Animal	People are driven by physiological requirements, from wanting food and water to avoiding pain to seeking sex. Personnel managers can help here!

Source: Adapted from Krech et al., *Elements of Psychology*

A whole range of needs is seen to exist: thirst, pain avoidance, hunger, sex, curiosity, affection, power, success, company and status. Maslow is one of the most famous authorities on needs.[8] Five levels of **need satisfaction** exist: physiological, safety, social, self-esteem and self-actualization. This could translate into the following examples at work:

Need	People management example
Physiological	Reasonable working conditions and a basic wage or salary
Safety	From safe conditions (non-hazardous) to job security
Social	Compatible teams and a reasonable boss
Self-esteem	An important job, recognition by your boss and a level of responsibility
Self-actualization	A challenge, with the facility to create and the opportunity to advance

These needs were seen as a hierarchy: the need at one level asserts itself when the previous, lower need has been met. Again, the needs were based on the deprivation principle.

McClelland and Steele examined the 'higher' needs of Maslow – achievement, power and affiliation. They suggested that we all have these three needs but that one need is dominant at any given time and affects our work performance. Thus high achievement needs lead to seeking responsibility and challenging goals; high power needs lead to liking to be in control and seeking recognition; high affiliation needs lead to liking people and group interaction. So the people manager must be aware of the dominant needs of his or her people and attempt whenever possible to accommodate these aspirations.

Alderfer took Maslow's needs and placed them in three broader categories: existence, relating to others and growth (personal) – hence the **ERG** theory.

Earlier, Herzberg had divided up the satisfaction of needs into two categories: the **motivators**, which led to job satisfaction, and the **hygiene** or **maintenance** factors, which did not lead to satisfaction but prevented dissatisfaction. Some doubts have been cast on the validity and transferability of Herzberg's research, but for our immediate purpose his division into motivators and hygiene factors is relevant

Motivators:

- achievement
- work itself
- responsibility
- recognition
- advancement

(not dissimilar to Maslow's, McClelland's or Alderfer's categories)

Hygiene:

- supervision
- money
- status
- security
- interpersonal relations
- company policy

People managers may be in the right position to facilitate the meeting of these needs.

Vroom started from a different perspective. **Performance** was the key and it was a function of both ability and motivation. So far as motivation is concerned the premise is self-interest and the process is that of rational decision making. Will the effort be noticed? Will it be fairly rewarded? So the action becomes a means to an estimated end. Individual expectations, which are more difficult for the people manager to cope with than needs, are prevalent.

Equity theory is another viewpoint, identified with Adams. Comparative analysis is to the fore: it is not enough to have your own needs satisfied, but outcomes are compared with the rewards others receive for their efforts. Inequity or equity can result. This 'felt fair' approach is particularly important in wage and salary negotiations and for treating people on an even-handed basis.

So where does this summary on individual needs and aspirations leave the personnel manager? The sociological work notes the diversity of what people want out of work, but a desire for some control over our job and its environment looks to be common. The people managers are better placed to meet some of the psychological needs. Basic physiological existence or working conditions are at the bottom of the hierarchy. Safety needs, salary, benefits and power could be the next level up. Affiliation, social needs, relatedness and fellow workers are in the next category. Then we have self-esteem, growth, achievement, recognition, advancement and responsibility, all coming before the apex of self-actualization and job challenge. Expectation of results, equity and comparability with others should not be forgotten.

For the personnel manager (line or staff), an awareness of the needs and aspirations of subordinates and clients is critical. The importance of decent working conditions, a basic salary, job security, financial incentives at work, safe and secure physical conditions, fringe benefits, a reasonable boss and reasonable colleagues, the facility to do an important job and have it recognized as such with merit pay, etc., and the possibility of achieving a challenging and creative job, as well as advancement within the organization, can be gleaned from this research on people's needs and aspirations at work. We will return to these points in the evaluation section. (See Activity PM6.1.)

ACTIVITY PM6.1

YOUR MOTIVATIONAL NEEDS

Activity code
- ✓ Self-development
- ☐ Teamwork
- ✓ Communications
- ☐ Numeracy/IT
- ✓ Decisions

Below you will find a series of statements. Consider these statements from your own perspective either at your place of work or at college. Low numbers represent disagreement, medium numbers represent partial agreement or partial disagreement, and high numbers illustrate greater agreement. It is not a validated test, merely an exercise on needs.

1	I like to control people.	1	2	3	4	5
2	The feelings of others are important.	1	2	3	4	5
3	Risks should be minimized.	1	2	3	4	5
4	My boss/tutor should always give me feedback.	1	2	3	4	5

5	Personal relationships are important to me.	1	2	3	4	5
6	People see me as forceful.	1	2	3	4	5
7	I am a natural leader.	1	2	3	4	5
8	I don't like conflict between people.	1	2	3	4	5
9	I like to plan my future career.	1	2	3	4	5
10	I like to solve my own problems.	1	2	3	4	5
11	I am a natural persuader of people.	1	2	3	4	5
12	I think about the feelings of my fellows.	1	2	3	4	5

Source: Extrapolated from the work of Steers and Porter, *Motivation and Work Behaviour*

We will consolidate this section by reinforcing several philosophies which have run through the book and which can be described as 'people-oriented'.

People Philosophies at Work

At the beginning of this work we traced several themes behind the growth of personnel management. We will draw upon this now and develop some current people-oriented work philosophies. These will include the following:

- welfare – human relations in practice;
- quality of working life;
- justice and equity;
- participative management: a lesson from Japan.

Welfare

We have touched on this philosophy in Unit One and consolidated its diverse manifestations under employee services in Unit Three, so there is no need for much discussion. The proposed perspective has been that welfare services from counselling to canteens, from transport to health and safety, have some part to play in effective personnel management as a form of 'safety net', particularly in non-union organizations, but 'industrial feudalism' is not being advocated, with 'cradle-to-grave' personnel policies and procedures. A benevolence mixed with commercialism lies behind welfare: it is better to be patted on the back than hit over the head, so there may be some mileage in these employee services.

Quality of working life

The term **Quality of working life** (**QWL**) represents a philosophy in which individual employees have the facility of satisfying key needs through their work experience. If anything the individual is placed centre stage and the organization adapts accordingly. This would be a case of fitting the job or the organization to the person and not the person to the job.

Examples of QWL could include:

- *training and development:* ongoing or continuous development of employees so that they can maximize their abilities at work;
- *compensation:* fair grading schemes, a reasonable 'cushion' above subsistence and rewarding effort ability;
- *selection and promotion:* careers open to talent irrespective of background, race, sex, sexual preference, etc.;
- *job redesign:* a serious attempt to build up the 'satisfiers' within a job;
- *health and safety:* minimizing hazards, from pollution to accident prevention;
- *equity:* fair treatment and access to management on grievances, counselling, etc.
- *job security:* so far as is practical, maintenance of this objective by the organization.

Walton broadens out the concept to include an ethical dimension, from the 'social value' of the products to wider responsibilities to the community.[9] This involves a move towards a vision of the wider social responsibility of management, which we have already discussed.

Justice and equity

To meet individual needs, personnel managers must be even-handed in their treatment of staff. Equity and fairness if not justice should be the aims of all managers when dealing with employees, but the specialist staff personnel manager has an important ethical role to perform across the organization. Uniformity of treatment and fair-mindedness should prevail. This is not to argue for the personnel manager to be the 'conscience of the organization', but if equity does not emanate from the personnel department, then we are in a sorry state.

French looked upon this concept of justice as the greatest good for the greatest number.[10] This justice was divided into two according to French: **distributive** and **corrective**. The argument revolves around human investment in skill, effort and seniority. There is a 'reward', such as wages or salary, job advancement and job interest, and a 'cost', such as boredom or the degree of danger in the job. The *in*justice occurs when the rewards are not proportional to the investment plus costs. Justice is therefore seen as a 'reward'. Adams continued the theme:[11] inequity occurs when the individual perceives him or herself to be losing out in his or her input-to-output ratio compared to the inputs/outputs of other people. So a comparison is made with others on the wage–effort–reward–cost equation.

This leads on to the make-up of rewards and costs (or penalties) and the physical allocation of rewards and costs (or penalties). This 'reward-and-punishment' viewpoint results in maximizing the incentives and the motivators at work, from money to the redesign of jobs, and in minimizing the disincentives, from work frustration to alienation.

Corrective justice is important to remedy ills, and includes a fair and reasonable treatment of disputes, grievances and disciplinary issues. The right to be heard, the right of representation and the facility to call witnesses must be aligned to the rights of appeal. The issues could be appraisal of performance, a problem of grading, a difficulty over promotion or selection, etc.

Correcting injustice is easier. The promotion of friends, the sacking of shop stewards, the ignoring of grievances, etc., can be remedied through procedural means if the manager is willing or is pushed. Distributive injustice is perhaps more difficult to remedy, as the individual may perceive an injustice which another, less sensitive person may shrug off. Line people managers aware of the sensitivities of their staff are best at handling these issues.

Either way, both forms of justice are required in order to meet individual needs. The reward–cost equation is not enough and neither is a fair procedure. This frame of mind demands uniformity of treatment, fair play without fear or favour, and an even-handedness when dealing with people. Policies and procedures back this up but they are no substitute for a progressive attitude. In spite of legislation in the UK, discrimination in employment still exists. We will use sex discrimination as an example of injustice which could be remedied in an organization. Please tackle Activity PM6.2.

ACTIVITY PM6.2

EQUAL OPPORTUNITIES

Activity code
✓ Self-development
✓ Teamwork
✓ Communications
◻ Numeracy/IT
✓ Decisions

The lecture was nearing the end:

As we have an international audience at this symposium for employers, I have tried not to be parochial in my approach. As the subject is equality at the workplace, it would not have been right to take a Eurocentric view. Having said this, the law must be embraced, but I considered the practicalities of the labour market rather than law – and, dare I say it again, some view of fairness.

Let us get rid of the law. I don't mean that literally, of course, for the law may be an ass but it is all that we have. Perhaps the fact that we need legislation in this area is indicative of the problem of negative attitudes in the first place, for these negative attitudes translated themselves into negative practices which enforced positive laws. Yet the law may not be the answer.

As we have seen, in the UK we have the Equal Pay Act, the Sex Discrimination Act and the Race Relations Act. The Treaty of Rome Article 119 gives a European dimension, and other directives have been added, such as 75/117 on equal pay, 76/207 on equal treatment and 79/7 on social security.

I am not going to reiterate the point on the lack of harmonization of the two legal systems, or the use of amendments, or the lack of compliance to the letter of the law. It may be that the law provides the answer. It does provide a stick to beat the less liberal employers into some submission, but this, as I've argued, is not the answer.

We could argue for equity and fairness. How does it feel to be a woman who is paid less than a man for doing the same job? Clearly natural justice is being flouted. Personnel managers have a crucial role in extending this fairness – selection, training, promotion, equal status, job evaluation graded schemes for money: a whole range of options allied to an equal opportunities policy. The buck stops at the managers of people.

However, the basis of industry is not human concern – it is greed: a lust for profit and a fetish for growth. Please excuse the terminology but it goes to the heart of the matter. To get equal opportunities on the agenda we must involve money – not penalties for not doing it, but pointing out the advantages of doing it.

By the end of this century, there will be a Western European demographic downturn. Fewer school-leavers are coming out of the system. Employers will need an alternative – and the obvious answer lies in female returners. My feeling, though, is that this is not enough – to paraphrase Marx, women are the slaves of the slaves. We are a source of cheap labour – that is the real issue.

So the law can help, but personnel managers at the *place of work*, working with the labour force and with unions, can ram the message home: women are not inferior to men and we must have equal personnel policies and practices. I ask you to go back to your place of work and implement these policies.

To quote a learned judge,[1] but to apply it to our context, remember 'If a woman upsets you, all right – it's part of their functions in life.' I ask you to go ahead and upset them.

The personnel manager was impressed and this issue, never far from the agenda, was item one on Monday morning. A new policy on equal opportunities governing all personnel management policies would be required. The company had some 1,500 employees, roughly 60 per cent of whom were women involved in the retail, distribution and packaging area. A draft policy would be a good starting point.

Your task is to construct a draft equal opportunities policy for the personnel manager (*c.*500 words). You may wish to include other opportunity-deprived areas, e.g. race etc. The policies should cover the range of personnel management dealt with in this unit, with the appropriate detail and criteria.

Source:
1 Judge John Lee quoted in the *Observer,* 4 October 1992

Participative management: a lesson from Japan

Cultural transferability from Japanese management may seem impossible or unacceptable to some. However, the post-war Japanese 'industrial miracle' should be given much credit, and participative personnel policies have been integral to that success.[12] While we are not advocating employees gathering round a company flag singing the company song, the Japanese can give us some lessons in personnel management:

- *Consultative decision making*: the aim is to seek some form of harmony or consensus before coming to decisions. It may slow the process of decision making down, but once an agreement is reached it is more likely to be unopposed.

- *Work groups:* there is a group rather than individual mentality, with a focus on group tasks and autonomous work groups more in control over their work task.

- *Communications:* a non-hierarchical vision at work and the removal of many artificial status and geographical or territorial barriers enhance the open communications of the Japanese.

- *Quality:* the personnel practices are linked to the task of production or operations, where a quality frame of reference dominates the labour force.

- *Flexibility:* job rotation and the possibility of eventual promotion of the core (non-peripheral) workers enhances job interest and organizational flexibility, with non-specialist employers.

- *People orientation:* it may be paternalism, but the wellbeing of the labour force is to the forefront of management thinking.

These are *some* of the main Japanese lessons for people managers. They are integrated totally with the culture of work and the technology system. However, if we had to choose one lesson, we would choose the people orientation – without the cultural and philosophical baggage.

Evaluation and Audit of Personnel Management

It has been proposed that personnel management has two 'clients': the organization and the employees – and perhaps a third: social responsibility to a wider community. The objectives as well as the aspirations and needs of these 'clients' or constituents, which we have covered, can provide the backcloth, if not the criteria, for the processes of evaluation and audit.

Evaluation concerns value while the **audit** process, not dissimilar to the financial process which we are accustomed to in companies, gives a check and a stocktake on policies, procedures and practices. (See Box PM6.7.)

Personnel management has tended to be evaluated from the perspective of the staff specialist and the impact on the staff function of the organization. Another variation has been to examine the various role sets

---

BOX PM6.7

Evaluation

Evaluation means determining the value of something. In turn, value means worth of usefulness. This can be seen in intrinsic terms of value 'within' something – for example, the beauty of Mona Lisa; as well as in utility terms of having a beautiful painting adorn a room; and finally, it can be seen in financial terms with the work of art being seen as a priceless painting. Clearly there are degrees of value – intrinsic merit, utility/usefulness and some financial benefit *vis-à-vis* costs and the potential or actual benefit accrued.

Source: Anderson, *Successful Training Practice*

---

and the parameters within these models. The administrative, the systems and business manager models, for example, have been suggested by Tyson.[13] The focus of these models is still based on the staff specialist, although different perspectives exist on this role, which, of course, would have an impact on the evaluation process. We are suggesting that evaluation can occur on the basis of the different clients.

The staff departmental vision of personnel management needs to be augmented by the line people managers' approach as well, to give us a **staff–line variable** in this evaluation process. The staff can be seen to service both the line and the wider organization, while the line services the latter.

The evaluation of personnel management can be viewed also from a **decision-making perspective**. Clearly the strategic–operational split can be used to gauge the impact of personnel management decisions, with a strategic perspective being geared to policy and an operational view examining procedures and practices on a more day-to-day level. An audit would be possible using this division.

The **efficiency–effectiveness division** can also be applied to the work of evaluating personnel management. 'Getting things done right' and 'getting the right things done' applies both to organizations and to some extent to people. Again, an audit may be used in this context.

Next we should consider how to conduct the evaluation. The list of methods is by no means exhaustive, but some suggestions include:

■ ratio analysis
■ human asset accounting
■ strategic capacity analysis
■ key objectives

- morale indices and surveys
- quality management
- functional approach.

See Box PM6.8.

Ratio analysis

Financial **ratios** are used in most organizations to gauge the state of 'health' and to trigger 'corrective action'. The example of personnel ratios can be seen in Fowler's analysis of the case of Granada TV Rental in the

---

BOX PM 6.8

The evaluation of personnel management

Table 6.1 Methods of evaluation

Possible criteria	Methods						
	Ratio analysis	Human asset accounting	Strategic capacity analysis	Key objectives	Morale indices and surveys	Quality management	Functional approach
Meeting needs of 'clients':							
Organization	✓	✓	✓	✓	?	✓	✓
Employees	–	–	–	?	✓	✓	✓
Community	?	✓	?	–	–	✓	✓
Staff and line management perspectives							
Staff (advisory)	✓	✓	✓	?	?	✓	✓
Line (executive)	?	✓	✓	✓	?	✓	✓
Decision-span							
Strategic	–	✓	✓	✓	–	✓	✓
Operational	✓	–	–	✓	✓	✓	✓
Efficiency (resources)	✓	✓	?	✓	✓	✓	✓
Effectiveness (goal-oriented)	–	?	✓	?	✓	✓	✓

Key: ✓ Probable use of method
? Possible use of method
– Improbable use of method

UK.[14] The idea here was to build an 'objective measurement system' to gauge the four main activities of the personnel department: recruitment, employee relations, remuneration, and training and development.

Fowler rightly argues that these ratios are not 'stand-alone', and an organization using them would need some comparative scale (from a past year or an industry norm). Again, the system is geared to company aims rather than to people aspirations per se. It may facilitate profit and organizational effectiveness, and will certainly assist the efficiency both of the personnel department and of the organization as a whole. Examples of these ratios analyses on training could include:

- $\dfrac{\text{management, craft or operator training costs}}{\text{number of managers, craftspeople or operators}}$ (£/head)

- $\dfrac{\text{total training costs}}{\text{total trainee days}}$ (£ per trainee day)

- $\dfrac{\text{actual training costs}}{\text{budgeting training costs}}$ and $\dfrac{\text{training costs}}{\text{sales turnover}}$

Ratio analysis does not have to stop at comparing personnel factors interrelating with one another: we can also compare payroll to profitability, etc.[15]

There are other examples of quantification which we can use apart from ratio analysis to assist us with evaluation. A summary in the context of training has been made elsewhere.[16] This quantified approach can be transferred to personnel management as a whole. (See Box PM6.9.)

BOX PM6.9

Quantification

- *Costs:* people costs can be budgeted for and variance analysis can be conducted.
- *Opportunity costs:* the staff personnel specialists can give an overview of this people cost by taking a view of resources allocated to, say, selection as opposed to training and determining the value of both.
- *Cost-effectiveness:* one salary incentive can be compared with another, but priorities need to be established.
- *Cost benefit:* the costs can be worked out, but the benefits may be more intangible and over a longer time span than the immediate costs.
- *Human investment:* some concept of 'value added' or appraisal can be used. Value added is used in some productivity schemes, as we have seen, while human asset accounting may be used as a separate entity.

Human asset accounting

We have seen that people are a key resource, if not *the* key resource, of the organization. **Human asset accounting** goes further: people, like capital projects, become an asset, so a monetary value can be placed on them. Of course, ownership will not occur unless the mode of production is slavery or serfdom, but the concept is intriguing.

When you buy a business – say, a shop or a pub – you often buy an element of the customers' 'goodwill'. Likewise, there is goodwill from within an organization: the training, the development schemes, the degree of job satisfaction and the level of employee commitment can be seen as 'benefits'. A monetary value is placed on those benefits. Likert is credited with introducing a system using this method.[17] The asset value is on an increasing spiral, of course, with experience, training and development all coming together.

The concept of 'pricing' people may not be acceptable to many, but it does give a 'feel', particularly to outsiders, of how management is treating its people. It can highlight difficult areas, such as high labour turnover or high recruitment costs, and perhaps it begins to put people in the same important category as finance. The idea of an asset and an investment is interesting, but the 'ownership', unlike capital, is never really there from the perspective of the manager.

Strategic capacity analysis

Walker takes a wider vision of personnel management.[18] His test, which we can use for evaluation, is 'the capacity to achieve strategic objectives'. He seems to view labour as a derived demand, as part of the implementation of the corporate plan, rather than as an input to, and a creator of, that plan.

His **capacity analysis** is a useful tool of evaluation, combining both qualitative and quantitative data. The analysis is classified into costs, the capacity to maintain current operations, and the capacity to undertake new enterprises and to handle change. Examples include:

- *costs:* employee replacement costs, net earnings per employee, sales per employee;
- *maintenance:* specializations required, the competencies of employees, the style of management;
- *change:* the adaptability to change, the totality of management resources, the untapped potential of human resources.

If we add another factor, the creative input by the planner, into the corporate plan this would be a very good coverage of 'hard' and 'soft' factors. It tends to serve the organizational client but, as it has an environmental interface, it may have an impact on the wider community as well. Considering people as an 'untapped resource' gives the employee angle, but it is organization-bound. It could apply to both line and staff personnel managers. It has a strategic definition and it tends to operate at such a level – although the costs and to some extent maintenance can be classified as operational.

Key objectives

Individual task objectives are usually integrated with, and derived from, departmental or functional aims. These in turn emanate from the overall corporate plan.

A whole series of objective-setting schemes are in operation: management by objectives (MbO), target setting, and key result areas (KRAs), to name but a few. By translating institutional aims into individual plans in whatever scheme, control and monitoring by management can be enhanced; 'variance' can be spotted and rectified, and people as a resource are seen to be directly contributing to the effectiveness of the overall corporate plan.

As we have spent a considerable time on such objectives in Unit Five, we can turn to their utility as a tool of evaluation. People objectives, whether task-oriented or more developmental, can be easily integrated into these targets. We can separate these two systems for the purposes of evaluation: **key aims**, usually task-based, and **developmental aims**, which involve more consciousness of motivational needs. The latter can be collated to give collective morale indices or left on their own to give a qualitative 'feel' for how people are developing as individuals. The harder task-based objectives involving people can be used across the organizations by both line and staff managers. Indeed, the specialists can also be given specified objectives to meet for their line clients. These objectives can cover strategic and operational issues as well as contributing to the efficiency and the effectiveness of the organization and its people. Such an objective-rated system covering task and development objectives is a useful way forward in the evaluation of personnel management.

Morale indices and surveys

We can have snapshots of morale to give us a more qualitative or 'softer' approach to evaluation. We can have a subjective analysis of, say, how well the personnel department is doing in meeting the needs of line managers, or perhaps vice versa. Subjectivity and open interpretations may vitiate such approaches. We should listen to feedback, certainly, but not to rumour and gossip.

Accident rates, labour turnover, productivity levels, scrap and wastage rates, sabotage incidence, and the number and duration of strikes and labour disputes may be symptomatic of low morale and a poor esprit de corps. A range of non-morale types of factor may also be involved, but these indices can be compared to industry norms and historical practice to get a feel for the morale of the employees as 'clients'.

Space does not permit us to cover each of these indices but we will examine the example of absence, or individual withdrawal from work, which has a fairly clear implication for morale and for people management practices in the organization. (See Box PM6.10.)

A specific attitude survey can give a reasonable analysis of the motivational state among employees. This in turn can be used to gauge the impact of personnel management on its employee-clients. We are going to use this survey method for our quality approach, so we will take the attitude and motivational aspect further in the following section.

BOX PM6.10

Absence

Absence costs billions of pounds per year. In 1986, for example, the Confederation of British Industry suggested that absence cost some £5 billion p.a.[1] The average employee has between seven and twelve days absence per year. This absence is non-attendance at work excluding sickness, statutory time off, strikes, holidays, bereavement leave, etc., and non-attendance through injury or accident at work. Taylor notes some of the detailed costs:[2] less experienced people covering the job, which may have an impact on output or quality; potential shutdowns of whole sections; others' resentment of covering absence; sick pay; and overtime cover.

Is this absence merely job dissatisfaction? Huczynski and Fitzpatrick[3] develop the earlier work of Steers and Rhodes[4] in examining a process model. Causation is usefully classified as follows:

- *The job:* the nature of the job situation covers the tasks and the working environment. The satisfaction with that situation is important.
- *The person:* length of service, age, sex and personality were all covered.
- *The attendance:* this includes the pressures to attend work, from work-group norms to incentive schemes, and the influences on ability to attend, from transportation to family responsibilities; and 'other factors', from past records to the time of the week or year.

The Incomes Data people followed up with an interesting survey in 1984.[5] A summary of their findings includes:

- *Age:* there was some incidence of 'young people' taking time off.
- *Sex:* women with children under the age of five were more likely to be ill.
- *Seasons:* some 'continued holidays', but there were most problems in winter.
- *Groups:* there was limited evidence that smaller groups meant less absence.
- *Hours:* flexitime removed lateness absence, which could often turn into a day off.
- *Sick pay:* it seemed to be related to the generosity of the sick pay scheme.

Is there a solution? People cannot help being ill. A war against 'malingerers' is often instigated by management, and controls and monitors must exist to prevent abuse. But the issue is not just poor health or management control, the core problem is morale. Much absence is a form of conflict, an individual withdrawal from work, and we need to motivate as well as control. This is a key role of the personnel function and of line managers.

Sources:
1   CBI, 'Absence from work'
2   P.J. Taylor, *Absenteeism*
3   Huczynski and Fitzpatrick, *Managing Employee Absence for a Competitive Edge*
4   Steers and Rhodes, 'Major influences on employee attendance'
5   Incomes Data Services, *Controlling Absence*

Quality management

This is really an internal market research-cum-customer-satisfaction process. We could use some tool to gauge how line managers felt about the 'service' from the staff personnel managers, how employees felt about people management (line and staff), how the personnel department felt about itself, and how the personnel department felt about line managers. This would be sensitive, perhaps, and unrealistic in some organizations, but such surveys would give a qualitative and quantitative evaluation of people management.

Activity PM6.3 gives some thoughts on the types of issues that we can address in our 'client' survey. It provides a useful balance to the hard quantitative data from the morale indices and continues along the motivational survey route.

Functional approach

Finally, we will use a functional analysis. By adapting the policy divisions used earlier, we can derive a useful client checklist for effective personnel management.

The main policy areas were seen as:
■ employment
■ training and development
■ remuneration
■ labour relations and welfare

ACTIVITY PM6.3

QUALITY PERSONNEL MANAGEMENT

Activity code
- ✔ Self-development
- ✔ Teamwork
- ✔ Communications
- ✔ Numeracy/IT
- ✔ Decisions

This is a survey on quality management. The results of the survey are shown below. In section (A) the line managers give their views on and approaches to the specialist personnel department. In section (B), the specialists in the personnel department give their views on and approaches to their own work.

Your task is to:
1 Analyse the statistics.
2 Derive themes from these statistics.
3 Attempt to marry up the views and approaches of sections (A) and (B).
4 Write a conclusion on this data with recommendations for the specialist personnel managers.

Section A Line managers
All results are in percentages; n = 100.

1 *In general terms, what do you feel about the work of the personnel department?*

	Totally	Fairly	Quite	Fairly	Totally	
Necessary	10	11	31	38	20	Unnecessary
Favourable	10	30	59	–	1	Unfavourable

2 *Note your involvement in the contact areas with the personnel department over the last year.*

	Frequent (weekly)	Often (monthly)	Never
Strategic assistance	1	2	97
Manpower planning	4	10	84
Recruitment	25	70	6
Selection	25	75	–
Training	8	63	29
Development	8	22	70
Welfare	15	85	–
Remuneration	13	60	27
Labour relations	20	30	50
General enquiries, e.g. pension	10	78	12
Other	–	–	–

3 *Give your specific views on this contribution made by the personnel department.*

	Totally	Fairly	Quite	Fairly	Totally	
Efficient	2	35	45	15	3	Inefficient
Helpful	34	40	15	1	1	Unhelpful
Supportive	31	41	23	3	2	Unsupportive
Effective	8	2	2	28	45	Ineffective

4 *What are your priorities in personnel management? Ranking is as follows:*
1   Recruitment/selection (equal)
2   Training
3   Welfare
4   Remuneration
5   Labour relations
6   Development
7   Manpower planning
8   General enquiries
9   Strategic assistance

5 *What are your views on the following?*

	Totally agree	Agree	Disagree	Totally disagree	No views
The personnel department is professional.	10	20	30	32	8
They are bureaucrats.	8	60	14	–	18
They have no real say around here.	18	50	26	8	8
They have great integrity.	51	26	2	14	8
We need a personnel department.	31	20	31	1	8

Section B: Personnel specialists
All results are in percentages; n = 10.

1 *In general terms, what do you feel that managers think about the work of the personnel department?*

	Totally	Fairly	Quite	Fairly	Totally	
Necessary	30	60	10	–	–	Unnecessary
Favourable	10	30	50	–	–	Unfavourable

2 *How often do you get involved in the following?*

	Frequent (weekly)	Often (monthly)	Never
Strategic assistance	20	60	20
Manpower planning	10	60	30
Recruitment	60	30	10
Selection	60	30	10
Training	10	50	40
Development	10	50	40
Welfare	10	70	20

	Frequent (weekly)	Often (monthly)	Never
Remuneration	10	70	20
Labour relations	–	30	70
General enquiries, e.g. pension	90	10	–
Other	–	3*	–

* Not named.

3 *Give your specific views on what you feel is the contribution made by the personnel department.*

	Totally	Fairly	Quite	Fairly	Totally	
Efficient	10	60	20	20	–	Inefficient
Helpful	10	70	10	10	–	Unhelpful
Supportive	10	80	10	–	–	Unsupportive
Effective	10	10	70	10	–	Ineffective

4 *What are your priorities in personnel management? Ranking is as follows:*
1 Recruitment
2 Selection
3 Training
4 Development
5 Strategic assistance
6 Manpower planning
7 Remuneration
8 Welfare
9 General enquiries
10 Labour relations

5 *To what extent do you agree with the following statements?*

	Totally agree	Agree	Disagree	Totally disagree	No views
The personnel department is professional.	40	60	–	–	–
They are bureaucrats.	30	20	30	20	–
They have no real say around here.	30	40	20	10	–
They have great integrity.	50	40	10	–	–
We need a personnel department.	100	–	–	–	–

ACTIVITY PM6.4

TOWARDS EVALUATION: OBJECTIVE SETTING FOR PERSONNEL MANAGEMENT

Activity code
✓ Self-development
✓ Teamwork
✓ Communications
✓ Numeracy/IT
✓ Decisions

Apply the functional list contained in the appendix to the scenario below to give qualitative and quantitative objectives which will make possible the evaluation of the personnel department.

You should cover all areas of employment, remuneration, services, and training and development within the objectives. You may wish to allocate some objectives to line managers and some to staff specialists.

Your role is to highlight key functional objectives for the personnel management of a large multinational firm. This should facilitate evaluation.

This book has given a focus on all of these issues (excluding labour relations). Criteria on how to judge or evaluate these functions are contained in the checklist in the appendix. You should now tackle the final activity, PM6.4.

Altogether this functional approach marries policy to practice and strategy to tactics, covers all people managers, and, most importantly, embraces all the clients of the services. Again, it not only leads to greater efficiency but to increased effectiveness – the main theme of this book.

Appendix: evaluation – a functional checklist

Employment

- Organizational plans and objectives take account of people.
- Departmental and job structures are designed and reviewed with the joint aims of implementing the plans and maintaining the job interests of employees.
- An ongoing manpower plan is available.
- External factors (PEST – political, economic, social and technological) and internal needs are married up in this plan.
- Succession plans and statistical information are updated regularly.
- Forecasts and budgets are prepared.
- Recruitment and selection occur on a systematic basis.
- Job analysis is done for all jobs.
- All people managers are trained in selection methods.
- Effectiveness checks occur in both recruitment and selection practices.

Remuneration

- Job analysis is covered systematically and used for job evaluation.
- The process of job evaluation is widely known and understood.
- Up-to-date salary and wage surveys are conducted and environmental changes are noted.
- Unions are involved. If no unions are evident, employees participate in the scheme.
- Fringe benefits are consistent with the market rates, and inconvenience pay applies as necessary.
- Incentives are used to motivate employees in addition to their core salary or wage.
- Merit and productivity are rewarded.
- The policy on remuneration is widely known and accepted.
- The schemes are fairly administered by management.
- Reviews, promotions and extraordinary payments can be accommodated fairly in the system.

Services (labour relations, employee services and welfare)

- Collective bargaining arrangements and/or systems of participation and communication exist.
- Employees are treated fairly and uniformly by management.
- The right of grievance and dispute exists, with appropriate representation.
- The right to fair discipline and equitable treatment exists.
- The right to job security is respected wherever possible and redundancy schemes operate in a fair manner.

- Services, from welfare to counselling, from pensions to medical advice, from social facilities to statutory requirements, are all provided.
- A safe and healthy workplace is in operation.
- The needs of individuals are met alongside the needs of the business.

Training and development
- Training needs analysis is made
- Individual jobs and tasks are clearly known and analysed for training.
- Induction is carried out.
- Programmes are 'scientifically' developed and designed.
- Implementation occurs, using a range of suitable methods.
- Evaluation is made.
- The needs of the individual are developed.
- The development of managers occurs.
- Self-development for all is encouraged.
- The policies on personnel, labour relations, training and development are widely known and acted on by all managers of personnel in good faith.

Notes

1 Terkel, *Working: people talk about what they do all day and how they feel about what they do.*

2 See Anderson and Barker, *Effective Business Policy*, and Anderson and Dobson, *Effective Marketing.*

3 Argenti, *Practical Corporate Planning.*

4 Warren, Gorham and Lamont Inc. in *Business and Society Review.*

5 See University of Westminster, *Business Ethics in the UK.*

6 K. Jones, *The Human Face of Change – social responsibility and rationalisation at British Steel.*

7 Terkel, *Working: people talk about what they do all day and how they feel about what they do.*

8 For the many leading motivational theorists referred to in this section, see: Maslow, *Towards a Psychology of Being*; McClelland and Steel, *Motivation Workshops: a student workbook for experiential learning in human motivation*; Alderfer, *Existence, Relatedness and Growth: human needs in organisational setting*; Herzberg, 'One more time: how do you motivate employees?'; Vroom, *Work and Motivation*; Adams, 'Towards an understanding of inequity'.

9 Walton 'Quality of working life: what is it?'.

10 French, *The Personnel Management Process – human resources administration and development.*

11 Adams, 'Towards an understanding of inequity'.

12 See Doré, *British Factory – Japanese Factory.*

13 Tyson, 'Is this the very model of a modern personnel manager?'.

14 Fowler, 'Proving the personnel department earns its salt'.

15 Ratio analysis is used extensively in Anderson and Nix, *Effective Accounting Management*, and Anderson and Ciechan, *Effective Financial Management.*

16 See Anderson, *Successful Training Practice.*

17 Likert, *The Human Organization: its management and value.*

18 Walker, 'Linking HR planning and strategic planning'.

Conclusion

If marketing is the business, people are the organization. This book has tried to show the importance of a systematic approach to people in an organization, taking account of the external environment and planning policies in line with the corporate plan. But this is not enough – the slaves have been emancipated and serfdom has broken down; the needs of people which are important in their own right must be married up with organizational need. Effective personnel management is concerned with the organizational management of people fusing with the needs and aspirations of employees. It is the responsibility of all managers who manage people, and the sooner we depart from scientific or neoscientific management the better. We need a committed and able labour force trained, motivated and rewarded. Someone once said managers get the shop stewards they deserve; perhaps personnel managers (line and staff) also get the people they deserve.

Bibliography and Further Reading

Adams, J.S., 'Towards an understanding of inequity', *Journal of Abnormal and Social Psychology*, 67 (1963).

Alderfer, C.P., *Existence, Relatedness and Growth: human needs in organisational setting* (Free Press, New York, 1972).

Anderson, A.H., 'Training and learning', in *Managing Human Resources*, eds A.G. Cowling and C.J.B. Mailer (Arnold, London, 1990).

Anderson. A.H., *Successful Training Practice: a manager's guide to personnel development* (Blackwell, Oxford, 1993).

Anderson, A.H., 'The learner without clothes', *Training Officer – The Independent Journal for the Professional Trainer*, 29, 5 (June 1993).

Anderson, A.H., 'Towards a training audit', *Training Officer – The Independent Journal for the Professional Trainer*, 29, 6 (July/Aug. 1993).

Anderson, A.H., 'Learning characteristics and learning theories', *Training Officer – The Independent Journal for the Professional Trainer*, 29, 9 (Nov. 1993).

Anderson, A.H., *Effective General Management* (Blackwell, Oxford, 1994).

Anderson, A.H., *Effective Labour Relations* (Blackwell, Oxford, 1994).

Anderson, A.H. and Barker, D., *Effective Business Policy* (Blackwell, Oxford, 1994).

Anderson, A.H. and Barker, D., *Effective Enterprise Management* (Blackwell, Oxford, 1994).

Anderson A.H. and Ciechan, R., *Effective Financial Management* (Blackwell, Oxford, 1994).

Anderson, A.H. and Dobson, T., *Effective Marketing* (Blackwell, Oxford, 1994).

Anderson, A.H., Dobson, T. and Patterson, J., *Effective International Marketing* (Blackwell, Oxford, 1994).

Anderson, A.H. and Kleiner, D., *Effective Marketing Communications* (Blackwell, Oxford, 1994).

Anderson, A.H. and Kyprianou, A., *Effective Organizational Behaviour* (Blackwell, Oxford, 1994).

Anderson, A.H. and Nix, E., *Effective Accounting Management* (Blackwell, Oxford, 1994).

Anderson, A.H. and Woodcock, P., *Effective Entrepreneurship* (Blackwell, Oxford, 1994).

Anthony, P.A., and Crichton, A., *Industrial Relations and the Personnel Specialist* (Batsford, London, 1969).

Argenti, J., *Practical Corporate Planning* (George Allen and Unwin, London, 1980).

Argyle, M., *The Psychology of Interpersonal Behaviour* (Penguin, Harmondsworth, 1967).

Armstrong, M., *Principles and Practice of Salary Administration* (Kogan Page, London, 1974).

Armstrong, M., 'HRM: a case of the emperor's new clothes?', *Personnel Management* (Aug. 1987).

Armstrong, M., *Handbook of Personnel Management Practice* (Kogan Page, London, 1991).

Armstrong, M. and Murlis, H., *Reward Management* (IPM/Kogan Page, London, 1981).

Ashton, D. and Easterby-Smith, M., *Management Development in the Organisation* (Macmillan, London, 1979).

Atkinson, J., *Flexibility, Uncertainty and Manpower Management* (IMS, University of Sussex, 1985).

Atkinson, J., 'Four stages of adjustment to the demographic downturn', *Personnel Management* (Aug. 1989).

Baldamus, W., 'The relationship between wage and effort', *Journal of Industrial Economics*, 5 (1961), pp. 192–201.

Bank, J., *Outdoor Training for Managers* (Gower Press, Aldershot, 1985).

Baron, B., 'Training', in *Managing Human Resources*, eds A.G. Cowling and C.J.B. Mailer (Arnold, London, 1990).

Barrington, H.A., 'Continuous development: theory and reality', *Personnel Review*, 15, 1 (1986), pp. 27–31.

Bartholomew, D.J. (ed.), *Manpower Planning: selected readings* (Penguin, Harmondsworth, 1976).

Bass, B.M., 'The leaderless group discussion', *Psychological Bulletin*, 51, 5 (1954).

Beckhard, R., *Organisational Development: strategy and models* (Addison-Wesley, Reading, MA, 1969).

Belasco, J.A. and Arlutton, J.A., 'Line and staff conflicts: some empirical insights', *Academy of Management Journal*, 12 (Dec. 1969), pp. 469–77.

Belbin, R.M., *Management Teams – why they succeed or fail* (Heinemann, London, 1981).

Bell, D.J., *Planning Corporate Planning*, (Longman, Harlow, 1974).

Bennis, W.G., *Organisation Development: its nature, origins and prospects* (Addison-Wesley, Reading, MA, 1969).

Bennis, W.G., Benne, K.D., and Chin, R., *The Planning of Change* (Holt, Rinehart and Winston, New York, 1969).

Blake, R.R. and Mouton, J.S., *The Versatile Manager: a grid profile* (R.D. Irwin, Homewood, IL, 1981).

Boydell, T.H., 'A guide to job analysis' (British Association for Commercial and Industrial Education (BACIE), London, 1970).

Brading, L. and Wright, V., 'Performance related pay', in *Personnel Management*, ed. C. Hogg, Institute of Personnel Management Factsheet No. 30 (IPM, London, June 1990).

Bramham, J., *Practical Manpower Planning* (IPM, London, 1982).

Burgoyne, J.G., 'Moving forward from self development', *Management Education*, 12, 2 (1981), pp. 67–80.

Burgoyne, J.G., 'Management development for the individual and the organisation', *Personnel Management* (June 1988).

Burgoyne, J.G., Boydell, T. and Pedler, M., *Self Development: theory and applications for practitioners* (Association of Teachers of Management, London, 1978).

Burns, T. and Stalker, G.N., *The Management of Innovation* (Tavistock, London, 1966).

Business Technician and Education Council (BTEC), 'Common skills and experience of BTEC programmes' (BTEC, London, n.d.).

CBI, 'Absence from work: a survey of non-attendance and sickness absence' (CBI, London, 1986).

Campbell, J.P., 'On the nature of organisational effectiveness', in *New Perspectives on Organisational Effectiveness*, eds P.S. Goodman, J.M. Pennings and Associates (Jossey-Bass, San Francisco, 1977).

Carroll, S.J. et al., 'The relative effectiveness of training methods – expert opinion and research', *Personnel Psychology*, 25 (1972), pp. 495–500.

Celinski, D., 'Systematic on the job training', *Training and Development* (Nov. 1986).

Clegg, H., *The Changing System of Industrial Relations* (Blackwell, Oxford, 1979).

Clegg, H., 'General Report No. 9 (Clegg Commission)', *Oxford Bulletin of Economics and Statistics* (Feb. 1983).

Clutterbuck, D., *Everyone Needs a Mentor* (IPM, London, 1985).

Cole, G.A., *Personnel Management: theory and practice* (DP Publications, London, 1986).

Connellan, T.K., *How to Improve Business Performance – behaviourism in business and industry* (Harper & Row, New York, 1978).

Constable, J. and McCormick, R., 'The making of British managers', *BIM* (1987).

Cowling, A.G., 'Manpower planning, information and control', in *Managing Human Resources*, eds A.G. Cowling and C.J.B. Mailer (Arnold, London, 1990).

Cunningham, M., *Non Wage Benefits*, Workers' Handbooks (Pluto Press, London, 1981).

Department of Employment, *Company Manpower Planning* (HMSO, London, 1972).

Department of Employment, *Glossary of Training Terms* (HMSO, London, 1977).

Digman, L.A., 'How well-managed organisations develop their executives', *Organisation Dynamics*, 7, 2 (Aug. 1978).

Doré, R.P., *British Factory – Japanese Factory* (George Allen and Unwin, London, 1973).

Drucker, P.F., *The Practice of Management* (Heinemann, London, 1955).

Drucker, P.F., *Managing for Results* (Harper & Row, New York, 1964).

Drucker, P.F., *The Effective Executive* (Harper & Row, New York, 1967).

Fairbairns, J., 'Plugging the gap in training needs analysis', *Personnel Management* (Feb. 1991).

Fletcher, C. and Williams, R., *Performance Appraisal and Career Development* (Hutchinson, London, 1985).

Fowler, A., 'Proving the personnel department earns its salt', *Personnel Management* (May 1983).

Fowler, A., 'New directions in performance pay', *Personnel Management* (Nov. 1988).

Fox, A., *A Sociology of Work in Industry* (Collier-Macmillan, London, 1971).

French, W.L., *The Personnel Management Process – human resources administration and development*, 4th edn (Houghton Mifflin, Boston, MA, 1978).

Goldthorpe, J.H., 'Attitudes and behaviour of car assembly workers: a deviant case and a theoretical critique', *British Journal of Sociology*, XVII, 3 (Sept. 1966).

Goodman, P.S., Bazerman, M. and Conlon, E., 'Institutionalization of planned organizational change', in *Research in Organisational Behaviour*, vol. 2, eds B.M. Staw and L.L. Cummings (JAI Press, Greenwich, Conn., 1980).

Grant, D., 'A better way of learning from Nellie', *Personnel Management* (1984).

Greiner, L.E., 'Evolution and revolution as organisations grow', *Harvard Business Review* (July/Aug. 1972).

Guardian, 'High flying plastic workers get paid in rows of beans', 11 January 1993.

Guest, D., 'Personnel and HRM: can you tell the difference?, *Personnel Management* (Jan. 1989).

Hackman, J.R. and Oldham, G.R., 'Motivation through the design of work: test of a theory', *OB and Human Performance*, 16 (1976).

Hackman, J.R., Oldham, G., Janson, R. and Purdy, K., 'A new strategy for job enrichment', *California Management Review*, 15, 3 (1975), pp. 96–7.

Hague, H., *Executive Self Development* (Macmillan, London, 1974).

Haider, M.L., quoted by *International Management* (Jan. 1966).

Hamblin, A.C., *Evaluation and Control of Training* (McGraw-Hill, Maidenhead, 1974).

Handy, C., *The Making of Managers* (National Economic Office, London, April 1987).

Harris, M. (ed.), *The Realities of Productivity Bargaining*, Industrial Relations Committee Report, reprint (IPM, London, 1969).

Heller, R., 'The change managers', *Management Today*, 25th anniversary issue (1991).

Herzberg, F., Mausner, B. and Snyderman, B., *The Motivation to Work* (John Wiley, New York, 1959).

Herzberg, F., 'One more time: how do you motivate employees?', *Harvard Business Review*, 46 (1968).

Hobsbawm, E.J., 'Trends in the British labour movement', *Labouring Men: studies in the history of labour* (Weidenfeld and Nicolson, London, 1963).

Honey, P. and Mumford, A., *Manual of Learning Styles* (Honey, Maidenhead, 1982).

Honey, P. and Mumford, A., *Using Your Learning Styles* (Honey, Maidenhead, 1983).

Huczynski, A.A. and Fitzpatrick, M.J., *Managing Employee Absence for a Competitive Edge* (Pitman, London, 1989).

Husband, T., 'Payment structures made to measure', *Personnel Management* (Apr. 1975).

ICI Organics Division, *Management Training and Development: investing in people*, Series No. 7 (Nov. 1987).

Incomes Data Services, *Controlling Absence*, Study 321 (London, 1984).

Industrial Training Research Unit, CRAMP, research paper TRI (Cambridge, n.d.).

Institute of Personnel Management, *Continuous Development: people and work*, 3rd edn (IPM, London, 1990).

International Labour Organization, *Job Evaluation* (ILO, Geneva, 1960).

International Labour Organization, *Teaching and Training Methods for Management Development* (ILO, Geneva, 1972).

Jaques, E., *Equitable Payment*, 2nd edn (Heinemann Educational, London, 1970).

Jones, J.A.G., 'Training intervention strategies: making more effective training interventions', ITS Monograph No. 2 (Industrial Training Services, London, 1983).

Jones, K., *The Human Face of Change – social responsibility and rationalisation at British Steel* (IPM, London, 1974).

Jones, M., 'Training practices and learning theories', *Journal of European Industrial Training*, 3, 7 (1979).

Katz, R.L., 'Skills of an effective administrator', *Harvard Business Review*, 52, 5 (Sept./Oct. 1974).

Kenney, J., 'Core competencies of a trainer', *Canadian Training Methods*, 9, 4, Supplement (1976).

Kenney, J.P.J., Donnelly, E.L. and Reid, M.A., *Manpower Training and Development* (IPM, London, 1979).

Kenney, T.P., 'Stating the case for welfare', *Personnel Management* (Sept. 1975).

Kolb, D.A., 'Towards an applied theory of experiential learning', in *Theories of Group Processes*, ed. C.L. Cooper (John Wiley, New York, 1975).

Kolb, D.A., Rubin, I.M. and McIntyre, J.M., *Organisational Psychology – an experimental approach* (Prentice Hall, Englewood Cliffs, NJ, 1974).

Kotter, J.P. and Schlesinger, L.A., 'Choosing strategies for change', *Harvard Business Review* (Mar.–Apr. 1979).

Krech, D., Crutchfield, R.S. and Livson, N., *Elements of Psychology*, 3rd edn (Knopf, New York, 1974).

Laird, D., *Approaches to Training and Development* (Addison-Wesley, London, 1978).

Leduchowicz, T. and Bennet, R., *What Makes an Effective Trainer?* (Thames Valley Regional Management Centre/Manpower Services Commission, Sheffield, 1983).

Legge, K., *Power Innovation and Problem Solving in Personnel Management* (McGraw-Hill, Maidenhead, 1978).

Lewin, K., 'Group decision and social change', in *Readings in Social Psychology*, revised edition, eds G.E. Swanson, T.M. Newcomb and E.L. Hartley (Holt, New York, 1952).

Lewin, K., *Field Theory in Social Science: selected theoretical papers*, reprint (Greenwood Press, University of Michigan, 1975).

Likert, R., *The Human Organization: its management and value* (McGraw-Hill, New York, 1967).

Littler, C.R., 'Deskilling and changing structures of control', in *The Degradation of Work*, ed. S. Wood (Hutchinson, London, 1982).

Littler, C.R., *The Development of the Labour Processes in Capitalist Societies: a comparative study of the transformation of work organisations in Britain, Japan and the USA* (Heinemann, London, 1982).

Livy, B., *Job Evaluation – a critical review* (George Allen and Unwin, London, 1975).

Livy, B., *Corporate Personnel Management* (Pitman, London, 1988).

Long, C.G.L., 'A theoretical model for method selection', *Industrial Training International*, 4, 11 (1969), pp. 475–8.

Long, P., *Performance Appraisal Revisited* (IPM, London, 1986).

Lupton, T., *Industrial Behaviour and Personnel Management* (IPM, London, n.d.).

Lupton, T., and Gowler D., 'Selecting a wage payment system', Federation Research Paper III (Engineering Employers Federation, London, 1969).

MCI, *Diploma Level Guidelines and Diploma Workshop Report* (Shell UK, London, n.d.).

McClelland, D.C. and Steele, R.S., *Motivation Workshops: a student workbook for experiential learning in human motivation* (General Learning Press, New York, 1972).

McGregor, D., *The Human Side of Enterprise* (McGraw-Hill, New York, 1960).

McKersie, R.G., 'Changing wage payment systems', Royal Commission Research Paper No. 11 (HMSO, London, 1968).

Maier, N.R.F., *The Appraisal Interview: objectives, methods and skills* (John Wiley, New York, 1958).

Makin, R.J. and Robertson, I., 'Management selection in Britain: a survey and critique', *Journal of Occupational Psychology*, 59 (1986).

Makin, R.J. and Robertson, I., 'Selecting the best selection techniques', *Personnel Management* (Nov. 1986).

Mangham, I.L. and Silver, M.S., *Management Training: context and practice* (ESCR/DTI, London, 1987).

Markwell, D.S., *Organisation of Management Development Programmes* (Gower, Aldershot, 1969).

Maslow, A.H., *Towards a Psychology of Being* (Van Nostrand, Princeton, NJ, 1962).

Mayfield, E.W., 'The selection interview: a re-evaluation of published research', *Personnel Psychology*, 17 (1964).

Miller, K.M., *Psychological Testing* (Gower, Aldershot, 1975).

Mintzberg, H., *The Nature of Managerial Work* (Prentice Hall, Englewood Cliffs, NJ, 1973).

Mintzberg, H., 'The manager's job – folklore and fact', *Harvard Business Review*, 53, 4 (July/Aug. 1975).

Mitchell, J.L. and McCormick, E.S., *Professional and Managerial Position Questionnaire* (Purdue Research Foundation, West Lafayette, IN, n.d.).

Mitchell, T.R., *People in Organisations* (McGraw-Hill, Tokyo, 1982).

Morris, M., 'The evaluation of training', *Industrial and Commercial Training* (Mar./Apr. 1984).

Mumford, A., 'Emphasis on the learner: a new approach', *Industrial and Commercial Training* (Nov. 1983).

Munro Fraser, J., *Handbook of Employment Interviewing*, 5th edn (Macdonald and Evans, London, 1978).

NEDO (National Economic Development Office) and MSC (Manpower Services Commission), *Competence and Competition, Training and Education in the Federal Republic of German, the United States and Japan* (NEDO/MSC, London, 1984).

Niven, M.M., *Personnel Management, 1913–1963* (IPM, London, 1967).

Observer, quoting Judge John Lee, 4 October 1992.

Oliver, N. and Wilkinson, B., *The Japanization of British Industry* (Blackwell, Oxford, 1992).

Owens, W.A. and Schvenfeldt, L.F., 'Towards a classification of persons', *Journal of Applied Psychology* (1979).

Palmer, G., *British Industrial Relations* (George Allen and Unwin, London, 1983).

Palmer, S. (ed.), *Determining Pay* (IPM, London, 1990).

Peach, L., 'A practitioner's view of personnel excellence', *Personnel Management* (Sept. 1989).

Pearson, R. and Pike, G., 'The graduate labour market in the 1990s', IMS Report (Brighton, 167, n.d.).

Pettigrew, A.M. and Reason, P.W., *Alternative Interpretations of the Training Officer Role: a research study in the chemical industry* (Chemical and Allied Product Training Board, Staines, Mar. 1979).

Pigors, P. and Myers, C.A., *Management of Human Resources* (McGraw-Hill, Maidenhead, 1973).

Pigors, P. and Myers, C.A., *Personnel Administration*, 8th edn (McGraw-Hill, 1977).

Plumbley, P.R., *Recruitment and Selection* (IPM, London, 1976).

Porter, H., 'Takes personality tests to task', *Observer Magazine*, 6 December 1992.

Purkiss, C., 'Manpower planning literature: manpower demand', Institute of Manpower Studies Course Document, 1976; reprinted in *Department of Employment Gazette* (Nov. 1976).

RBL (Research Bureau Ltd), 'Research on external and internal influences in training report' *Manpower Services Commission* (Sheffield, The Review Team, Research Bureau Ltd, 1979).

Ray, M.E., *Practical Job Advertising* (London, IPM, 1971).

Revans, R.W., *The ABC of Action Learning* (Bratt, Chartwell, 1983).

Robbins, S.P., *Organisation Theory: structure, design and applications* (Prentice Hall, Englewood Cliffs, NJ, 1987).

Rodger, A., *The Seven Point Plan*, revised 1968 edn (NIIP, London, 1952).

Rogers, C., *Freedom to Learn* (Merrill, Columbus, OH, 1969).

Rogers, C., *Freedom to Learn for the 80s* (Merrill, Columbus, OH, 1983).

Rogers, J., *Adults Learning*, 2nd edn (Open University Press, Milton Keynes, 1977).

Roy, D.R., 'Banana time: job satisfaction and informal interaction', *Human Organisation*, 18 (1960).

Schein, E., *Career Dynamics: matching individual and organisational needs* (Addison-Wesley, Reading, MA, 1978).

Sidney, E. and Brown, M., *The Skills of Interviewing* (Tavistock, London, 1961).

Silverzweig, S. and Allen, R.F., 'Changing the corporate culture', *Sloan Management Review* (Spring 1976).

Starbuck, W.H., *Organizational Growth and Development: selected readings* (Penguin Education, Harmondsworth, 1971).

Starbuck, W.H., 'Organisations as action generators', *American Sociological Review*, 48, 1 (Feb. 1983).

Steers, R.M. and Porter, L.W., *Motivation and Work Behaviour* (McGraw-Hill, New York, 1979).

Steers, R.M. and Rhodes, S.R., 'Major influences on employee attendance: a process model', *Journal of Applied Psychology*, 63, 4 (1978), pp. 391–407.

Stephenson, T., 'O.D.: a critique', *Journal of Management Studies* (Oct. 1975).

Stevens, C., 'Assessment centres: the British experience', *Personnel Management* (July 1985).

Stewart, R., *Managers and their Jobs: a study of the similarities and differences in the ways managers spend their time* (Macmillan, London, 1967).

Storey, J., 'Developments in the management of human resources: an interim report', Warwick Papers in Industrial Relations No. 17 (Nov. 1987).

Tannehill, R.E., *Motivation and Management Development* (Butterworth, London, 1970).

Taylor, F.W., *Scientific Management* (Harper, New York, 1947).

Taylor, P.J., *Absenteeism – causes and control* (Industrial Society, London, 1982).

Terkel, S., *Working: people talk about what they do all day and how they feel about what they do* (Pantheon, New York, 1979).

Thomason, G., *A Textbook of Personnel Management*, 3rd edn (IPM, London, 1978).

Thakur, M., *OD: the search for identity* (IPM, London, 1974).

Titbits, 'A Thousand Ways to Earn A Living' (London, 1888).

Training and Development Lead Body, *How Do You Spot Good Trainers?: consultation document*, circulated 1991 (TDLB, London, n.d.).

Training Agency with Deloitte, Haskins, and Sells, *Management Challenge for the 1990s – the current education, training and development debate* (Sheffield, Training Agency, July 1989).

Training Agency, *Training in Britain: a study of funding activity and attitude* (HMSO, London, 1989).

Training Commission/Council for Management Education (CMED), 'Classifying the components of management competencies' (Training Commission, London, 1988).

Training Services Agency, 'An approach to the training of staff with training officer roles' (Training Services Agency, Sheffield, 1977).

Tyson, S., 'Is this the very model of a modern personnel manager?', *Personnel Manager* (May 1985).

University of Westminster, *Business Ethics in the UK* (London, Jan. 1993).

Vant, J.H.B., 'Reducing lost time accidents in North Sea drilling companies', research paper at the 1982 Oil Safety Congress and Exposition, 8–9 Nov., Lafayette, LA.

Velasquez, M.G., *Business Ethics: concepts and cases* (Prentice Hall, Englewood Cliffs, NJ, 1982).

Vroom, V., *Work and Motivation* (John Wiley, New York, 1964).

Walker, J.W., 'Linking H.R. planning and strategic planning', unpublished paper to Institute of Management Services, 1977.

Walton, R., 'Quality of working life: what is it?', *Sloan Management Review*, 15, 1 (1973).

Warren, Gorham and Lamont Inc., *Business and Society Review* (Summer 1984).

Watson, T.J., *The Personnel Managers* (Routledge and Kegan Paul, London, 1977).

Williams, A., 'Organisation development and change', in *Managing Human Resources*, eds A.G. Cowling and C.J.B. Mailer (Arnold, London, 1990).

Wilson, B., 'The role of the personnel function in a changing environment', in *Personnel in Change*, eds M. Thakur, J. Bristow and K. Carloff (IPM, London, 1978).

Wright, V. and Brading, L., in 'Performance Related Pay', ed. C. Hogg, *IPM Factsheets* (IPM, London, n.d.).

Index